INN SEARCH OF BIRDS

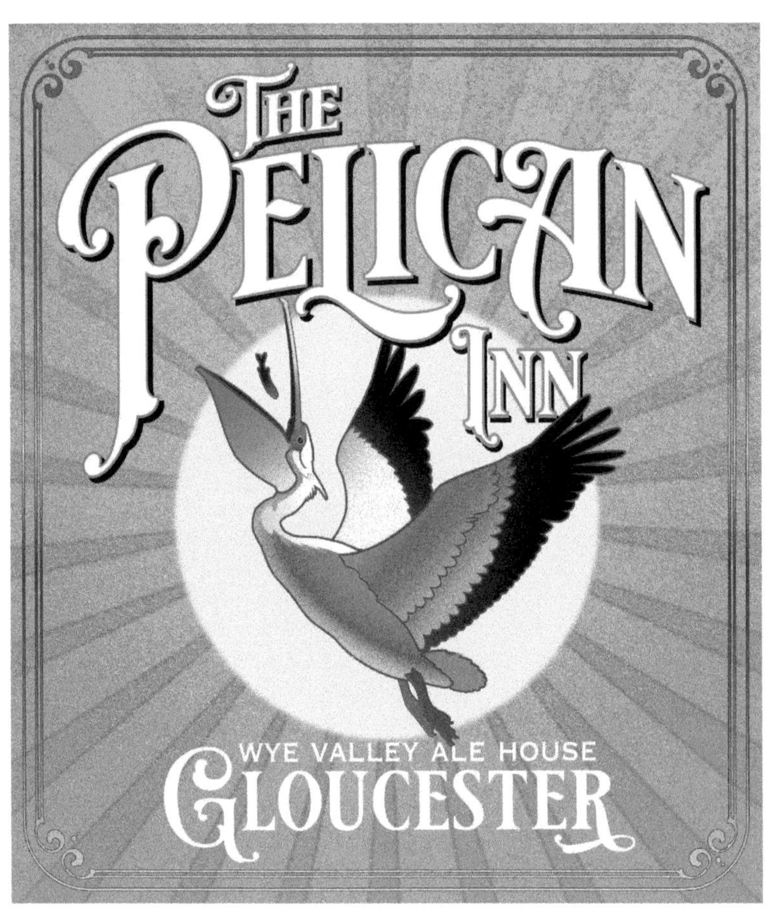

The Pelican Inn, Gloucester

INN SEARCH OF BIRDS

PUBS, PEOPLE AND PLACES

JOHN LAWTON

Whittles Publishing

Published by
Whittles Publishing Ltd.,
Dunbeath,
Caithness, KW6 6EG,
Scotland, UK

www.whittlespublishing.com

ISBN 978-184995-506-5

Printed and bound by
CPI Group (UK) Ltd, Croydon, CR0 4YY

CONTENTS

PREFACE

Most birders (we used to be called bird-watchers) enjoy pubs. I certainly do. This book is a ramble through the world of pub birds. That is the birds that appear in the names and on the signs of pubs, bars and inns in England, Scotland and Wales (and 'bird-associated' things like feathers or bird-cages). The ramble has four entwined themes. How the pubs acquired their names, the memories they evoke in me from a lifetime of birding, the natural histories of the birds themselves, and the stories (and sometimes un-natural histories) of the pubs.

There is much more to go at than you might imagine. There are 117 identifiable species, seven non-specific kinds of birds and four mythical species on my list in a sample of just over 700 pubs, collected between 2010 and 2021. It's not to be taken too seriously, but it is meant to be fun and entertaining, as well as accurate and informative. It is also quirky – at least I hope it is.

There are many areas in the story of pub birds that I do not understand, and I may have said so too many times in the book for readers who want simple explanations. But life isn't simple, particularly in the range and types of material I have tried to deal with, where no one person can be an expert on all of it. So I see *Inn Search of Birds* as work in progress, to be picked up and re-worked by others, to correct my mistakes, and add to the sum of human knowledge. And enjoy doing it.

The book was started and a substantial chunk written during the Covid-19 lockdowns in 2020-21. During this time all pubs were closed, and this sector of the economy was among the hardest hit by the pandemic. It remains to be seen how many pub birds sadly didn't survive, and this book is their obituary.

Cheers.

John Lawton
York, November 2021

ACKNOWLEDGEMENTS

Many friends, colleagues and correspondents have tolerated my obsession with pub birds and helped me with my research. You know who you are, and some of you are mentioned (but not everybody) in the text. But to all of you, "thank you!" The following people were particularly helpful:

Tadhg Carroll (University of York) for preparing the two figures in Chapter 8.

Alastair Fitter, particularly for information about his father Richard Fitter.

Bob Holt, for suggesting the new game *Ticks and Tipples.*

Chris Perrins, particularly for guiding me to W.B. Alexander's paper on pub birds, and for correspondence about Black Swans.

Roger Riddington, without whose help and enthusiasm my initial exploratory note on pub birds in *British Birds* would never have been published.

York Ornithological Club members, who have tolerated me talking about pub birds for a long time, made numerous useful suggestions and never complained (at least within earshot).

Keith Wittles, of Whittles Publishing for his endless patient and sound advice.

My wife Dot was typically patient and supportive as my obsession with pub birds grew but, as always, made it very clear when I needed to back off. In what should have taken 30 minutes in the car, what turned out to be a four-hour fruitless marathon to find *The Barn Owl Inn,* reputedly in Kingskerswell outside Newton Abbot in Dorset, was not one of the high points of our 55 years of marriage. We have two grown-up kids (Anna and Graham) who tolerated their father's new hobby with mild amusement, put me right about the pub in *The Hitchhikers Guide to the Galaxy*, and Graham (a Feature Writer for *New Scientist*) made invaluable professional comments on the first draft.

PHOTO-CREDITS

Most of photographs in the book were taken by me between 2010 and 2021. I am extremely grateful to friends, correspondents, and pub managers, landlords, landladies, and owners for sending me additional photographs and giving me permission to reproduce them. They are:

Bald Buzzard Micropub, Leighton Buzzard. Bald Buzzard Micropub (Chapter 3).
Bird in Hand, Hayle. www.birdinhandhayle.co.uk. Nick Reynolds (Chapter 4).
Bird in Hand, Wreningham. Alex Brake, Director (Chapter 3).
Bonny Moorhen. Stanhope. Michael Leakey (Chapter 3).
Bustard Inn, South Rauceby. Julian Lonsdale, The Bustard Inn Ltd (Chapter 3).
Crown and Liver, Ewloe. Gareth Lambert, Marstons Brewery (Chapter 4).
Curlew, West Parley. Sara Parsons, Mitchells & Butlers (Chapter 3).
Firecrest, Wendover. David Gantzel (Chapter 7).
Fox and Pelican, Hindhead. John Childs, vice-chairman (via Lauren Green, manager), Grayshott Heritage (Chapter 4).
Fur and Feathers, Herriard. Chris Spooner (Chapter 6).
Harte and Magpies, Coleshill. David Gantzel (Chapter 7).
Lamb and Lark, Limington. Rob and Jane Chapman (Chapter 3).
Magpie, Combs Ford The Magpie, Combs Ford (Chapter 2).
Magpie (Inn), Little Stonham. Indre Butcher (Chapter 2).
Merlin, Billingham. Michael Leakey (Chapter 5).
Mole and Chicken, Easington. The Heather family and Kelly Cherry (Chapter 7).
Ostrich, Colnbrook. Sarah Morgan, Ostrich Colnbrook Ltd (Chapter 3).
Pelican Inn, Gloucester. pelican.glos@icloud.com. Michael Hall (artist Ian Coleman) (Frontispiece).
Phoenix Inn, Twyford. Chris Spooner (Chapter 4).
Red Kite, Winlaton Mill. Keith Bowey (Chapter 1).
Redstart, Barming. David Gantzel (Chapter 7).
Three Pigeons, Ruthin. *Three Pigeons Inn*, Graigfechan (Chapter 2).

CHAPTER 1: OPENING TIME

Most birders I know keep lists of the species of birds they have seen, ranging from where they live to the entire world, with time periods as short as an hour or two, to weeks, months, years or lifetimes. I keep a cumulative weekly garden list, a UK list, a list for the Western Palaearctic – a technical biogeographical term that roughly corresponds to Europe, North Africa and the Middle East – and a list for each country outside the Western Palaearctic that I have been privileged to visit. It is standard stuff, and like many birders one of the ways I keep track of what I have seen is to 'tick off' species on printed lists. My grand total of ticks is just over 3,000 from a possible global total of about 11,000 species. It may seem a lot, but my life list is very modest compared with the serious listers, some of whom have seen many thousands of species more than me (although nobody has seen all 11,000). However, I may well be unique among living birders (or if not unique then very unusual) in that I also keep a list of pub birds – birds on pub signs and in pub names – that I started in 2010[1.1]. This book is about these pub birds, their natural histories and folk histories, and the histories of the pubs that bear their names, some of the people involved in the stories, and the memories that pub birds have evoked in me about my own birding life And in case you are wondering, only very rarely do I have to actually go into the pub. Mostly it is an outside job, and not a very exciting one at that, or done by searching on Google. But in Edinburgh I once asked a taxi driver to take me to the *Doocot* (dovecote). "What do you want to go there for?" he asked. I explained. "It's burned down – insurance job" was his reply. It was being rebuilt, and it's the only pub I've been chased away from when taking a photograph.

There is a rich literature on the history of pubs and their names, but I know of very few previous attempts to write about pub birds. The most significant is by one of the great doyens of UK ornithology, W.B. Alexander, who published a paper in *Bird Notes* (the house magazine at the time of the RSPB) in the 1950s, entitled *The Ornithology of Pub Signs*[1.2]. The second is a one-page, 1955 article[1.3] in the *Birmingham Daily Post* called 'Bird Inn Signs' by R.S.R. (Richard) Fitter, one of the great English natural historians of the pre- and post-war periods. The third is by T. Hyde-Parker in 1940 in *The Naturalist*[1.4], which pre-dates both Alexander and Fitter but which is an altogether less substantial effort.

The only other serious compilation of pub birds of which I am aware is an impressive list (without text) of pubs bearing bird names assembled by Steve Shaw over a 20-year period and published as an appendix in the wonderful book *Birds Britannica* in 2005, so the data probably spanned a period roughly between 1980 and 2000, well before my own interests were sparked. The list is invaluable[1.5].

How did I get into this admittedly niche bit of birding? Of course, like most birders I like nice pubs, not only for their own sake but also because, in the days before the internet and mobile phones, pubs in good birding spots were often the best place to find out from other birders "What's about?", preferably over a pint. One that will be familiar to many birders is *The George* at Cley next the Sea on the north Norfolk coast, with a stylised Brent Goose on its sign[1.6]. You can stand at the door and listen to the Geese out on the marshes nearby. But it isn't how I got into pub birds; that came later. On the eastern edge of the Yorkshire Dales at the entrance to Wensleydale are four pubs all named after Black Swans. They lie roughly within a five-mile radius of one another in Bedale (*The Old Black Swan*), Fearby near Masham (*Black Swan)*, Leyburn (*The Black Swan Hotel*) and Middleham (another *Black Swan Hotel*). When I encountered them on holiday in 2010 I was intrigued. Why here? I still don't know for certain, but they sparked my interest in pubs with birds on their signs or named after birds, and pubs with bird-related names such as the *Doocot* in Edinburgh or *The Fur and Feathers* and

Black Swan Hotel, Middleham

the *Bird Cage*, both in Norwich, Norfolk. I've been keeping my list ever since. It spans 11 years, from 2010 until nearly the end of 2021. And unlike my list of living, breathing real birds I don't have to have seen or heard them; many of them have been ticked off using Google.

My first serious foray into publishing something on pub birds was in *British Birds* in 2020[1.7]. I was planning this book and I wanted to gauge peoples' reactions to the idea, and hopefully prompt some "Do you know about the pub called..." type responses.

The reaction to the article was remarkable, and I was told about several pubs I didn't know of. As well as identifying new (to me) pub birds, readers also sent me some interesting anecdotes. One (from Charles Gallimore, who lived in a village with the appropriate name of Wing in Rutland for 45 years) illustrates particularly nicely the link between birders, pubs and pub birds. Most birders have at some time visited the famous Bird Fair held annually for the last 30 years at Rutland Water. Charles used to set the questions for the Mastermind-like quiz 'Bird Brain of Britain' and in 2006 one of the questions was: "*The Cuckoo, The Kingfisher, The Old Pheasant* and *The Finch's Arms* are all pubs in Rutland. Which is nearest to the Bird Fair at Egleton?" To get the answer right you had to know about pub birds, and in those days I wouldn't have had a clue. Charles tells me it's *The Finch's Arms*, but that's cheating because the name refers to a notable local family, not a bird. So, it would not have made it into this book under my own 'house rules', which I will now explain.

For the *British Birds* article, I complied a database of pub birds from two sources: random[1.8] samples of all the pubs in an area, initially by consulting *Yellow Pages* and *Thompson Directories* (remember those?); and latterly using Google, by searching "pubs, bars and inns in [say] York". It turns out that in the sample of 6,846 pubs searched in this way, 307 (4.5%) qualified as pub birds. (This is a useful percentage for reasons I will get to later.) The *British Birds* article also included pub birds ticked off haphazardly as I travelled about or those that were sent to me by friends.

For this book I augmented the *British Birds* database with new pub birds, sent by readers and found during extensive internet searches, with a focus on finding new species rather than yet more examples of the commonest. The resulting main database is in Appendix 2. In a sample of 711 pubs there are 117 identifiable species of birds, 17 non-specific kinds of birds (for example "Duck") and four mythical species, plus 35 pubs named after what I have called "bird paraphernalia" such as "birdcage" and feathers.

Just over a dozen species or kinds of birds are very common (Chapter 2) – that is, there are numerous pubs named after them. Examples include Mute Swans, Red Jungle Fowl (Hens to you and me), Eagles and Pheasants[1.7]. Trying to list all of them would not only be very time consuming but also uninteresting. It becomes the birding equivalent of watching little else but Mute Swans for day after day. The website Pubs Galore lists the 256 most frequently used pub names in the UK (of all types, not just birds)[1.9]. I used this extensively to 'sample' the commoner birds[1.10]. The website was also helpful for locating rarer species, as were the lists produced by W.B. Alexander[1.2], Richard Fitter[1.3] and Steve Shaw[1.5], but I checked that these pubs were still open before 'ticking' them (many no longer exist or have changed their names). Then for other possible UK species I simply worked through a comprehensive list of UK birds, Googling species names and pubs. The resulting aviary of 117 species doesn't quite range from A to Z. I have not been able to find a pub called *The Avocet* (despite the bird's striking appearance) and *The Albatross* in Redhill (Surrey) was renamed *The Joshua Tree* in 2001. At the other end of the alphabet there are no pubs called *The Zebra Finch* or *Zitting Cisticola*, but the list does run from *The Blackbird* on Earls Court Road in London to a *Yellow Wagtail* in Yeovil.

To re-emphasise, this is still a *sample* of pubs, not a complete inventory of pub birds. And it is strictly time limited. Numbers differ in different sources, but according to *The Guardian* newspaper (11 July 2020), between 2010 and 2019 the number of pubs in the UK fell from roughly 55,400 to 47,200. Split the difference and assume that over the period of my study (2010–2021) there were about 51,000 pubs in the UK.

Now go back to that 4.5% figure. If approximately 4.5% of the roughly 51,000 pubs in Britain are named after birds or have bird-related names, a comprehensive database of pub birds should have about 2,295 pubs in it, so 711 is a sample. But it excludes Northern Ireland[1.1] and, as I have just explained, is one that makes no attempt to include all the examples of the commonest pub birds. So, the *species* coverage will be very much better than roughly a third of British pubs. However, it would be very foolish to say I have discovered all possible species of pub birds extant at some point between 2010 and 2021. And finally, not every pub named after a bird (even some of the rarer ones) finds its way into the book; every species does, but not every example. If I fail to mention your favourite pub, I apologise.

The Little Owl, Charlton Kings

Pitfall 1: Birds That Aren't

Several pubs apparently named after birds (as we have just seen with *The Finch's Arms*) are not – at least not directly. Other examples include *The Ostrich Inn* in Bristol and *The Swallow* near Cheltenham (both sailing ships, presumably themselves named after birds). *The Little Owl* (also just outside Cheltenham) is named after a racehorse; I once drove 50 miles out of my way to photograph it and was not pleased when I found it. If I had known about Steve Shaw's list[1.5] at the time I could have saved myself a lot of trouble, because he marks it as not referring to a bird. There are 24 pubs called *The Crow's Nest* also on Steve Shaw's list; in the absence of evidence that any of them are named directly after Carrion Crows I have assumed they refer to the lookout on a ship's mast and have ignored them. Nor is a near-relative of the Carrion Crow, a Rook, commemorated in *The Rook and Gaskill* on Lawrence Street in my home city of York. Peter Rook and Leonard Gaskill were hanged for sheep rustling on St Leonard's Gallows nearby on 1 May 1776; they were the last two men to be executed in York[1.11].

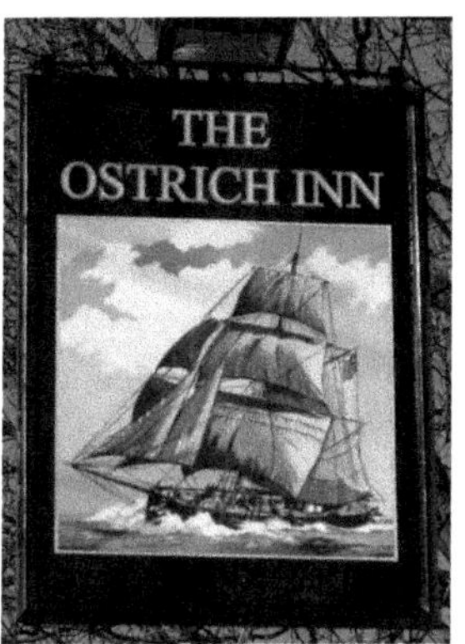

The Ostrich Inn, Bristol

Some non-bird pubs come close. There are two called *The Grouse and Claret*, one in Rowsey on the edge of the Peak District and the other at Heatheryford in Kinross. So, the habitat is right. Except a grouse and claret is wet fishing fly used to hook Trout and Sea Trout, but it does

The Crow's Nest, Hull

(I am told) have 'wings' made from the tail feathers of a Red Grouse. *The Merlin* in Swindon isn't named after a small Falcon; the sign has Merlin the wizard on it. Nor can you always assume that a pub called *The Cock and Bottle* (there are several, including one in York and one in Skipton, North Yorkshire) is named after a Cockerel; it can signify that a pub sold both draft and bottled beer, the "cock" being another name for the spigot on a beer barrel[1.12]. Alternative origins for the name include "Cock Ale" which was "popular throughout England in the sixteenth century"[1.13] and was a type of beer flavoured with spices and chicken. Not my cup of tea. The signwriters or the landlord of the pubs in York and Skipton appear to have preferred a bird over a spigot, and their signs now show a hansom Cockerel (Skipton) and a Cockerel's head on a wine bottle label (York).

Cock and Bottle, York

The great W.B. Alexander[1.2] had the same kind of problem. For example, he thought the *Blue Cap* near Northwich in Cheshire may be a Blue Tit, "but Mr. A.W. Boyd informs me that it actually commemorates a celebrated hound". In similar vein, Richard Fitter included *The Harriers* (plural) in Witney (Oxfordshire) which is much more likely to refer to either cross-country runners or a breed of dog than to a flock of Hen or Marsh Harriers (which Alexander did realise[1.19]).

Riverside, Saltford (Wood Duck)

Pitfall 2: The Name Doesn't Apparently Relate to a Bird

The opposite is also true: a pub can have a name that is apparently nothing to do with birds, but the pub sign has a bird on it. I've already mentioned *The George* at Cley with a stylised Brent Goose on its sign. Others include the *Riverside* near Bath (Wood Duck), *The Scolt Head* in London (Oystercatcher) and *The Leaking Tap* near Shrewsbury (Carrion Crow).

The most difficult pub in this category is *The Live and Let Live* in Pegston (Bedfordshire) which used to have a Hobby (a type of Falcon) and a Dove on its sign, a photo of which was sent to me by my birding colleague Jono Leadley. Hobbies are one of the fastest Falcons in the world. They specialise in catching dragonflies, Swifts, Swallows and House Martins on the wing and they may be capable of catching a Dove, although neither Pigeons nor Doves are listed as prey in standard ornithological references. On the sign the two birds were shown peaceably coexisting on what looks like a bird table, reflecting the sentiment in the pub's name. I say "were" because Jono's photograph is undated. The pub changed hands in 2016 and when I Googled it in 2021 the sign was birdless. I have included it in the database on the assumption that it probably existed in 2010. Inevitably I have had to make similar assumptions about other pub birds, whilst erring on the side of caution.

The Leaking Tap, Cockshot (Carrion Crow)

Where I have seen the pub sign, either in reality or virtually, and the bird is clearly identifiable, it takes precedence over the name. If the pub only has a bird's name and no sign[1.14] I've been pragmatic and just accepted it, though sometimes even that can be a bit tricky.

The Pyewipe in Saxilby just outside Lincoln has no sign and doesn't obviously refer to a bird, unless you know that this is one of many vernacular names for a Lapwing[1.15]. In Norfolk there are two pubs called *The Harnser,* which is local dialect for Grey Heron[1.15], one in Stalham on the edge of the Broads (with a sign, which in this case is how I first identified it) and the other without a sign in Cley overlooking Cley Marshes and the famous windmill. "Nest" gives the game away for *The Spink's Nest* in Huddersfield: "Spink" is an onomatopoeic vernacular name for a Chaffinch, based on its call[1.15].

For a time I had no idea what a Hauser is (or was). Hyde-Parker[1.4] says: "One Broadland village I know possesses both *The Hauser* and *The Grebe.*" That's presumably Stalham and I have assumed that '*Hauser*' is a misprint for *Harnser*, and that *The Grebe* refers to a Great Crested Grebe (Chapter 3).

I will have undoubtedly overlooked other pub birds named in the vernacular, and pub birds named in Welsh or Gallic will have definitely been missed. *The Gockett*, three miles south of Monmouth, apparently had a fine portrait of a Black Grouse on its sign. "Gockett" is possibly an old Welsh name for Black Grouse (although this is not the Welsh name for this species in *Birds Britannica*)[1.16]. Whatever, the pub closed in 2003 so it isn't in the database.

W.B. Alexander[1.2] also recognised that vernacular names could be a problem, specifically mentioning the *Blue Back* in Warrington (Cheshire) "but Mr. Boyd assures me it is the local name for the Fieldfare", a large, handsome winter visitor related to Thrushes and Blackbirds. The pub was demolished in the redevelopment of Warrington town centre in the 1970s and 80s. (There is still a pub in Chorley, Lancashire called the *Fieldfare* and another in Postwick, near Norwich. Neither appears to have a sign.) Other vernacular names that caused Alexander some problems included *Iron Devils*, said to be a corruption of the French Hirondelles (Swallows) – doubly difficult to spot and now closed; and *Spink's Nest* (which as we have seen still exists) and *Yutick's Nest* (Whinchat) in Blackburn, which doesn't.

The Sign has Priority over the Name

Giving the bird on the sign priority has consequences. It means that a pub with a name unrelated to birds can still be classified as a pub bird if its portrait is on the sign, and that if a pub is named after a bird but the sign is a different species, the sign again takes priority. For example, the *Tawny Owl* in Hurworth Moor near Darlington has an Owl on its sign, but it isn't a Tawny Owl because it has conspicuous, slightly floppy 'ears'; if the picture were better, it might be identifiable as an Eagle Owl. And the signs for the *Falcon* (in York) and the *Falcon Inn* (in Prudhoe, County Durham) are not Falcons at all but some sort of unidentifiable larger Eagle, or in the case of *The Old Falcon* in Driffield, East Yorkshire, a stylised North American Bald Eagle. It looks like the Driffield sign may have been copied from that of another pub just around the corner called the *Spread Eagle*, which is clearly a Bald Eagle.

The Old Falcon, Driffield

I have had to be pragmatic about names such as *Swan* or *White Swan* (a very large number of pubs[1.10]), or *Dog and Partridge*[1.9], where I have not actually seen numerous examples of the pubs named after either species. Others don't have a sign anyway. For these and other similar examples I have assumed that they refer to Mute Swans and Grey Partridges respectively, ruling out rarer or less likely relatives (Whooper Swans or Red-legged Partridges for example). Most do, but some may not. Similar remarks apply to other species with rarer or less likely relatives, unless there is clear evidence to the contrary. For example, I have assumed that two pubs called *The Sparrow* (in Ansty near Coventry and in Bradford, West Yorkshire) are House Sparrows and not Tree Sparrows or even Hedge Sparrows (Dunnocks), whilst the *Black Sparrow* in Glasgow (with a sign depicting a black, cartoon-like, dishevelled small bird) is classified as an unidentified 'kind of bird'. But *The Lamb and Lark* in Limington near Yeovil is not a reference to a Skylark (the most likely species) but has an accurate representation of a Woodlark on the inn sign (p. 83).

Spread Eagle, Driffield

Black Sparrow, Glasgow

If these self-imposed rules strike you as odd or unnecessarily restrictive, all I would say is that most birders who make lists have their own rules for the real birds they encounter. For instance, if you are on the road outside your house and not in the garden when a new bird flies over, you can't put it on your garden list (unless you are fast on your feet). For lists more generally, some birders only count species they have seen; others tick hard-to-see species they identify by call. I fall into the latter group, with a small number of 'heard-but-not-seen' on my life list. On one memorable occasion I was on Tiritiri Matangi Island just off Auckland in New Zealand. Introduced rats, stoats, foxes and cats have played havoc with New Zealand's birds and many only now survive on offshore islands such as Tiritiri Matangi that lack alien predators. The island is host to Spotless Crakes (somewhere between European Spotted and Little Crakes in size and just as hard or even harder to see). A New Zealand birding friend and I stood about a yard apart whilst a Spotless

Crake called loudly from a grass tussock between our feet. Somehow it disappeared without us seeing it. But it's on my life list, and we celebrated hearing it when we got back to Auckland by going to a pub.

Pub Closures and Name Changes

It would be impossible to explore and document the names of the thousands of pubs that have closed their doors since the 17th century or changed their names (sometimes multiple times). Several of the pubs included here are now closed, but were open in 2010 and closed or changed their name before late 2021. And early estimates of the impact of the 2020–2021 Covid-19 pandemic suggest that as many as 2,500 pubs may have closed permanently because of it. The potential list is also dynamic for the opposite reason: new pubs get built and named after birds, or older pubs have their names changed to that of a bird. In other words, there is no simple static list to be discovered, however thorough I have tried to be.

To drive home the point of the sheer impossibility of taking into account all the pubs that have closed or changed their names, take two examples, one anecdotal, the second drawing on a local but quite large database.

Of the four pub birds sent to me by Charles Gallimore, *The Kingfisher* used to be called *The Karozzin* and he thinks possibly *The Plough* before that, and anyway it is now closed. *The Cuckoo* had been so named since 1860 but was originally *The Red Lion* and then the *Noel Arms* (or perhaps the other way around; I'm not sure) but is now also closed. *The Old Pheasant* used to be called *The Monkton Arms* and is the only one that is still in business (or was in 2020).

Four years after I started to collect pub birds I came across a little book called *The Old Inns and Inn Signs of York*[1.12], published in 1897. It cost two shillings and six pence in 'old money', or roughly 12.5p in decimal currency; it cost me £5 in 2014, which I regard as a bargain. At the back of the book are two appendices: 'Past Hotels, Inns and Taverns' in York that had closed or their signs had "disappeared since the beginning of this century", i.e. just three years short of the entire 1800s; and 'Present Hotels, Inns and Taverns, etc.' Both lists give their current (or last) name and earlier names. There are 232 'extant' pubs, 13 of them named after birds (or 5.6% – slightly higher than my 4.5%), and of these, 58 used to be called something else, some with more than one change of name. Many of these no longer exist. I have not attempted to count how many still do, but it is way fewer than 232. What we do know is that 112 York pubs that existed at the start of the 19th century had disappeared by the end (five of these were pub birds or 4.5% – exactly the same as my modern 'random' sample[1.8]) and, again, that there are a lot of name changes.

Alternatively, look at the changes to the names of the pubs in York that were in existence in 1897. There are pubs that started off being called something else but which metamorphosed into a pub bird: The *Labour in Vain* became *The Phoenix* (a mythical bird, of which more in Chapter 4), which still exists; the *Ruben's Head* became the *Eagle and Child* (now gone); and the *Bricklayer's Arms* was renamed the *Spread Eagle* (which also survives). One pub bird became something else: a *Black Swan* on the Hull Road became, and still is, the *Bee's Wing*, which happens to be another racehorse. And the *Magpie and Stump* had its name shortened to just plain *Magpie*, before it too was closed. Even in one small northern city, it would be very difficult to incorporate all these changes and losses into a sensible, comprehensive list, and quite impossible at a national scale. So I haven't tried.

However, if (largely by chance) I do know that a pub that existed in 2010 and later permanently closed some time before I finished writing this book in 2021, I will say so.

Changes to Signs

Not only do pubs change their names or close, but their signs can also change. Much of the research for this book has been done on the web and a pub's website can have several different images of a bird on it, usually undated. As we shall see, some even metamorphose from one species to another. All I can say is that whatever I say about the bird's identity or however I describe the sign or illustrate it, it existed in this form sometime between 2010 and 2021. It may not be like that now.

Back to W.B. Alexander

W.B. Alexander was one of three birdwatching brothers born in England towards the end of the 19th century. Christopher was killed in Flanders in the First World War, Wilfrid Blackhouse Alexander was born in 1885 and his younger brother Horace Gundry four years later. The latter two are almost always identified individually as W.B. and

H.G. Their pioneering contributions to ornithology were enormous. This brief summary of W.B.'s life is taken from a book by H.G. and W.B.'s obituary[1.17].

After an early career working abroad, primarily in Australia, both as an entomologist and an ornithologist, W.B. Alexander was appointed director of the Oxford Bird Census in 1930. The Census became the Edward Grey Institute of Field Ornithology (EGI) in 1938, via two re-christenings: Oxford University Research in Economic Ornithology in 1931, and the Institute of Field Ornithology funded by the newly formed British Trust for Ornithology in 1933. He retired as director of the EGI in 1945 to take up the post of its librarian, where he remained until 1955. His personal bird books formed the original nucleus of the library that was named after him in 1947. I like to think (but have no evidence) that once he retired as director he took up pub birding. If so, he accumulated the list in less than ten years.

His list is both impressive and at first glance puzzling. It is impressive because in his words: "For some time past, with the assistance of numerous friends, I have been collecting information about inns and hotels named after birds, and now have a list of over a thousand." That is roughly one-and-a-half times the number of pubs I have, without anything remotely as efficient as Google. But the puzzle is that in a much larger sample of pub birds than I have been able to accumulate, he has far fewer species. He summarises "the complete list of birds named on inn-signs known to me at present" at the end of the paper. There are just 62, including both identifiable species and non-specific groups of species such as Owls, Geese and Parrots. That compares with 117 identifiable species and 17 non-specific groups of species on my list. Why did he only find half the species that I have ticked, when his sample of pub birds is significantly larger than mine? It has nothing to do with the fact that he explicitly did not include mythical species, feathers and apparently not eggs, birdcages etc., which only add another 25 pubs to my list (excluding ten *Bird in Hand* pubs in my core database). Rather, Alexander did not have the benefits of Google, which allowed me to make targeted searches of specific bird names. He had to rely on haphazard discoveries by colleagues and himself, so he accumulated numerous examples of commoner species and missed many rarer ones.

One of the curious features of these 'missing species' are some seabirds. Curious because among his many accomplishments he was a world authority on seabirds and I might have expected his correspondents to have been aware of his interests. In 1926 he spent most of the year in the American Museum of Natural History preparing his pioneering book on the world's seabirds[1.18], a forerunner of modern field guides. The seabirds on his pub list number just two, namely Gull or Seagull, and Kittiwake. The seabird pubs on my list do include *The Gull Inn* in Framlington Pigot, Norfolk, *The Gulls Nest* in Edinburgh, *The Seagull* in Abergele, North Wales and *The Kittiwake* in Whitley Bay, Co. Durham, some or all of which may be the same pubs that Alexander had on his list. But he missed *The Stormy Petrel* in Market Drayton, Staffordshire (sadly now demolished), *The Cormorant* (Portchester, Hampshire), the delightfully named *Pig and Puffin* near Tenby (this one in south-west Wales, and now also closed), and two *Seabirds,* both on the Yorkshire coast in Bridlington and Flamborough respectively. They are quite old, and must have existed in the late 1940s and 1950s.

He does have five species on his list that I do not: non-specific Harriers (some of which he admits could refer to "hounds"[1.19], but one is definitely a Hen Harrier), Quail, Condor and Whinchat (as the vernacular *Yutick*). None of these seem still to exist.

He lists his pub birds "beginning with the commonest". From that perspective his and my lists are broadly similar, and I consider the most abundant pub birds (i.e. the species or types of birds appearing most frequently in the name of a pub) in Chapter 2. Alexander is also intrigued by several characteristics of pub birds which had also occurred to me quite independently (I only became aware of his paper in 2020[1.2], after my article in *British Birds* was published[1.7]). Our shared insights include the varied origins for the names of pub birds, for instance those located in appropriate habitats or geographical regions; birds from the heraldic devices of wealthy or notable local families, royalty or medieval guilds; sporting interest (i.e. killing things); religious symbolism; and puns and other plays on words. I discuss these and other sources of the names of pub birds in later chapters.

The Seabirds Bridlington

The Red Kite, Winlaton Mill

Alexander noticed two things that I had not. First there are differences in the frequency of pubs named after birds in different parts of the UK, which I will discuss in Chapter 3. The second is his comment "that birds never seem to be red, since this is a common colour for sign-board animals: bears, bulls, cats, cows, deer, dogs, foxes and horses may all be red, and *The Red Lion* is one of the commonest signs." *Red Lion* is currently the commonest name for a pub in the UK according to the Pubs Galore website[1.9] (555 pubs). Alexander clearly had in mind creatures that are not naturally red in real life, so that would exclude Red Kites, which are red(ish). There are several Red Kite pubs, including *The Red Kite* with a splendid 'cut-out' figure of a Kite on its sign at Winlaton Mill, Blaydon on Tyne. *The Red Hawk* in Brough, East Yorkshire appears currently to be a Red Arrow display jet manufactured by BAe systems at their factory in the town, although a correspondent (Erich Hediger) tells me that for a time the inn sign was of a Red Kite. *The Red Hawk* in St Ives just has a name, so it is impossible to know what it is.

Richard Fitter

Richard Fitter's short article[1.3] was published in 1955, at least a year after Alexander's paper appeared, and yet he doesn't explicitly cite it. However, his article is a good synopsis of Alexander's paper and covers much the same ground. He does say: "There are many queer hobbies in the world. But I have only ever met one person who had mine…and he got the idea from me." Fitter started listing pub birds during a car journey on 18 November 1940, whilst on a birding trip between London and Tring Reservoirs "during the second winter of the [second world] war, as a kind of light relief from the somewhat grim preoccupations of those days". He admits "I am a born collectomane, and a new hobby was born".

Richard Fitter was not a professional ornithologist like W.B. Alexander. He was an all-round naturalist with a special interest in British plants and birds. His *London's Natural History* was published at the end of the war[1.20]. It is a tour de force spanning the geology, geomorphology and pre- and post-Roman history of London as well as detailed accounts of its plants, animals and people. Among its many unique contributions is Appendix F, a "List of Flowering Plants and Ferns Recorded from Bombed Sites in London". Appendix B is a scholarly summary of "The Birds of the London Area". It has some mouth-watering entries (at least for other birders) of species now long lost to 'development'. With R.A. Richardson he pioneered a totally new approach to bird identification in two books organised not by taxonomy (pages of Ducks, pages of Finches and so on) but by habitats (land, waterside and water), body size and a bird's general appearance (e.g. "uniform brown with darker streaks, thick bill")[1.21]

Richard Fitter's son Alastair[1.3] confirms that in the small world of distinguished British naturalists and ornithologists during the Second World War and the immediate post-war years Fitter and Alexander knew one another. It therefore seems highly likely that Alexander was the one person who shared Fitter's queer hobby of collecting pub birds and that he did indeed get the idea from Fitter. The timing is right. Fitter started in 1940 and Alexander retired as director of the EGI in 1945. At some point after 1940 when Fitter started his new hobby the two men must have met, leading to Alexander joining the club.

"In the intervening 14 years or so", between 1940 and 1954, Fitter "amassed a collection of several hundred names of inns based on birds." Unlike my list (and W.B. Alexander's), he had to have seen the sign or name himself, but of course he didn't have the means of seeing it on the web. In total he "listed some 38 different British birds' names", far fewer than his 'pupil', but covering much the same ground as Alexander. Unlike Alexander, Fitter did include (as I have done) bird-related objects such as feathers, birdcages and so on, as well as mythical species, which Alexander ignored. Alexander looks from his portrait to have been a rather austere figure, but quipped "I do not count *Angels*, though they conform to the well-known definition of a bird as a feathered biped." I don't count angels; Fitter did, and called them "honorary birds". But these are minor details. They make little or no difference to the big picture.

T. Hyde-Parker

Compared with Alexander's paper and Fitter's short article, Hyde-Parker's[1.4] 1940 effort is lightweight. Like Alexander, Hyde-Parker does identify pub birds in appropriate localities, others derived from heraldry, religious symbolism and so on, and he has some literary allusions that Alexander doesn't make. But his own description refers to it as "rambling remarks" adding "Needless to say, the foregoing makes no pretension to completeness, and readers could probably add many further examples which I have either omitted or never even heard of." I can only agree. If nothing else, his short paper reaffirms how many of the pubs he mentions can no longer be traced.

Pub Birds and the Scientific Method

I'm a scientist. For readers who are not, you may regard science as a huge body of 'facts' about the world, crammed into very thick books. Well, it is that, and I have used the information in two wonderful books to underpin this one[1.22 & 1.23]. But as much as science is about reliable information it is also about a way of working and thinking. The nearer you get to new areas the less certain the facts become, and ideas (hypotheses and theories) about the way the world works are much more important. Science progresses by showing that an idea is wrong and suggesting a better one, only for that one to be rejected until a consensus gradually emerges. I am not saying that *Inn Search of Birds* is serious science. It isn't. But I have approached it using the scientific method, with numerous possible explanations (hypotheses if you like) about how pubs acquired their names and/or histories, with frequent admissions that things are unclear (at least to me) or that I do not know. But for many (even most) of these, somebody must know another or better explanation and can show that I am wrong. Good. That way the story of pub birds and their pubs and publicans will only improve and grow. So, think of the book as work in progress.

In Praise of Pub Birds

Technical stuff aside, pub birds are fun. Whilst I want to be as accurate and informative as possible, this book is not meant to be too serious. Whilst 'plain vanilla' Swans get boring, the *Swan and Cemetery* (in Bury), the *Swan and Railway* (in Wigan) and three pubs called *The Swan with Two Necks* (in Bristol, Clitheroe and Wakefield) cry out for an explanation, as do two Welsh pubs called *The Goose and Cuckoo*, in Llanover (Monmouthshire) and Llangadog (Carmarthenshire) respectively.

Some pub birds changed their identity between 2010 and 2021. We have already encountered *The Gull Inn* at Framingham Pigot in Norfolk. When I first 'ticked' it in September 2011 the Gull on the sign had olive-green legs, feet and bill and looked more like the middle-sized and quite delicate Common Gull than anything else. In May 2019 it had transformed into a rather stylised, much larger, thuggish, ice-cream stealing Herring Gull sort of bird. There are several others that have transformed from one species to another, which we will encounter later.

The old and new signs for The Gull Inn, Framington Pigot

A few pubs have amusing names, or names that are a play on words. I wonder if the *Night-jar Bar* in Hebden Bridge (West Yorkshire) or *The Swallow* between Grimsby and Lincoln are meant to be puns? We shall see. But more often than I would like with such names I have had limited or even no success in explaining them[1.7]. Asking the person behind the bar too often generates an unhelpful shrug of the shoulders, and if you Google almost any pub name you get an avalanche of photographs of food, drink and happy customers, but typically nothing about how the pub got its name or history. So, the six chapters that follow are an attempt to summarise what we do (and do not) know about pub birds and the pubs that bear their names.

Chapter 2 deals with 13 of the commonest pub birds. (You will see why it is 13 when we get to it.) For the pubs in my core database (Appendix 2), just over half (353 from a total of 676) are named after one of these 13 identifiable species or kinds of birds. (Including 'bird-related' things such as feathers and 'bird paraphernalia' reduces the proportion to just under half – 353 out of 711 pubs.) Chapter 2 tries to identify what makes these 13 species so dominant as pub birds and explores their natural and cultural histories.

Chapter 3 focuses primarily on the geography of pub birds, but starts with history – how old are the oldest, and what kinds of birds they are. Among these old pubs are claims to be the oldest in the country when clearly they are not. The geography of pub birds is intriguing and confirms W.B. Alexander's and Richard Fitter's observations that pubs in large parts of northern and western Britain are rarely named after birds. The chapter also explores how pubs play an important role in giving us a sense of place. Bob Holt, a birding and work colleague, has invented a new, potentially competitive birding game he calls "Ticks and Tipples", which is centred on the geographic ranges of pub birds and the location of their pubs. You will find the rules at the end of the Chapter 3.

Aliens, foreigners and mythical pub birds are the subjects of Chapter 4. To put it bluntly, we don't much favour funny foreigners on our pub signs. There are a few exceptions (Hens, Peacocks and Pelicans for example) but not many.

The two shortest chapters are 5 and 6, but for different reasons. Chapter 5 covers areas that I am not well qualified to deal with, namely pub birds that make an appearance in art, music and literature. Of these I probably know most about art (which is still not much). The chapter does include a 'gallery' of some of my favourite signs if they have not already appeared earlier in the book. The art of pub signs is celebrated in *Inn-Signia*[1.24], published in 1948, and it currently has a society devoted to their appreciation[1.25]. There are some very beautiful and accurate depictions of pub birds (*The Peacock* in Stepney, East London is particularly lovely p. 56). There are also some (but really not many) that leave a great deal to be desired, apparently painted by somebody who might more profitably try their hand at a different job. Tracing the sources for some of the artists can be intriguing, but I could have done with an art historian who was also a birder to help me.

Chapter 6, on nests, baby birds, feathers and 'bird paraphernalia' (birdcages and the like) is short because there are relatively few pubs named after them. Nests and baby birds are particularly scarce. They are for softies. They lack aggression; being big, bold, fierce, forceful or hunted are all characteristics of many much commoner pub birds.

Chapter 7 is one last twitch of the species we have still not encountered. It has further views on some that we have come across, including some very odd couples, and the general conclusion that most pub birds lead solitary lives.

The final chapter wraps up the story and incorporates the book's only two graphs. Only including two graphs was a real effort on my part – scientists often think of using graphs, which I know is sad, but it is also true. However, after the *British Birds* paper appeared (it had a precursor of one of the two graphs here) one of my former postgraduate students emailed me to say he loved the article but didn't understand the graph. So I have tried really, really hard to make both of them intelligible. Just don't look at them after a beer or two.

In a nutshell the book is about the where, when, what and why of pub birds. Sometimes one can only wonder "Why?" It is difficult to believe that calling a pub *The Dead Pigeon* was a good idea. But somebody did. It's in Rochester, and looks nice from the outside. I haven't been in. At least not yet.

CHAPTER 2: THE COMMONEST PUB BIRDS

Which are the commonest pub birds? Or, more precisely, which species of bird, or types of bird, feature most frequently in pub names? We have already seen that Mute Swans dominate, but by how much, and what else is up there with them? This chapter explores the natural history of the commonest pub birds, the history of some of their pubs and what they tell us about the origins of pub names.

Rankings from 1–12 in four different databases are summarised in Table 1 (those of W.B. Alexander[1.2], Steve Shaw[1.5], pubsgalore[1.9] and my own database). Suffice to say that whilst there are some puzzling differences between the lists, and differences in the protocols of the different authors, 13 species or types of bird feature in at least three of the four. Thirteen is a 'baker's dozen', not an unlucky number.

The 13 species or types of birds in alphabetical order are: Black Swans; Domesticated and Wild Ducks (Mallards), Domesticated and Wild Geese (Greylag Geese) , Doves and Pigeons, Eagles, Falcons, Magpies, Mute Swans, Partridges, Peacocks, Pheasants, Ravens and Red Junglefowl (Cockerels and Hens). These are a mixture of single species, and groups involving both unspecified species and/or several identifiable species. Eagles are a good example which I explore further below. When the 332 Eagles in Steve Shaw's list are unpacked into their constituents, none of them (specific or non-specified Eagles) are more numerous than Mute Swans.

Despite the remarkable number of pubs and species on Steve Shaw's list it has two puzzling features compared with the other three. There are only four pubs with Hen in their names, and eight with Cock (or possibly 17 if you add nine pubs called *Black Cock*, because the Grouse species of that name is usually called a Blackcock – one word). Peacocks are even more poorly represented, with just one, the *Peacock and*

Table 1

The rankings of the commonest pub birds in four different data sets. Each data set uses subtly different criteria for including a species. 'Bird-related' pub names (see Chapter 1) are not included.

	W.B. Alexander (his ranking and classification)[1]	**Steve Shaw** (all pubs with this bird in name, alone or in combination as a 'double-barrelled' name)	**Pubs Galore** (pub birds exactly as named on website)[3]	**My data**[4] (all pubs with this bird in name, alone or in combination, or sign depicts bird with this name)
1	*Swan*[2]	*Eagle (332)*	*Swan* (287)+*White Swan* (40) = 396	*Mute Swan* (124)
2	*Cock (and Hen)*	*Swan* (assume *Mute* 296)	*Eagle* (55)+ *Spread Eagle* (48) = 103	*Eagle* (44)
3	*Eagle*	*Pheasant* (148)	*Cock* (78)	*Cock, Hen* (40)
4	*Falcon*[6]	*Falcon* (123)[6]	*Black Swan* (64)[2]	*Pheasant* (29)
5	*Pheasant*	*Duck, Drake, Mallard* (120)	*Falcon* (53)	*Black Swan* (28)
6	*Peacock (and Peahen)*	*Bird in Hand* (115)[6]	*Phoenix* (50)[5]	*Falcon* (26)
7	*Raven*	*Black Swan* (114)[2]	*Bird in Hand* (48)[6]	*Duck, Mallard* (23)
8	*Duck (and Drake)*	*Partridge* (80)	*Pheasant* (47)	*Goose, Geese* (18)
9	*Magpie (and Pie or Pye)*	*Dove* (43)+ *Pigeon* (29) = 72	*Peacock* (42)	*Raven* (17)
10	*Partridge*	*Raven* (50), tied with *Goose, Gander, Geese* (50)	*Dog and Partridge* (34)	*Dove, Pigeon* (12)
11	*Dove + Pigeon*	________	*Raven* (27)	*Peacock* (12)
12	*Goose (and Gander)*	*Magpie, Pye* (44)	*Fox and Goose* (18)	*Magpie* (11), tied with *Kingfisher* and *Pelican*

1. Alexander does not say how many birds of each species or group of species there were. He appears to put them in rank order "beginning with the commonest".
2. Alexander does not appear to distinguish between Mute Swans and Black Swans, even though many pubs called *Black Swan* were in existence when he was gathering his data. Shaw includes *Black Swan* among his compilation of Swans in general, but he does clearly identify them as two entries (*Black Swan* 113 and *Old Black Swan* 1); whether any others lie hidden in his overall list of Swans is unclear.
3. Data collected from the web in October 2020; the site is continually updated. Pub birds in other forms (e.g. *Swan and 'Something'*) are not included, so if pubs are named after a species but in a different format they will not be counted, making the Pubs Galore data minima for each species.
4. As explained in Chapter 1, I have made no attempt to produce comprehensive lists of the commonest pub birds.
5. W.B. Alexander and Steve Shaw do not include mythical species in their lists. I have recorded them, but they do not make it into my most common list.
6. Pubs Galore lists *Bird in Hand* as a separate category. W.B. Alexander explicitly says, "*Bird in Hand* is commonly represented as a hooded falcon on a gauntlet", and he appears to have included these under Falcon. Shaw lists *Falcon* and *Bird in Hand* separately. However, the falconer's bird can also be an Eagle, and some (as we shall see later) may not be a bird of prey at all. I have chosen to discuss pubs called *Bird in Hand* under *Falcon* later in this chapter.

Magpie, which was closed when Shaw added it to his list. It is difficult to understand how he missed so many other Cocks, Hens and Peacocks. For completeness, readers may have noticed that I have not included Richard Fitter's short article[1.3] in these preliminary analyses because he does not provide enough numerical information. But he does include "Cocks" as one of the commonest birds on his list and says that *Hen and Chickens* are also "not uncommon". He is silent about Peacocks.

Pubs, Inns, Taverns, Hotels and Bars

Before getting back to the commonest pub birds, I want to take a short diversion to explore the origins of pub names in general, not just those named after birds, starting with the difference between just a plain old "pub" (or "public house"), an "inn", a "tavern" and a "hotel". No, that's not a joke. You can find the answer in Albert Jack's book[1.13] about the names of pubs. They are all public houses, which means they are not private drinking holes or clubs, but are open to anybody (during opening hours, above a certain age and sober-ish) to walk in and buy a drink. Most pubs just have a name, and do not carry the epithet "Inn" or "Tavern". But where they do "An inn differed from a tavern in that it was usually located along the ever-growing road network, providing overnight accommodation, food and shelter for travellers." That is, they were coaching inns and tended to be a bit posher than a tavern. Hotels were grander still, often with longer licensing hours and catering for long-distance travellers arriving and departing any time of the day or night. But as Jack nicely puts it: "Many early pubs labelled themselves hotels simply to benefit from the more lenient [licensing] laws. Calling itself a hotel gave a pub the legal right to open for business on the Sabbath, even if the only real place it provided for sleeping was face down in the beer garden."

The ubiquitous Mute Swan illustrates the frequency of just a simple pub name, versus those with the epithet "Inn", "Tavern" or "Hotel". In my sample of the 124 pubs named after Mute Swans 39 are inns (32%); among them is *The Swan Inn* in Clare (Suffolk) with a gloriously carved medieval inn sign of a Swan with a golden ring around its neck in the form of a crown, reputed to be the oldest carved inn sign in Britain[1.22]. Another five (4%) are hotels and just three (2.4%) are taverns. Black Swans are similar. Twenty-six are just plain *Black Swan*, two in North Yorkshire are hotels and one (in Culgaith near Penrith) is an inn. Curiously, but for no obvious reason (except perhaps just small sample sizes and chance) Red and Black Grouse are exceptions. All three Red Grouse pubs in my database are inns (the *Moorcock Inn* in Upper Wensleydale (p. 74), and two *Grouse Inns*, one on the edge of, and the other in, the Peak District National Park) and both Black Grouse pubs are inns (*The Blackcock Inn* just below the Kielder Reservoir in Northumberland (p. 75) and another *Moorcock Inn*, this one in Middleton-in-Teesdale). I will return to the identity of Moorcocks later, because it isn't simple[1.22] and Moorcock has been used both for Red and Black Grouse; as explained in Chapter 1, it is the identity of the bird on the sign that matters.

Some modern inns can also provide exceptions because they were never coaching inns. *The Woodpecker Inn* at Washwater near Newbury in Berkshire was renamed in the 1970s, having started life as the *Derby Arms*. The century-old pub was originally a cider house, and the inn sign now carries a picture of a Green Woodpecker, the logo for Bulmers Cider. The pub's website, incidentally, has a Great Spotted Woodpecker on it, so I guess that their marketing team are not birders and that one Woodpecker looks pretty much like any other, just a different colour.

For no other reason than to vary the text I have referred to pub-bird signs as either "pub signs" or "inn signs" indiscriminately, whether the hostelry is a pub, an inn, a hotel or a bar.

Albert Jack doesn't mention "bars", which tend to be public houses in urban areas and some more remote rural parts of the country. The name is particularly frequent in Scotland. At the end of Chapter 1 I mentioned *The*

The Swan, York

The Swan Inn, Morton in Marsh

The Swan Inn, Seaton, Hornsey

White Swan Hotel, Alnwick

Nightjar Bar, and individual pubs named after birds sometimes advertise themselves as a bar. They are included on my list, but I have not counted cocktail bars.

Finally, Eagles enjoy a unique additional kind of premises – vaults. There are (or were) three of them. The two *Eagle Vaults*, in Witney (Oxfordshire) and Liverpool, respectively, are permanently closed; the one in Worcester (West Midlands) survives and has a Golden Eagle on its sign. A vault can be a cellar, burial chamber, a strongroom or some other form of underground room, or a roof or ceiling in a normal room. Why Eagles and no other pub bird should inhabit any of these structures is a mystery.

During the survey period between 2010 and 2021 new public houses began to open styling themselves as "microbreweries", "café-bar kitchens" or similar: they were small, sometimes very small, and often delightful niche pubs selling specialist beers and other beverages and good food. Several are named after birds, but they can be a bit of a grey area. In general, I have treated them as pubs, not least because CAMRA[2.1] does. Examples include *The Starling* in Harrogate (North Yorkshire) and an *Owl and Pussycat* in Northfields, London. It's good to know that *The Dodo* micropub (p. 118) in Hanwell (also London) which opened in 2017 is not extinct.

A Brief History of the Origin of Pub Names

From at least the end of the 14th century (during the reign of Richard II in 1393) the law of the land in Great Britain compelled every publican to display a sign advertising his (and it usually was "his") pub[2.2]. There is a record of a landlord in 1393 being in trouble from the authorities for not showing the required sign[1.24]. There were no pubs or inns in the modern sense of the word in Roman or Anglo-Saxon times, although the good citizens of these islands certainly drank alcohol, and the Latin *taberna* gives us "tavern". When the *taberna* was fully stocked with wine, some grapes would be hung outside the building as an advertisement[1.13], the apparent origin of pub signs. By the 12th century naming public houses was common, and their signs were frequently actual objects (such as grapes) rather than pictures; with a largely illiterate population there was no point in having a written name. Some of these actual objects hung from poles and posts, 'ale stakes' projecting from a building, or carved on a wall still survive as pub names in the modern world[1.24]. They include, as well as *Grapes*, numerous pubs called *Plough, Copper Kettle, Boot and Shoe, Bush, Hollybush* and *Bull and Bush*. I am unclear whether any *Bulls, Cows, Horses* or *Bears* were living animals and whether any were living pub birds (at least I can find no documentary evidence to this effect, although it seems likely that some were). However, there is one remarkable exception, the *George and Vulture* in Castle Court, Cornhill in the heart of London. But that story comes later (Chapter 3).

Great ingenuity and creativity went into the signs selected, to make a pub stand out from the crowd with a local identity that was easy to remember and that indicated "good cheer". The origins of some kinds of pub names[1.12, 1.24] can never be applied to a bird: famous people (for instance *The Lord Nelson*) cannot feature among pub birds. But there are many other sources that can and do. They include:

- birds on the coats of arms and badges of royalty, the great and good, livery companies and guilds, and other crests and heraldic devices
- religious symbols
- falconry, usually as some variant of *Bird in Hand*, which is often (but not always) a Falcon.

Specifically named birds or types of bird can be associated with:

- hunting and shooting
- cockfighting
- local landmarks, habitats and places
- art and literature
- plays on words and other types of humour
- some modern pub chains also name their pubs after birds, for no other apparent reason than the names are catchy and often unique. The names of some older pubs also appear to have been chosen to make them memorable.

Pub birds may be so named for more than one of these reasons. If we work through the names of the commonest pub birds we can find numerous examples of most, but not all, of these reasons.

'Double-barrelled' names are common and have several potential origins, most frequently when two formerly separate establishments merged into one. Alternatively, the name could be taken from the heraldic device of a local dignitary, which may involve two species[1.24]. And there are other explanations, although sometimes it is impossible to find any reason other than somebody thought it was a good idea. There is even one 'triple-barrelled' name (the *Bush, Blackbird and Thrush* in East Peckham, Kent), with only a partial possible explanation for its origin (Chapter 3).

The rest of this chapter explores what the commonest pub birds tell us about the origins of pub names, the history of some of their pubs and aspects of the natural history of the birds. I will work through them according to their order in my database.

Mute Swan

What makes Mute Swans *the* bird of first choice on pub signs? I think it is a combination of several things[1.22]. They are huge (one of the largest flying birds in the world) and extremely beautiful but also brutally strong, capable of killing or doing serious damage to rival Swans and pets with a blow from their wings. That is impressive enough, but uniquely they are royal birds that historically belonged to the king or queen (and their favoured subjects) and semi-domesticated for the table[2.3]. No other wild UK species of bird has ever been owned by royalty (which is why this is not one of the general criteria given for attributing names to pubs). Being royal gives a huge boost to your CV. For this reason Mute Swans also feature prominently on the coats of arms and crests of the great and the good. Any pub sign featuring a Mute Swan would be easily identified and remembered. It does not seem to have been a disadvantage to have so many of them; it hardly makes any pub called *Swan* or *White Swan* (Table 1) stand out from the crowd. Nor can many be named to give a sense of place. Although there are numerous Swan pubs along rivers and canals, there are just as many if not more nowhere near water.

Swan Inn, Stalham

The White Swan, Fence

Mute Swans were semi-domesticated and managed for the table from at least the

15th century under 'swan laws' dating from 1482, but much earlier statutes probably existed to control their ownership, management and exploitation. From the 16th century onwards Mute Swan cygnets were caught and marked to signify ownership, primarily with notches, brands or other marks cut into the upper mandibles. By the reign of Elizabeth I there were at least 900 such registered marks in Britain. The tradition of catching and marking Swans, known as 'swan upping', continues annually to this day during the third week in July, on the River Thames between Sunbury-on-Thames and Abingdon[1.22]. The Swans are now only ringed, not mildly mutilated, and their ownership is divided equally between the crown and two livery companies (which are direct descendants of medieval trade guilds), the Vintners and the Dyers. Swan upping was and is carried out by teams known as 'swan uppers'; *The Old Swan Uppers* pub in Cookham Rise, north of Maidenhead on the Thames, celebrates the tradition. It currently has a flying Mute Swan on its sign.

Swan upping is a curious expression and I have always assumed it is derived from the same linguistic roots as rounding *up* cattle and sheep. But apparently not. My *Collins English Dictionary* tells me it is derived from a two-letter 16th-century word that looks vaguely like a U and a P and which means "to catch and mark swans". Swan upping also gives us the names of at least four more pub birds. *The Swan with Two Nicks* (in its bill) in Worcester is correctly named. The Vintners had business connections with taverns and hostelries around the country and "Two Nicks" as a name on a pub sign advertised their wine. But the names of two other pubs have been corrupted over time to the very strange *The Swan with Two Necks* in Pendleton near Clitheroe and in Wakefield[2.4]. A third *Swan with Two Necks* on Little Ann Street in Bristol is even stranger. It shows a pair of Mute Swans with necks entwined on one side of the sign and a pair of Black Swans on the other (though they look more like two black Mute Swans than real Black Swans – see Chapter 5). If they are meant to be Mute Swans and Black Swans it would be a rare example of one pub contributing two pub birds. Swans with two nicks or necks are of course memorable and undoubtedly make the pubs stand out from the crowd.

Swan upping is not just an eccentric tradition. The long-term data on Mute Swan numbers on the Thames is an invaluable time-series on the health of the population and revealed a dramatic decline in numbers between about 1960 and 1980. Post-mortem examination of

94 dead Swans from the Thames towards the end of this period showed that 57% had died from lead poisoning[2.5], with the lead derived from the lead weights used by anglers. The use of lead weights has since been banned and Swan numbers have recovered.

Their semi-domestication and royal ownership have led some authors to question whether Mute Swans are genuinely wild birds in Britain, but the evidence is unequivocal[2.6], with archaeological records stretching back to the late-Glacial, late-Pleistocene-Holocene and Mesolithic periods. There are both Roman and Anglo-Scandinavian records from York. However, that such a huge, edible bird survived at all to the present day in Britain may well be because of the protection proffered by royal ownership and semi-domestication.

The core of the Mute Swan's world range is in the Western Palaearctic, but many of the populations in mainland Europe owe their current existence to human introductions. They have also been introduced (with varying success) to Japan, South Africa, Canada, the USA, Australia and New Zealand[2.7]. They are only tenuously established in Australia. The Black Swans imported into the UK from Australia are similarly also only tenuously established as a self-sustaining population here (see later this chapter).

Mute Swans are a common feature on coats of arms and other insignia, from where they may be transferred to the name of a pub, not least in an attempt by the landlord to honour, flatter or curry favour from a local dignitary. "The insignia of royalty, the badges of nobility, the arms of countries, the heraldic devices of cities, livery companies and guilds – the innkeeper has ransacked them all to find an attractive sign to make his house known to customers."[1.24] Swans featured on the crests and badges of many Lancastrians (descendants and supporters of John of Gaunt, Duke of Lancaster), and doubtless gave rise to the names of some pubs in the north of England, although I cannot find specific examples from that part of the world[2.8]. I long puzzled over The *Swan and Talbot* in Wetherby (North Yorkshire), which I discovered early in my search for pub birds. A Talbot is an extinct breed of large, white hunting dog, said to have been brought here by William the Conqueror (and on its own is not an uncommon name for a pub). The *Swan and Talbot* dates from the 17th century and was originally called *The Dog and Swan*. The pub was later upgraded by it being allowed to bear the coat of arms of the Swann family, who lived at the nearby

Askham Manor; their crest shows two Mute Swans with above them a large white dog atop a helmet and visor.

Bishops' mitres are a feature of ecclesiastical heraldry and it is possible that The *Swan and Mitre* in Bromley (London) was (like The *Swan and Talbot*) taken from a coat of arms. We will revisit this pub in Chapter 7. The *Swan and Helmet* (Northampton) similarly has an heraldic ring to it, and the sign is armorial. But there is nothing on that pub's website (which describes it as a "traditional Irish pub" established in 1864) about the origin of the name. A merger of two pubs is almost certainly the explanation for the *Swan and Railway* in Wigan, but not for the *Swan and Cemetery* about 15 miles away in Bury (you wouldn't imagine that anybody is going to call a pub *The Cemetery*, but you never know). However, for once the website is informative about the origin of the name. It was a pub selling beer at least as early as 1838 when it was called *The Old Swan* and later *The Swan Inn.* The adjacent public cemetery was opened in 1869 with access immediately opposite, and the pub changed its name soon after to the *Swan and Cemetery.* However (again from the pub's website), a merger is the explanation for *The Swan and Bottle* in Uxbridge, Greater London. It is situated by the River Colne and Grand Union Canal, dates from the 17th or early 18th century and was originally two pubs, *The Olde Swan* and *The Leather Bottle.*

Whatever the origins of these 'double-barrelled' names there is no denying that they ensure the pubs stand out from the crowd.

Cockerels, Hens and Chickens (Descendants of Red Junglefowl)

On a late afternoon in mid-December 2010 Dot and I were in India, riding on the back of a 40-year-old Elephant called Lucky in the Corbett National Park at the end of a wonderful two weeks of trekking, botanising and birding in the foothills of the Himalayas. The final three days were to be spent in Corbett looking for Tigers. We heard them roar quite close to our camp, found their scats and tracks but failed to see any. However, the birding in Corbett was brilliant, particularly from the back of an Elephant where it is a bit like trying to watch seabirds from a swaying boat in a heavy swell as the huge animal walks along. But the bird's eye view you get more than makes up for it. That late afternoon and early evening I saw a bewildering variety of new birds. Three stand out: flocks of striking, red-and-black (male) and yellow-and-black (female) Scarlet Minivets about the size of a slim Song Thrush; a single male Small Niltava, an unbelievably blue Robin-sized bird with a brilliant blue forehead; and wild Hens *aka* known as Red Junglefowl. The first Junglefowls I saw were two Bantam-sized females, flushed by Lucky's enormous feet and then, just as the light was fading, a very beautiful Cockerel crossed our trail. He was about two-thirds the size of a barnyard Cockerel, bronze, gold and deep glossy blue overall, resplendent with a red comb and wattles and a graceful plume of arched, dark glossy-green tail feathers. I never imagined I would find Hens so engaging. Seeing them from the back of an Elephant probably has something to do with it.

Domestic Hens descended from Red Junglefowl somewhere in Asia, with a pedigree that extends back at least 8,000 years. Domestication may have happened more than once[1.23 & 2.9]. There is also evidence of bits of DNA in Hens derived from the closely related Grey Junglefowl, but where or how it entered their genome is uncertain[2.10]. In this domestic form, Hens are now the most numerous species of bird on the planet and humanity's primary source of animal protein. In the early years of the 20th century, for instance, the global annual consumption of chicken meat and Hens' eggs was about 90 million and 57 million tons, respectively. With a rising global human population and increasing consumer affluence, current consumption of both meat and eggs must by now be even more mind-boggling. Every year, the UK alone slaughters over one billion Hens for food[2.11]. Most of these unfortunate birds (by one recent estimate over 90%) are kept and reared in massive indoor chicken and egg factories in conditions that I personally regard as appalling. The only good thing to say about the whole factory farming industry is that the poor birds don't live very long. Nor is this the first time in history human beings have been unbelievably cruel to Hens. We have been doing it for a long time in the form of cockfighting. And it is cockfighting, not food, that captured the imagination of pub owners and landlords when choosing a name for their pub and to enhance its business.

Ye Olde Fighting Cocks, Arnside

The idea is as simple as it is cruel. Put two specially bred Cockerels together in a confined space and they will fight for dominance, sometimes to the death and almost always suffering serious injuries. Make the fight even more exciting by fitting the birds with taylor-made long, pointed (and sometime sharpened) spurs as appendages to their own hind claws (which they naturally use to attack their rival) and build an arena (a cock pit) around which spectators can sit, watch, gamble on the outcome and of course drink – preferably a lot. The result is a plethora of pubs named after either the birds or the arena and is the first of several examples of pub names that rejoice in 'sport' – killing things in plain English.

Cockfighting was made illegal in England and Wales in 1835 but not until 60 years later in Scotland[1.13]. It continued illegally, at least in England, until 1857 when (reputedly) the last cockfight took place in an old pub (still extant) with the intriguing name of the *Lion and Pheasant* in Shrewsbury (p. 66). According to contemporary accounts on the pub website about 200 birds were involved, with a large audience ready to wager on each fight. The event was broken up by the police and the promoters taken to court and fined. There appears to be no record of what happened to the poor birds.

In my own database there are 40 pubs with names derived from the domesticated descendants of Red Junglefowl. All but four of them are males. There are two called the *Hen and Chickens* (in Highbury, London (p. 153) and Longden near Shrewsbury), a single *Hen Hoose* (p. 157) in Aberdeen and the *Mole and Chicken* in Easington, Buckinghamshire (p. 171). In other words, pubs are not generally named after nice, gentle, harmless females. Among the 36 males, one is explicitly named *The Cockpit* (St Pauls in London), "fighting cocks" in various guises feature in six others[2.12], and among the remaining majority (variously called just plain *Cock*, or *Cock and 'Something'*, *'Something' and Cock*, with or without adding *Inn* or *Tavern*) the sign often depicts a fighting cock. I briefly discussed *Cock and Bottle* in Chapter 1. The *Cock and Greyhound* in Whitchurch (Shropshire) implies a double dose of betting on outcomes. *The Cock and Pye* (Ipswich, Suffolk) doesn't appear to have anything to do with cockfighting and again may well be the result of another pub merger. It is also another uncommon example of two species of pub birds ("Pye" is a vernacular name for a Magpie) depicted on one sign.

The Cockpit, St Pauls, London

Eagles

In my database Eagles (44 pubs) just outnumber Cocks and Hens (40), but the Eagles involve several identifiable species as well as generic Eagles, whilst the descendants of the Red Junglefowl constitute just the one species. In other databases (Table 1) Eagles (generic and specific) substantially outnumber Cocks and Hens. It matters little. A large number of pub birds are Eagles.

It is hardly surprising. Eagles are fantastic birds. *Birds and People*[1.23] points out that "Eagles probably feature on more flags and coats of arms than any other kind of bird". Their prominence as pub birds (as with Mute Swans) may come from two directions: the sheer power, aggression and beauty of the living bird, and their association with the coats of arms, badges and insignia of armies, royalty and the great and good. And yet, paradoxically, as *Birds and People* points out, whilst human beings are apparently besotted with the power and beauty of these magnificent birds in symbolic form, we have in the past mercilessly persecuted them, and in many parts of the world continue to do so, because we believe they kill things that we also want to kill and/or eat, for example gamebirds and lambs.

I saw my first Eagle, a Golden Eagle, soaring above Loch Dhughaill on the Isle of Skye in the Inner Hebrides. It was July 1959 and I was 15 years old and on holiday with my parents and younger brother. I can still see the huge bird in my mind's eye. It blew me away. Skye is still a great place to see Golden Eagles and in Scotland overall there are a little over 500 pairs of adults[2.13] (plus non-breeding immature birds) but there should be many more. In my lifetime they have been exterminated or greatly reduced in number over large parts of their former range in the central and eastern Highlands of Scotland by relentless illegal persecution on land dominated by Grouse moors, where they are systematically shot, trapped or poisoned. The moor owners and their gamekeepers deny it of course, but the evidence is unequivocal. A landmark report[2.14] published in 2017 showed that between 2004 and 2016 "Of 131 young eagles [satellite] tracked as many as 41 (31%)… disappeared (presumably died) under suspicious circumstances…. These disappearances occurred mainly in six areas of the Highlands (predominantly in the central and eastern Highlands)…. Some, but not all, areas managed as grouse moors were strongly associated with the disappearance of many of the tagged eagles." The report concludes that "the persecution of young eagles is supressing the...population [of eagles] in the central and eastern Highlands".

Unfortunately, the persecution of birds of prey of all kinds, not just Eagles, is still practised (illegally) all over the UK, and particularly on Grouse moors and some lowland shooting estates. There are currently no Golden Eagles breeding in England[2.15], although there used to be before bird of prey numbers were greatly reduced in the 19th and 20th centuries by the relentless persecution of 'vermin'. They are OK on pub signs, but they are not OK on my shooting estate.

Many of the Eagles on pub signs are not identifiable to species, but a few are. There is a *Golden Eagle* in Lincoln and one in Castleford, and three pubs called the *Spread Eagle*, in Camden (London), Sawley (near Clitheroe in Lancashire) and York, depict Golden Eagles. The *Eagles Nest* in Kidderminster in the West Midlands (now closed) had a lovely sign with a pair of Golden Eagles at their nest. The *Eagle and Sun* in Droitwich has one of the most dramatic pub signs I have ever seen and shows a large bird of prey diving out of the sun towards its potential prey (it is illustrated in Chapter 5). It is completely the wrong colour for a Golden Eagle and, if anything, I have always assumed it depicts a New World Harris's Hawk[1.7 & 2.16]. It doesn't. As Keith and Alison Noble informed me after publication of my *British Birds* article, it is indeed a rather colourful Golden Eagle copied to perfection (except for the colour) by the signwriter from the cover of *Birds of Prey* by Glenys and Derek Lloyd, published by Hamlyn in 1968. On the cover of the book it is diving at a wolf. Golden Eagles can kill foxes, as one of the stunning images in *Birds and People* shows. But a wolf strikes me as ambitious.

All the signs I have seen for pubs called the *Spread Eagle* depict a real bird, albeit not one necessarily identifiable to species. The name, however, is very old and derived from the spread Eagle as an heraldic device in which a highly stylised Eagle with one (or sometimes two) heads is displayed with wings, tail and legs splayed. Commonly used in Europe, the coat of arms of the German nation (adopted in 1950 but derived from the much older coat of arms

Spread Eagle, Camden

of Prussia) is a black spread eagle with red beak, tongue and feet on a yellow background. As the name of a pub, it may originally have been used to indicate that it sold German wine[2.17].

Eagle and Child, Oxford

The Eagles depicted on signs for *The Eagle and Child* have a varied pedigree. The *Eagle and Child* on St Giles in Oxford is a Grade II listed building and is reputed to have been the lodgings of the Royalist chancellor of the exchequer during the English Civil War, but it probably wasn't (see Chapter 3). The Eagle on the current sign is identifiable as a Golden Eagle, whilst the *Eagle and Child* in Leyland (Lancashire), the town in which I grew up, is an American Bald Eagle (or almost; it has a striking white head but its tail is brown and should be white[2.18]). My first experience of underage drinking was in this pub, with the school rugby team and the games' master. Polite nicknames for *Eagle and Child* include "Bird and Baby". We used to call the pub "The Bird and Bastard", for reasons I didn't understand at the time, but do now.

Eagle and Child, Leyland

In a Google search I can find 13 pubs currently called *Eagle and Child*, all but four of them in what was the historic county of Lancashire[2.19]. Why? W.B. Alexander[1.2] is quite coy, saying: "The *Eagle and Child* is the badge of the house of Stanley, from the legend that their ancestor was carried off by an eagle when a baby." Well, yes and no. The legend is more raunchy[2.20]. The Stanley family (or Audley-Stanley) has many notable members, including the Earls of Derby, which is why *Inn-Signia*[1.24] is able to say (in apparent contradiction to Alexander) that the name comes "from the armorial bearings of the Earls of Derby". One of their 14th-century ancestors was Sir Thomas Latham. (Just to add to the confusion, the name is variously spelled Latham, Lathom, Lathum and even de Lathom, which makes searching their genealogy for a non-expert like me very confusing. Anyway, back to the main plot). Sir Thomas had a daughter (Isabel in some versions, Isabella in others) but no sons, and his wife was beyond childbearing age, so he had no male heir. The couple are reputed to have found a baby boy lying in the grass below an Eagle's eyrie (or in another version in the nest) in a wild section of their estate known as Tarlescough Woods near what is now Lytham St Anne's in Lancashire. (If you are following this you will realise that Lytham and Latham have the same linguistic roots.) The couple adopted the child and brought him up as their own. Inn signs for *The Eagle and Child* variously depict the baby in the nest or being carried by an Eagle. On his deathbed (1382 or 1383) Sir Thomas admitted that the baby was in fact his illegitimate son by a young lady with whom he had had an affair. You can see why Alexander (and the Stanley family) might be a bit coy. It also explains the cluster of pubs with this name in Lancashire.

Despite being even larger and more impressive (they have been described as "flying barn doors"), White-tailed (or Sea) Eagles do not, as far as I am aware, have any pub named after them or depicted on their sign. White-tailed Eagles were persecuted to extinction in the UK when the last pair bred on Skye in 1916, but they have now been successfully reintroduced in a project that started in the 1960s. The reintroduction programme was a huge and complex effort and the first successful breeding attempt by a pair in Scotland in 1985[1.22]. Eagles live a long time and breed slowly, but just over 30 years later in 2017 the UK population had reached 123 pairs[2.13], all of which were in Scotland (plus an unknown number of non-breeding young birds). Further reintroductions are now being carried out on the Isle of White and are planned elsewhere in England. These wonderful birds surely deserve to have a pub named after them.

Last but by no means least there are at least two Eagle pubs graced by species that do not occur in the UK. The *Black Eagle* in Hockley, Birmingham seems to be this African species (also called Verreaux's Eagle), which has a range that extends through South Africa and up the Rift Valley to the Red Sea; there are also occasional records from Israel and North Africa. I have watched them many times in South Africa (the first being a pair flying over the Oribi Gorge in the Eastern Cape in April 1983) and they are if anything even more impressive than Golden Eagles; they are certainly on average larger birds. The pub was built in 1895, but nowhere can I find an explanation for the choice of name. The sign is of a black Eagle diving towards the observer. It has accurately depicted buttercup-yellow legs and feet and a characteristic wing shape in which the secondaries (inner flight feathers) bulge out along the rear of the wing and are pinched in near the body. However, if it is a Black

The Eagle, Shepherdess Way, City Road, London

Words from the nursery rhyme as a pub sign

Eagle the bird on the sign should have white bases to the undersides of the primary (outer) flight feathers. If it isn't supposed to be a Black Eagle, I don't know what it is.

I cannot identify the second foreign Eagle, but I can identify where the name comes from. Virtually all children in the UK know the nursery rhyme *Pop! Goes the Weasel.* The first verse goes:

Half a pound of tuppenny rice,
Half a pound of treacle.
That's the way the money goes,
Pop! goes the weasel.

And the third verse:

Up and down the City Road,
In and out the Eagle,
That's the way the money goes,
Pop goes the weasel.

The key lines here are: "Up and down the City Road, in and out the Eagle". The pub (*The Eagle*) is still there, at the corner of City Road and Shepherdess Way in London, and it has an Eagle on its sign, but not any old Eagle. My best guess is that it could either be a Harpy Eagle (from South America) or a Martial Eagle (from Africa); if I knew which field guide the artist had used identification would be easier. The meaning of the nonsense verse has been much debated[2.21]. The rhyme may have originated in the 18th century (but did not become popular until Victorian times). However, the pub most probably also dates from the 18th century, although exactly when is unclear. We do know that it closed as a pub in 1825 and did not reopen until 1901. I discuss this and other old pubs in Chapter 3.

Black Swan

The 'discovery' of Black Swans by Dutch explorers on the west coast of Australia in the 17th century was sensational. As every right-minded person knew, Swans were supposed to be white. Indeed, the term "Black Swan events", particularly in history and economics, first coined by Nassim Nicholas Talib, has come to be shorthand for extreme, highly improbable events[2.22]. The first living Black Swans were brought to England in 1791[2.22 & 2.23] but by that date pubs here had already been christened *Black Swan*. For example, Cooper points out in *The Old Inns and Signs of York*[1.12], published in 1897, that *The Black Swan* on Coney Street (now demolished) "has flourished above 200 years, taking its name long before the actual bird was brought from Australia". W.B. Alexander[1.2] goes further, saying (without offering any proof) that "the *Black Swan* was depicted on English inn-signs before the discovery of Australia". Since that European discovery was in 1606 (with Black Swans spotted in 1636), Alexander's comment would imply that a pub or pubs so named existed in the late 1500s or early 1600s. I have seen no evidence that this was the case and will (for now) assume that the birds were found by Dutch explorers in 1636 and that pubs named after them quickly followed. But there may be another explanation for a pub called *The Black Swan* pre-dating their discovery by Europeans, which I will touch on in Chapter 5.

A landlord or landlady wanting to choose a name for their pub might well settle on *Black Swan* for two reasons: the cachet of the regal links with 'normal' white Swans (even though Black Swans have never been royal property) plus the startling thought of them being black. At least this is a reasonable explanation for a single pub. It doesn't begin to explain why there are four *Black Swans* within a small area of Wensleydale, which set me on this story of pub birds (Chapter 1). One possibility, which I have found impossible to verify or refute, is that a wealthy local landowner imported some Black Swans in the early years of the 19th century that greatly impressed the locals; both Constable Burton Hall and Bedale Hall lie between Leyburn and Bedale and a few miles north of Middleham and Masham. They are fine country seats, both currently with small lakes in their grounds. But there the trail goes cold and I have no evidence that they were ever graced by Black Swans.

The Black Swan Inn, Alnwick

Old Black Swan, Bedale

Black Swans themselves are striking birds, with all-black plumage that is peculiarly 'frizzed' over their backs and (visible when they open their wings) startlingly white primaries and secondaries, all set off by a red eye and pinkish-red bill to die for, which has a bold white ring near the tip. They first 'jumped over the fence' and bred in the wild in this country in 1891 in Surrey[2.7], and despite them being the most frequently recorded 'feral' species of bird in the UK[2.24] the population is not thought to be self-sustaining, despite being recorded away from captivity in 111 locations during the breeding season in comprehensive survey work between 2007 and 2011[2.25]. It is very unclear why (unlike Canada Geese, for example) the number of breeding pairs remains so low (with just 19 pairs recorded between 2010 and 2014)[2.26]. Black Swans introduced into New Zealand from about 1864 onwards have thrived, and the population now numbers many thousands[2.7].

I live close to the University of York, which has two large lakes within its Heslington East (new) and Heslington West (old) campuses that are part of my local birding patch. A pair of Black Swans bred (unsuccessfully) on the West Campus lake in 2014 (the first and only time they have done so) but the male died from unknown causes. His surviving mate, or a second, wandering Black Swan appeared on the new campus in early September that year, and joined the resident pair of Mute Swans and their well-grown cygnets. For the next five years the Black Swan followed the Mute Swans and a succession of cygnets wherever they went, with no signs of aggression from the Mutes. This unlikely *ménage a trois* remained on Heslington East, with occasional visits to Heslington West until April 2019 when the female Mute Swan was found dead on her nest. The male found another mate by early May, and the new pair were again being accompanied by the Black Swan throughout the rest of 2019 and 2020. It is easy to be anthropomorphic and find it touching that a widowed, alien Black Swan, far from its native home, has found solace with a pair of white relatives (they are in the same genus, *Cygnus*). But we can have no idea what is actually going on in their heads, or indeed why the Mute Swans tolerate the Black Swan when they are so fiercely aggressive to members of their own species that invade their territory. And it may not be entirely innocent. Black Swans and Mute Swans can hybridise[2.25], but I would hate to spoil a lovely story.

Pheasant

The most famous line in the Monty Python film *The Life of Brian* is "What have the Romans ever done for us?" The answer it doesn't give is "Pheasants". Whether or not the Romans brought Pheasants to Britain appears to be a matter of dispute. *Birds Britannica* [1.22] says simply: "the Greeks first brought pheasants...to Europe, and the Romans eventually took them to Britain, although it is unknown whether these birds established a feral population. The first reliable written reference to the species concerns pheasants eaten at Waltham Abbey just prior to the Battle of Hastings." However, this latter assertion appears to be based on a document written over 100 years later (1177) in an account of rations for the household of the Abbey's cannon in 1058–59[2.7]. Oliver Rackham[2.27] is even more sceptical, saying simply: "The pheasant is an oriental bird thought to be native in Central Asia and south-east Russia. It was well known to the Romans and is often alleged, though not on good evidence, to have been kept by them in Britain. Roman introductions, if any, did not survive: no Anglo-Saxon writer mentions pheasants...[which]...could not have escaped record had it been present." A more recent analysis by Yalden and Albarella[2.6] supports Rackham's conclusions. The first evidence of Pheasants occurring in the wild in England is in a charter of 1089. By the 12th century the species was probably naturalised, and was sufficiently abundant by the early 14th century to be regarded as game[2.27].

It is as a gamebird, to be hunted and shot, that Pheasants feature as a pub bird, although the slaughter is usually implicit. Explicit references to hunting are *The Dog and Pheasant* in Shrewsbury, and, as with all other Pheasant pubs, the bird on the sign of *The Game Bird Pub* in Beverley (East Yorkshire) is male. It seems likely that some of the inn signs for pubs called *The Sportsman* or *Dog and Gun*[2.28] and their variants probably have a Pheasant on them, but it could be another species of gamebird and I have not checked all of them to see.

The number of Pheasants now released into the UK countryside with the intention of shooting as many of them as possible is staggering. It is basically factory farming on an industrial scale. According to Mark Avery[2.29] roughly 43 million young Pheasants are released annually and about 13 million of these are shot. The rest must die of 'something else'. To put this in perspective, by late summer, Pheasants (mainly the released birds, but including some wild ones) make up about half of the total biomass of *all* birds in the UK. The environmental consequences of this unregulated bonanza (for what is after all a non-native species) are largely unknown. Among the main concerns are the impacts of the living birds on the populations of the plants, insects and reptiles they consume as food, and the inevitable boost such a huge biomass of food must give to their own predators (Foxes for example) and carrion feeders (such as Carrion Crows and Magpies, as well as Foxes) that feed on the Pheasants that die from 'something else'. It is inevitable that there will be potentially damaging knock-on effects elsewhere in the food web. A quite different worry focuses on the amount of lead (an extremely toxic and persistent metal) scattered over the countryside from shotgun cartridges. Illegal persecution of birds of prey is also far too common on Pheasant shoots, particularly in the vicinity of the mass rearing pens. Given these concerns, towards the end of 2020 Mark Avery and colleagues from an organisation called Wild Justice successfully challenged the Department of Environment, Food and Rural Affairs (Defra, in the Westminster Government) in the High Court. The Court ruled that Defra must issue licences for the release of Pheasants (and Red-legged Partridges), with the intention of limiting the numbers of these alien "problem species" and undertake research to better understand their impacts. You can hear the "garumphing" in *The Pheasant* and *The Sportsman's Arms* throughout the land.

The Pheasant Inn, Falstone

The Pheasant, Dubwath

The birds themselves are not, by any stretch of the imagination, very exciting creatures. *Birds Britannica* [1.22] points out that in the last 55 years of *British Birds* (my favourite birding journal) there are only about a dozen brief references to the species and that "no other wild bird has been so ignored". Mark Avery's paper[2.29] and the subsequent High Court ruling[2.30] (and other associated reports in *British Birds*) are probably the most extensive coverage the species has received in the last (now) 65 years. But its taxonomy is worthy of attention, and is still debatable. Two sorts of male Pheasant appear on inn signs, those with a white ring on their necks (for instance two called *The Pheasant Inn*, in Falstone, Northumberland and Keswick, Cumbria) and those without (such as *The Pheasant* at Dubwath near Bassenthwaite in the English Lake District). *Birds of the World* [2.10] lists 30 different subspecies across Europe and Asia that are distinct enough in appearance to warrant recognition as being 'different' but not different enough to be given the status of separate species. The evolutionary relationships among them are still unresolved. The subspecies brought into Britain in the 11th or 12th century (see above) from what are now Georgia, Azerbaijan, Armenia and Iran were *Phasianus colchicus* (the scientific name for all Common Pheasants), subspecies *colchicus*, known as Black-necked Pheasant because it lacks a white neck ring. Ring-necked Pheasants with bold white neck rings came into Britain much later and involved two subspecies (*torquatus* from Eastern China and *mongolicus* from Western China, Kazakhstan and Kyrgyzstan). The two subspecies, although they look different, freely hybridise, so the UK Pheasant population is now a veritable melange, potentially further complicated by the addition of other subspecies to the mix. And that is probably the most interesting thing we can say about Pheasants.

Ducks (Both Wild Mallards and Their Domestic Descendants)

Wild Ducks (Mallards) and their domestic descendants feature on pub signs in two main ways. As wild birds they are (like Pheasants) celebrated because we hunt them. As domesticated birds pubs signs tend to favour humour.

Wild Ducks are (or were) hunted in two ways. They are still shot, but they also used to be killed in Duck decoys (more on decoys in a moment). The decoys are now used to catch wild birds in order to ring them; in a nice turning of the tables the data so gathered helps to sustainably manage and conserve Duck populations. Pubs called *The Dog and Duck* celebrate (if that's the right word) both forms of hunting. Shot Ducks are often retrieved for their owners by gun dogs ("Retrievers" for obvious reasons, numbering about six large and broadly similar breeds), and a Retriever with a Duck

The Drake, Hull

features quite widely on pub signs; three examples include two pubs, one in and the other just outside Beverley in East Yorkshire, and another in Walthamstow, London.

The alternative form of hunting uses decoy dogs such as King Charles Spaniels, which are much smaller than Retrievers. Decoys are a cunning way of catching Ducks in large numbers and they were often caught using used specially trained dogs. The decoy itself is a natural or artificially constructed lake to which, usually, at least four long, curved, spiral arms called pipes have been added. The arms taper from a mouth on the lake to a point at the end about 75m away, roofed over with netting supported on hoops and screened along their length with reeds. The screens have peepholes in them, so the decoy operator can see what is happening inside[2.27]. Any wild Ducks (of several species, including Mallards) that landed on the lake were attracted into the pipes either by tame Ducks trained for the purpose or by decoy dogs that the wild Ducks treated as Foxes, and in an attempt to keep the pseudo-predators in view followed them down the pipe. Once safely in a pipe the Ducks were driven to the end by the hunters and slaughtered. *The Decoy Tavern* in Fritton, Great Yarmouth is the only pub, as far as I am aware, that celebrates (if that's the right word) this clever but brutal hunting technique. At its height it is said that over 100 decoys were operating in England, resulting in the slaughter of half a million Ducks a year[2.27]. The *Royal Dog and Duck* in Flamborough (East Yorkshire) and the *Dog and Duck* in Soho, London, both have a King Charles Spaniel and a Mallard on their sign to commemorate these activities.

Royal Dog and Duck, Flamborough

Dog and Duck, Babbacombe

Humour and hunting come together on the sign of the *Dog and Duck* in Babbacombe (Devon), which shows a stylised Retriever gazing up at a Duck sipping beer from a pint pot just out of reach of the dog. It isn't alone in being humorous.

My favourite is *The Drunken Duck Inn* in the English Lake District. The story goes[1.13] that the wife of the landlord at *The Station Hotel* in Ambleside, finding a Duck apparently dead in the backyard and thinking it would make a good meal, took it inside and plucked it to cook. However, the very bald Duck eventually woke up and the landlord soon discovered the problem. A barrel had broken and beer had flooded the yard where the Duck had been feeding. It wasn't dead, just drunk. The landlady, full of remorse, knitted it an outfit to keep it warm until some of its feathers grew back, and the unusual sight of a Duck in a cardigan attracted customers from far and wide. Not surprisingly *The Station Hotel* became *The Drunken Duck.*

There is a *Scruffy Duck* in Norton, Stockton on Tees[2.31]. The sign is a stylised cartoon of a fat, whitish Duck in flight. The pub was originally a coaching inn built around 1870 and called (unimaginatively) *The White Swan*, but (along with some other pubs named after Mute Swans) it was known locally as "The Mucky Duck", a nickname which is the exact opposite of an elegant, regal Mute Swan. It was recently formally renamed the *Scruffy Duck.* The origin of the *Dirty Duck* in Stratford-upon-Avon is similar, albeit a bit more complicated. It was originally (and still is) called *The Black Swan* and has a sign showing that species. According to the pub's website American GIs christened it the *Dirty Duck* during the Second World War, which is as good a nickname as any for a Black Swan. The name stuck, and the pub now has a second image of a stylised Duck sitting on a stool painted on the reverse of the Black Swan sign.

The sign of the *Strawberry Duck* in Clayton, Manchester, depicts a male Mallard apparently trying to eat three strawberries. As usual, it is not at all clear how or why the pub is so named, but it is an amusing sign. And quite bafflingly it has an (almost) namesake in *The Strawbury Duck* in Entwistle, Lancashire. The Duck is a Mallard, and from Google we learn the origin of the name of the village: it is derived from Old English *ened* and *twisia*, meaning "a river fork frequented by ducks" which is an appropriate sense of place for a Mallard. But why *Strawbury*? (notice it is not "Strawberry"[2.32]). I can find no explanation.

Falcons and Bird in Hand

Falcons are beautiful, the larger species are impressive, and they are all highly refined killing machines, with a long history of human use in

Bird in Hand, Saltford

the ancient art of falconry. By now you should have realised that it is little wonder that they are popular pub birds. Taken together, *Falcon* and *Bird in Hand* (widely cited as a reference to falconry, to which we will come shortly) number 101 pubs in Pubs Galore and 123 and 115 respectively in Steve Shaw's list (Table 1). But not all *Bird in Hand* pubs are Falcons (some are Eagles or an indeterminate raptor, others not a bird of prey at all). For that reason, *Bird in Hand* is not included in my own top 13 in Table 1.

The *Bird in Hand* was adopted as a pub name in England in the Middle Ages. The most frequent derivation does indeed refer to a Falcon perched on the gloved hand (gauntlet) of a falconer[2.33]. These birds of prey are carefully trained over many months and there develops a strong and close bond between the handler and the bird. The bird is then flown against potential prey for human consumption or just plain 'sport'. The birds are 'paid' for their efforts with food from the handler on returning to them. When not hunting the Falcon or Eagle is frequently hooded so it cannot see; the whole skilful ritual is enmeshed in its own private vocabulary, equipment and codes of conduct, which survive to the present day[1.23] even though few people need to hunt with a bird of prey to obtain food in the 21st century[2.34].

The proverb[2.35] "a bird in the hand is worth two in the bush" refers back to medieval falconry in which a bird in the hand (the Falcon or Eagle) was a valuable asset and certainly worth more than two other birds in the bush (the prey). The first citation of the expression in print in its currently used form is found in John Ray's *A Hand-book of Proverbs*, 1670. By how long the phrase pre-dates Ray's account is not clear, as variants of it were known for centuries before 1670. The earliest of those referring to birds is in Hugh Rhodes' *The Boke of Nurture or Schoole of Good Maners*, circa 1530: "A byrd in hand – is worth ten flye at large." John Heywood, the 16th-century collector of proverbs, recorded another version in his ambitiously titled *A dialogue conteinyng the nomber in effect of all the prouerbes in the Englishe tongue*, 1546: "Better one byrde in hande than ten in the wood."

So far, so straightforward. But there are also competing explanations. For example, Cooper's[1.12] history of pubs called *Bird in*

Hand in York in the 19th century describes a pub (long closed) with "an old-fashioned sign, with a man's arm…holding a bird between his fingers [i.e. not a bird of prey], and in the background two birds in a bush." A second origin Cooper suggests may have been due to competition between rival innkeepers in the same district. *Bush, Holly Bush* (and similar) are very old and still quite common names for a pub. A landlord competing with a pub called (or nicknamed) *The Bush* may have decided to call his own pub *The Bird in Hand* to make the point that a drink in his pub was worth two in that of his inferior rival[1.24]. So, *Bird in Hand* may not always be a reference to falconry.

Realising that I did not know how common the alternatives are, or indeed what species of birds could be involved, I undertook a Google search for "pubs called *Bird in Hand*" on a wet Sunday afternoon in January 2021. The results of this small but essentially random sample of 25 pubs are in Table 2[2.36].

They are instructive. Fewer than half (ten) are bird of prey, of which eight are Falcons or Falcon-like) and one is an Eagle. Cooper's suggestion (where the sign clearly does not depict a bird of prey) has six examples. At least another five have just a name with no sign. In contrast, the website for one *Bird in Hand* at Sonning Common near Reading has no less than three different signs (all of which are unlikely to be contemporary); two clearly refer to falconry and the third to Cooper's alternative of a small bird cupped in a hand. Peregrine Falcons dominate the identifiable birds of prey. Some of the other smaller birds are also clearly identifiable and the sign for the *Bird in Hand* at Wreningham is particularly delightful, depicting a Wren perched on a human hand (p. 94). The inn sign for *The Bird in Hand* in Hayle is the head of a Scarlet Macaw (no hand in sight)(p. 110). There is clearly a great deal more to learn about *Bird in Hand* that is not just about falconry.

The Falcon Inn, Nottingham

The Falcon, Chester

Table 2

Pubs called *Bird in Hand*, giving the location of the pub, a brief description of the bird on the inn sign (if there is one) and its identification if that proved possible.

Kind of Bird	Location of Pub	Description of Sign (if any)	Species
Falcon			
	Bromley, Greater London	Falcon on a gloved hand	?
	Long Ashton, Bristol	Large Falcon	Probably Peregrine
	Lower Stondon, Henlow, Bedfordshire	Hooded Falcon on a gloved hand	Peregrine
	Mayford, Woking, Surrey	Stylised Falcon-like bird of prey in flight	?
	Mobberley, Knutsford, Cheshire	Unhooded Falcon on gloved hand	Peregrine
	North Curry, Taunton, Somerset	Unhooded Falcon on gloved hand	Peregrine
	Sonning Common, Reading, Berkshire	Web has three different signs: (1) Large raptor, wings spread on an uplifted arm and hand; (2) Large Falcon on a gauntlet, above door; (3) See Other kind of bird, below	?
	Urmston, Greater Manchester	Cut-out sign of a Falcon on gloved hand. Pub is called *The Bird I'th Hand* (dialect)	?
Eagle			
	Saltford, near Bath Somerset	Flying Eagle	(Golden?) Eagle
Generalised Bird of prey			
	Witney, Oxfordshire	Large, Buzzard-like raptor on falconer's gauntlet	?
Other kind of bird, not a Bird of prey			
	Blidworth, Mansfield, Nottinghamshire	Goldfinch, held in an outstretched hand	Goldfinch
	Guilden Sutton, Chester	A Pigeon/Dove sitting on the palm of an outstretched hand, carrying an olive branch in its bill	Pigeon/Dove
	Hayle, Cornwall	The red and white head of a large Macaw (Chapter 4)	Scarlet Macaw
	Sonning Common, Reading, Berkshire	Third sign for this pub on web. Stylised yellow (?) passerine on an upstretched blue-green hand	?
	Stourport-on-Severn, Worcestershire	Baby duckling held gently in two hands	Duckling

	Wreningham, Norwich, Norfolk	A Wren perched on the first finger of an upstretched hand (Chapter 3)	Wren
Unknown or no visible painted sign, just name			
	Beck Row, Bury St Edmunds, Suffolk		———
	Ironbridge, Shropshire		———
	Knowl Hill, Reading, Berkshire		———
	Dartmouth Road, London		———
	Long Ashton nr Bristol		———
	Sandhurst, Berkshire	Website has a sign, but too small and distant to see what is on it	———
	Shrewsbury, Shropshire		———
	Stafford, Staffordshire		———
	Westhay, Somerset		———
	Wigton, Cumbria		———

Falcons also appear on the signs of pubs that are not called *Bird in Hand*, either (again) as a falconer's bird, or just as the bird itself. The bird on the gauntlet of a falconer on the sign of the *Falconers Rest* in Leeds is too small for me to identify using Google. Where the Falcon can be identified, Peregrines again dominate. They are truly wonderful birds, and arguably one of, if not *the* fastest bird in the world[1.22]. The Peregrine on the sign for *The Falcon Inn* in Nottingham sits on a falconer's glove. *The Falcon* in Chester has two signs, a stylised golden carving of a falconer's bird, and a portrait of a Peregrine. *The Falcon Inn* in Arncliffe, Warfedale depicts a rather brown Peregrine on a crag, not far from one of the known breeding sites in the Yorkshire Dales (where they are also still illegally persecuted).

The history, biology and ecology of Peregrine Falcons are summarised in a monograph by Derek Ratcliffe[2.37], whose brilliant research in the 1960s established how persistent organochlorine insecticides (in the UK particularly aldrin, dieldrin and heptachlor seed-dressings) accumulating up the food chain were responsible for breeding failures in Peregrines, the death of adult birds and massive population declines throughout their global range. Since the pesticides were banned Peregrine populations have recovered, so much so[2.38] that they are no longer only birds of wild uplands and sea cliffs, but increasingly of our towns

The old sign for The Kestrel, Harrogate

The new sign for The Kestrel, Harrogate

and cities (where they nest on tall buildings) and lowland countryside (where they typically nest on electricity pylons). They breed on York Minster and on several pylons near my home on the Vale of York, something that was absolutely unthinkable when I was growing up in the 1950s and 1960s. Although I have been keeping my life list of birds since 1954 (when I was ten years old) I did not see my first Peregrine until October 1963 (at the age of 20), a wintering male that was hunting Ducks on Longton Marsh on the Ribble Estuary in Lancashire. The site is now part of a major RSPB reserve and has regular wintering Peregrine Falcons. It isn't all bad news.

Other, smaller species of Falcon also feature on inn signs. The smallest UK Falcon, the Merlin, was the falconer's bird of choice for female monarchs such as Mary, Queen of Scots and Catherine the Great. Its larger cousin the Kestrel, on the other hand, came lowest in the feudal hierarchy of falconers, flown by "the servant or nave"[1.22 & 1.23]. As pub birds they can be found in Edinburgh (*The Merlin*) and Harrogate, North Yorkshire (*The Kestrel*). The latter is a rare example of a pub bird changing species during the period of my main database. In 2012 the sign depicted a Common (European) Kestrel; by 2019 it had transformed into an American Kestrel (smaller than 'ours' with a characteristic boldly patterned 'moustache and sideburns' head pattern). This little foreign Falcon now sits on a falconer's gauntlet.

Geese

As with Pheasants I find it quite hard to get enthusiastic about geese as pub birds (wild geese are a different matter). But they are still an important source of food and were much more so historically. Greylag Geese (the most abundant Goose in the wild in the UK) are depicted on Egyptian frescoes dating from about 2000BC, where they were first domesticated[2.39]. These birds are the ancestors of the familiar, usually white, 'farmyard geese' with pink bills; wild Greylags in Europe (subspecies *anser*) have orange bills whilst those from further east (subspecies *rubirostris*) have pink bills[2.10], revealing the deep historical origins of the domesticated birds. It is a subtlety too far for a pub sign.

The prevalence of *Fox and Goose* as a pub name reflects their importance as food for people and the battle against foxes that also wanted to eat them. When there is a sign it invariably depicts a domestic Goose, for instance the *Fox and Goose* in Hebden Bridge (West Yorkshire) or Ealing in London. Other 'Goose pubs' are more difficult to explain. There are two Welsh pubs called the *Goose and Cuckoo*. They lie just around 40 miles apart as the Peregrine flies, on the north-west and south-east edges of the Brecon Beacons National Park, in Llangadog, Carmarthenshire and Llanover in Monmouthshire respectively. The pub in Llangadog just has a name, no sign and no history on its or other relevant websites. The pub sign in Llanover depicts a white farmyard Goose, wings spread, facing a Cuckoo, and the pub itself has several informative websites[2.40]. It was built in at least 1780 as a cider house formerly called the *New Inn* and was renamed (in 1947 in one account and in the 1880s in another) after a couple who ran it in the 19th century called each other a "silly old goose" and "a silly old cuckoo" during a marital argument. It is not clear, at least to me, who was the Cuckoo and who was the Goose. This matters, because although it sounds innocent enough, "goose" in Elizabethan times was slang for a prostitute[1.22]. I do not know whether that meaning survived in Wales into the 19th century.

Moving hurriedly on, one other species of Goose has been domesticated, the Swan Goose[2.39]. The bird is now threatened with extinction in the wild with only small numbers still breeding in Central Asia, from Siberia to Mongolia and Northern China, and wintering in North and South Korea and parts of China[2.10]. It was formerly much more widespread, and domesticated by the Chinese, the domesticated birds being known as Chinese Geese. As with Greylags they are larger and heavier than wild

Gaping Goose, Garforth

birds, but unlike Greylags their bills differ markedly from those of their wild ancestors, having a highly distinctive large knob at the base of the upper mandible and forehead (not dissimilar to the knob in the bill of a Mute Swan). This distinctive knob identifies the bird depicted on the sign for the *Gaping Goose* in Garforth, Leeds as a Chinese Goose.

Raven

Ravens have a party trick. They can fly upside down or more precisely from level flight they can flip over onto their backs and glide, feet up, for surprising distances "with evident enjoyment" as part of "aerial play"[2.41], particularly early in the breeding season. I remember watching with astonishment the display for the first time, below the summit of Harrison Stickle in Langdale in the English Lake District in 1959. In those days Ravens were more or less confined, because of relentless persecution by farmers and gamekeepers, to the mountains of the north and west of the UK, even though they are primarily scavengers and in particular carrion feeders. However, they are perfectly capable of killing their own prey and do occasionally take lambs and sheep, particularly sickly ones that would probably have died anyway[2.42]. In the absence of persecution Ravens live more or less anywhere and are summed up in *Birds of the Western Palearctic*[2.41] as being "so wide-ranging that [the] concept of habitat is hardly applicable". Globally, Ravens occupy vast swaths of land of all sorts across the whole of the Northern Hemisphere. With a reduction in persecution in the UK they have now reoccupied many of the former lowland haunts in eastern and southern England, and continue to spread, accompanied by a move to nesting in trees (as they used to[2.43]) rather than on mountain crags.

There is rarely anything fancy about Ravens as pub birds. Most are simply called *The Raven* with no obvious local association, except *The Raven* on Tower Bridge Road in London (see below). The most flamboyant is *The Raven* in Bath, which depicts the bird in a dress coat and top hat on its sign (p. 147). There are three *Raven Inns* (Sheffield, Welshpool and just outside Mold) and a *Tilley Raven* in Tilley near Shrewsbury. One pub has a more unusual name and history. The *Ravenscourt Arms* in the London Borough of Hammersmith closed in 2018, but a Googled image shows a coat of arms above the door. The adjacent Ravenscourt Park was originally part of a much larger medieval estate called Palingswick (or Pallenswick). In 1746 the then owner Thomas Corbett (secretary to the Admiralty) changed its name to Ravenscourt as a pun on his coat of arms, which depicted a Raven. The family motto – *Deus pascit corvos* – translates as God feeds the ravens[2.44].

The Raven, Tower Bridge Road, London

Ravens mostly speak for themselves. They are big birds, the largest passerines (perching birds) in the world, impressive in appearance, highly intelligent and steeped in folklore; it is not hard to see why they are common pub birds. They have the richest cultural heritage of any of the 105 species in my database, a status summarised in *Birds Britannica* [1.22] and in more detail by Derek Ratcliffe in his monograph[2.42] (the same Ratcliffe of Peregrine fame). What follows is primarily taken from Ratcliffe. They are one of 12 species of bird depicted in Neolithic paintings in the cave of Tajo Segura in the Province of Cadiz (some 6,000–8,000 years old). There are several references to Ravens in the Old Testament – spring chickens by comparison – and they are also mentioned in the Koran. Both the Ancient Greeks and the Romans saw them as an adjudicator of human affairs. Throughout history they have been regarded as prophets, soothsayers and magicians, capable of transforming into human form and vice versa. In Anglo-Saxon England the legendary King Arthur didn't die but was magically transformed into a Raven, and for centuries afterwards it was illegal to kill a Raven in the West Country. For Norsemen they were sacred birds; Odin, their war god, had two Ravens called Hugin and Mugin (Thought and Memory) and used them to gather intelligence throughout his domain. Norse war banners themselves were fashioned in the form of a Raven. And so it goes on, through Norman times and the Middle Ages. Shakespeare mentions them at least 50 times, usually in some sombre context, although in later history the bird has also gradually acquired more peaceful connotations. Echoing this changing attitude, *Birds Britannica* says "Modern life has drained the bird of its symbolic significance" but echoes of darker associations persist to this day (albeit taken with a pinch of salt by most people). The tradition of keeping seven Ravens in the Tower of London dates only from Victorian times, and that of their keeper, the raven master, from just 1968. They are pinioned and cosseted like Kings and Queens, because, as rumour has it, if their numbers fall below six the White Tower will collapse and the monarch will be in mortal danger.

Mute Swans aside, no pub bird can get close to Ravens for their cultural significance.

Pigeons and Doves (Both Feral and Domestic) Derived from Wild Rock Doves

We will get to Pigeons and Doves in a minute, albeit by a circuitous route.

As well as being one of the most important and influential books ever written, Charles Darwin's *On the Origin of Species by Means of Natural Selection*, first published in 1859, has generated a number of persistent myths about how he arrived at his groundbreaking insights. One is that he had an epiphany on the Galápagos Islands where he first observed the amazing ecological and morphological radiation in a group of small, drab (mainly brown, grey, olive or black) birds we now call Darwin's Finches and concluded that they must all have evolved by natural selection from a common ancestor[2.45]. He didn't[2.46], at least not whilst he was on the Galápagos. Whilst on the islands he did not understand their significance, failed to keep a careful record of which Finches he had collected on which islands, and seriously miss-classified them[2.47]. Fortunately, Robert Fitzroy (the captain of Darwin's ship, the *Beagle*) had also collected specimens of the Finches and had accurately labelled them. In March 1837, about five months after returning to England, Darwin visited John Gould (the great ornithologist of the day) to discuss his collection of birds. Based on Fitzroy's material Gould told Darwin that there were 13 species of Finch, all closely related, all unique to the Galápagos and unmistakably of South American origin. Darwin, we are told[2.46] was "stunned" that he could have got it so wrong, but at some point soon after he did finally 'get it'. These unique little birds must have evolved and radiated from one species of ancestral Finch that was blown out to the islands from South America. Some species are confined to just one island, others to several islands, and between them they span an amazing variety of ecologies, ranging from tiny, Warbler-like birds to larger Finches with different-sized bills used for cracking open different-sized seeds; ground-feeders and species that feed in bushes, cacti and trees; species that feed on nectar and one that feeds on the blood of Nazca Boobies (a kind of Gannet); and even one species that regularly and a second that occasionally use tools to extract insect prey from crevices.

There are now thought to be 17 species of Darwin's Finches[2.48 & 2.49] in three genera. I have reliably seen eight of them; some can be notoriously hard to identify in the field. They are, without question, one of the most thoroughly documented examples of the evolution by natural selection of life on Earth[2.50]. Yet *On the Origin of Species* has nothing whatsoever to say about them. It does discuss some of the Galápagos Islands' other plants and birds, but these occupy only about 1.1% of the text in the whole book[2.46]. Darwin, it would seem, felt unable to use the Finches as evidence because of his collecting errors and no doubt a sense of embarrassment. Instead, by way of at least partial compensation, he chose Pigeons, devoting no less than six (hardly gripping) pages to the numerous varieties of domestic Pigeons and Doves, the descendants of wild Rock Doves, created by the artificial selective actions of human beings.

He did this to illustrate how numerous very different kinds of birds can evolve from a common ancestor. In his own words from Chapter 1 of *The Origin*[2.51]: "The diversity of breeds [of Pigeon] is something astonishing", and tellingly by way of an example: "The short-faced tumbler [one of the many varieties of Pigeon] has a beak in outline almost like that of a finch." To show just how different these selected varieties could be: "The fantail has thirty or even forty tail-feathers, instead of twelve or fourteen – the normal number in all the members of the great pigeon family." And: "I do not believe that any ornithologist [if they were told they were wild birds] would place the English carrier, the short-faced tumbler, the runt, the barb, pouter, and fantail in the same genus." You can almost hear him muttering in desperation "I wish I could talk about Galápagos Finches."

According to *Birds Britannica* (it does not say how this number was arrived at) Darwin estimated there were 228 named varieties of Pigeon. This remarkable diversity is not reflected in the Pigeons and Doves in pub names and on pub signs, not by two orders of magnitude. As far as I can tell, pub birds feature just two varieties, plus dovecotes.

As well as *The Doocot* in Edinburgh (from which I was chased away – Chapter 1) the buildings (dovecotes) specially created to house domesticated Pigeons and Doves for food or pleasure are discussed in Chapter 6.

Of the birds themselves *The Liverpool Pigeon* in Waterloo (Liverpool) is a micropub, with a sign that shows a handsome, glossy, greenish Pigeon marked with white spots and black bars that can only be a prized Racing Pigeon. Racing Pigeons and the Feral Pigeons of towns and cities throughout the world are descendants of wild Rock Doves. They come in all sorts of colours, although the majority are grey, black and white, and more heavily chequered and barred with black than Rock Doves; all invariably have white rumps[2.52]. Darwin describes their wild ancestor ("rock-pigeons" as he calls them) as "slaty-blue with white loins". Properly depicted wild Rock Doves or Feral Pigeons would be quite easy to identify on a pub sign but are surprisingly rare (or I have missed them). An old sign for *The Three Pigeons Inn* in Ruthin (Denbighshire) depicted three Feral Pigeons, but now has a lovely new sign depicting three stylised white Doves. In general we neither like nor appreciate Feral Pigeons, despite their spectacular success globally (Woody Allen's oft-repeated description of Feral Pigeons is "rats with wings")[1.22], but we love the white ones, which we generally call Doves, although they are both the same species. *The Dove* in Hammersmith depicts Noah's white Dove framed by a rainbow and carrying an olive branch; it is a lovely sign, with a clear religious origin. But at least in my own database the most frequently recurring name is the *Three Pigeons,* which (in all the signs I have seen) depicts three white Doves. As well as Ruthin, there are pubs of this name in Bolton (Lancashire), Halifax (West Yorkshire), Halstead (Essex), Oswestry (Shropshire) and Richmond upon Thames (Surrey). I have struggled to understand the reason for its popularity or the origin of the name[2.53], with one possible exception.

The old sign for the Three Pigeons Inn, Ruthin

The new sign for the Three Pigeons Inn, Ruthin

The Dove, Hammersmith, London

The website for the *Three Pigeons Inn* tells us that "the name is surrounded in mystery".

But it then goes on to suggest that the Doves may symbolise the Three Graces, which according to poetic and literary tradition were eternally young and lovely ladies representing (depending upon which website you consult) charm, beauty and human creativity; honesty, fidelity and loyalty; or faith, hope and charity. And (deep blushes) they are often depicted naked in paintings or as statues, or at best vaguely clothed. Now you couldn't possibly have that on an inn sign, could you? So Doves were a nice safe way of hinting at it, without actually depicting naked ladies. Maybe. I have no idea.

Indian Peafowl (Peacock)

Peacocks are natives of the Indian subcontinent, widely admired and introduced mainly as domesticated, bling 'pets' in many parts of the world. The Romans also relished them as exotic food, including their tongues, although this may have been more for show than gastronomic delight. There appears to be better evidence that the Romans brought Peacocks to Britain than there is for Pheasants but despite Peacocks being widely featured in Roman art (for example as motifs in mosaic floors) there is only a "scattering of early British records from Roman and Anglo-Norman times" in the form of reliably identified archaeological remains, with "rather more in Mediaeval and later times"[2.6]. And unlike Pheasants, the general view is that Peacocks never established themselves as self-sustaining populations in the wild in this country[2.7]. In other words, most people, inn keepers and their customers alike, would know Peacocks only as domesticated birds, not as gamebirds or food. But as domesticated birds they epitomise style, wealth and exotic, expensive luxury, which almost certainly explains their popularity as a pub bird, despite the tail feathers (actually the upper tail coverts) of the males having a reputation as bringers of bad luck because they are thought to resemble evil eyes[1.23].

Pubs simply called the *Peacock* (a majority – the one with the most beautiful sign is in Stepney, London), *Old Peacock* (Radford, Nottinghamshire), *Peacock Hotel* (Liverpool) and *Peacock Inn* (Shrewsbury, Shropshire), if they have a sign at all and in common with most other pub birds, are all males. Given the male bird's high coefficient of bling, that is hardly surprising. But there is one lonely, dowdy *Peahen* in St Albans (Hertfordshire), which is anything but boring. It may be the only female of its type but it is also one of the oldest pubs in Britain and without any doubt at all the oldest pub bird

The Peacock, Stepney

(Chapter 3). I have been unable to find out why she was chosen as the pub's name rather than the male.

Despite their size, the spectacular appearance of the males and their loud, exotic-sounding, bray-like calls, plus a general familiarity to most people (not just birders), it also transpires that the general notion that the species has never established a self-sustaining population in the wild in Britain may be plain wrong. Anthony Cheke[2.54] describes a well-established feral population at Nuneham Courtenay in Oxfordshire and provides convincing evidence of other apparently self-sustaining populations. For example, he points out that "far more Peacocks are reported found [by members of the public] than are reported lost, suggesting there are many unknown birds on the loose". His research revealed "96 groups of free-ranging Peacocks" all over the UK. Confronted with Cheke's evidence, it seems highly probable that Peacocks are much more firmly established in the wild in the UK than Black Swans, but more likely to be ignored by birders, who 'know' that they cannot be wild birds.

So, if you are lucky enough to encounter a Peacock wandering down a road or in a wood you may not have spent too much time in the pub. It may well be wild and living happily in its adopted country.

Magpie

I have to confess that I was surprised (and still am) to find that the Magpie makes it as the penultimate species in my baker's dozen of most common pub birds. It is on three of the four lists (but not Pubs Galore). And it is yet another species admired and striking enough to feature strongly as a pub bird but also to be reviled and persecuted by gamekeepers in the flesh.

It was not always so. As Tim Birkhead explains in his monograph on Magpies[2.55] Chaucer wrote about the "joly pie" in his *Parlement of Foules* (ca 1381) and it shares the habit of giving human names to popular birds in the late Middle Ages: "Jack"-daw, "Tom"-tit, "Jenny"-wren and "Mag"-pie, "Mag" being the diminutive of Marguerite. Its present name was first recorded in 1605. The bird has a rich folk history as a bird of good omen. *The Old Inns and Inn Signs of York* records[1.12]:

"In some parts of the North they say-
Magpie, magpie, chatter and glee,
Turn up thy tail, and good luck befalls me."

There are several versions of the rhyme that tells you what to expect if you see one or more of them[1.22]:

"One for sorrow, two for joy
Three for a girl and four for a boy
Five for silver, six for gold
Seven for a secret never to be told...."

And so on. In some versions there are up to 12 (although gatherings of Magpies can be substantially larger than a dozen).

These pleasant connotations and associations, together with the bird's striking appearance, probably account for its popularity as a pub bird, rather than the reputation it later acquired as 'vermin' because it predates the eggs and young of songbirds and gamebirds, although the impacts of this predation on the populations of these birds appears to be essentially negligible[2.55].

The Magpie, Combs Ford

Several pubs are just plain *Magpie*, for example in Sunbury-on-Thames (Surrey) and Stapleford (Nottingham), others the more upmarket *Magpie Inn* (for example in Carlisle). The *Magpie Inn* (now just *The Magpie*) in Little Stonham (Suffolk) has an amazing sign in the form of a football goalpost that spans the main A140 road outside. The sign is a Grade II listed structure, described by Historic England as "traditionally believed to have originally been used as a gibbet for hanging highwaymen"[2.56]. About four miles away from this pub is another *Magpie*, in Combs Ford, on the other side of Stowmarket. I have no idea why two Magpies feature as pub birds in this corner of Suffolk.

The gibbet at The Magpie, Little Stonham

Magpies also get paired with other birds, possibly through pub mergers. In two cases these are with Hens (the *Cock and Magpie* in Bewdley, Worcestershire, and the *Cock and Pie* in Ipswich, Suffolk) and one involves a Yellow-headed Amazon parrot (the *Magpie and Parrot* in Shinfield near Reading, Berkshire), though surely the latter must have a more interesting origin.

Partridge

Two species of Partridge are (or were) common in Britain, the native Grey Partridge and the introduced (for hunting) Red-legged Partridge. As far as I know no Partridge pubs explicitly take their names from Red-legged, which were initially introduced into this country in 1673, although they did not become established here (in Suffolk) "until about 100 years later"[2.7], and they are now widespread throughout England and the eastern side of Scotland[2.25]. Grey Partridges were always a popular gamebird but agricultural intensification, particularly the 'chemicalisation' of farming[2.57] (in which insecticides and herbicides have drastically reduced the insects on which Partridge chicks depend for food[2.58]) has resulted in a major decline[2.25]. They are still shot in much-reduced numbers; their legacy is a plethora of Partridge pubs in the first three lists in Table 1 (W.B. Alexander, Steve Shaw and Pubs Galore), but not mine. My database has only had ten[2.59], but six of them are called the *Dog and Partridge*[2.60], which is top of the list for the species in Pubs Galore and makes up all but seven of the 80 Partridge pubs on Steve Shaw's list. No other pub bird comes remotely close to so many pairings with gun dogs (or paired with anything come to that), to which we will return in Chapter 7.

The Partridge, Bromley

With that we complete an exploration of the 'baker's dozen' of the 13 most frequent pub birds. I will revisit some of them again in later chapters, but the primary focus from now on is on the 100-plus other species and types of birds that make up the aviary. What are they? Where are they? And what do we know about the birds, pubs and people involved?

CHAPTER 3: TIME AND PLACE

If things were the same everywhere life would be very dull. A sense of place is built upon comparisons (good or bad) between different towns, different buildings and different landscapes. We treasure old buildings (for example cathedrals or castles), ancient landscapes and veteran trees, preferably the older the better, and old pubs, provided they sell good beer, wine and food. The name of the pub itself can also help create or enhance a sense of place. *The White Swan* doesn't cut it, but *The Old Swan Uppers* on the River Thames or pubs such as *The Seagull* in Abergele on the coast of North Wales, do. This chapter starts by briefly exploring differences in the frequency of pubs named after birds in different parts of the country – the regional geography of pub birds – before moving on to some of the oldest pub birds and where they are located. The bulk of the chapter is an exploration of pub birds in particularly appropriate places or regions, of some that are puzzling because they seem out of place, and how some pub birds have contributed to a sense of place.

Geographical Differences in the Frequency of Pub Birds

In his short but influential paper in *Bird Notes*[1.2] W.B. Alexander observed: "Finally I may mention a fact for which I can provide no explanation, that inns named after birds are much commoner in the Anglo-Saxon parts of England than in Celtic Areas. There are comparatively few in Scotland or Wales, or in Cumberland, Westmorland, Devon and Cornwall." Richard Fitter[1.3] made the same point: "There are some interesting regional differences in the number of bird inn signs in a country. The Midlands are on the whole very good, especially the more southern counties such as Bedfordshire and Oxfordshire. Scotland and Wales are definitely bad."

There is probably enough material in these statements for a PhD thesis by a student of geography or cultural history, and I don't propose to delve into it in depth here. I do have pub birds on my list from the "Celtic" counties of England, and from Wales, but I have a general feeling that Alexander and Fitter are right. They do not occur as frequently in these regions as they do in the rest of Great Britain. Their observations are definitely true for Scotland.

My own data from two of Scotland's great cities, Edinburgh and Glasgow, and their hinterlands reveal very few pub birds. Recall that in a Great Britain-wide sample of 6,846 pubs, 307 (4.5%) qualify as pub birds (Chapter 1). These data include Edinburgh (eight pub birds in a sample of 417 pubs, or 1.9%), and Glasgow (one pub bird in a sample of 200 pubs, or 0.5%)[3.1], well below the average number for Great Britain as a whole. Aberdeen has a single pub called *The Hen Hoose* (Chapter 6). Thinking more about this I realised that despite spending recent holidays on both Orkney and the Outer Hebrides I had no pub birds from any of these enchanted islands. There are none. Googling "pubs, bars and inns on [name of Scottish island]"[3.2] comes up with far more pubs dubbed "hotel" or "bar" (the latter often as part of the hotel) than is the case in England, and it is sometimes difficult to be sure that the establishment is really a pub (Chapter 1) and not a fancy restaurant. But that doesn't matter. If I include them all, there is still not one named after a bird in a sample of 146 pubs, bars and inns across the whole of Orkney, Shetland, the Outer Hebrides (Harris, Lewis, North and South Uist and Benbecula) and the Inner Hebrides (Mull, Skye, Coll, Tiree, Jura, Islay and Arran). If this was England there would be at least six or seven pub birds. Not many, but enough to be reasonably confident that the absence of any pub birds on these islands isn't just down to chance. But like W.B. Alexander I am not at all sure why. Richard Fitter's explanation is blunt: "Scotland and Wales are bad [for pub birds], natural history never having appealed to the Celts even in their cups… but in both Wales and Scotland the inn signs are so obscurely placed compared with England that I have probably overlooked a good many." There really must be at least a master's thesis in this for somebody.

There is also one exception that proves the rule. Scottish islands have some of the finest seabird colonies in Europe, but (unlike England) no pubs named after them, with one striking exception. *The Puff Inn*, on St Kilda[3.2] was a deliberate pun. It was the most remote pub in Great

Britain (at least 2.5 hours or about 40 miles from the Outer Hebrides) on an island with spectacular seabird colonies, including Puffins. The inn was the watering hole for military personnel from the Ministry of Defence's missile tracking station on the island and visiting National Trust volunteers (the NT is the islands' custodian), birders and other naturalists. It closed in August 2019 after 50 years. *The Puff Inn* was so named by the military not by the last of the original inhabitants, who were evacuated in 1930, nearly 40 years before it was built.

What Are the Oldest Pub Birds and Where Are They?

Age gives a sense of place. If pubs have been named since at least the end of the 14th century, what are the oldest pub birds still extant? Although the question sounds simple, the answer is "it depends". What is certain is that *Ye Olde Fighting Cocks* in St Albans (Hertfordshire), which claims to be the oldest pub of any name in England, isn't. Not by a long chalk[3.3]. This section looks at what I think are the oldest pubs named after birds. To qualify there must have been not just a building but clear evidence of a pub on that site since the date in question. But it can still get quite complicated, as we shall see. They are in approximate date order, starting with the oldest in 1480 and finishing arbitrarily at around 1775.

The oldest pub bird I can find is the *Peahen* on the London Road in St Albans (Hertfordshire). As explained in Chapter 2, not only is this pub very old but it is also very unusual in being named after, and having on its sign, a female bird. All other *Peacocks* (there are over 40) are male, as with so many other pub birds. The first written record of the *Peahen* dates from 1480, way ahead of any other pub bird. Towards the end of the 18th century it became an important coaching inn on the road from London to St Albans. The original half-timbered building burned down towards the end of the 19th century, when the present pub was rebuilt. So there has been a pub bird on this site for over 500 years. There appears to be nothing older, and it has always been a female Indian Peafowl. I know of no explanation for the name.

The 'also rans' are generally more complicated in one way or another, because the name has changed, or the original building (which may itself be very old) wasn't a pub.

The *Ostrich Inn* in Colnbrook, Buckinghamshire is a case in point. Its website claims that it is "more than 900 years old" and

Ostrich Inn, Colnbrook

hence "the fourth oldest pub in the entire country", and that it opened in 1106 when Henry I was on the throne. But a careful and thoughtful analysis of the evidence by Mike Dash[3.4] reveals that the pub probably dates from about 1500. Dash's research suggests that it started life as a hospice – which was gifted to Abingdon Abbey in 1106 and only later became *The Hospice Inn* – and that the name was subsequently corrupted to *Ostrich*. But other possible origins of the name are also in Dash's article, including corruptions of Oyster Ridge and *Eastridge Inn*. Dash pours cold water on the claim that the inn was the site of a series of 60 brutal murders of overnight guests, perpetrated by the landlord and his wife in the 12th century. History aside (I am in no position to easily evaluate these rival claims), the current pub has a splendid portrait of an Ostrich on it. It is worth a visit just to see the sign.

I have been unable to discover any historical details about the *Fox and Goose* in Greywell (Hampshire). Its website simply says it is a "superb example of a 16th century pub". It is difficult to tell from photographs whether the current building is at least in part original. It is certainly old. The same is true of the *Falcon Inn* in Denham (Buckinghamshire), described on its website as a "16th century inn overlooking the village green" but with no specific date. It is in a designated conservation area (for the village architectural heritage, not its wildlife) and has a real sense of place. It shares its delightful setting with *The Swan* on the same road (Village Road), which is Georgian and so could date from any time after 1740 up to ca 1830. Both have lovely signs, a well-executed Peregrine and an unusual carved wooden Swan stained black, which is clearly a Mute Swan.

The oldest pub bird arising from a name change, *The Jackdaw* in Denton in Kent (which dates as a pub from 1645), started its long life as *The Red Lion*. As we have seen there are hundreds of pubs so named, and in 1962 (or 1963 – accounts differ) then owners Whitbread renamed it after *The Jackdaw of Rheims*, one of *The Ingoldsby Legends* written by the Reverend Richard Barham who lived in the village. We will return to The Jackdaw of Rheims in Chapter 5.

Next up we have the *Eagle and Child* on St Giles in Oxford, also discussed in Chapter 2. It is a Grade II listed building and reputed to have been the lodgings of the Royalist chancellor of the Exchequer during the English Civil War, between 1642 and 1649, and so would just pip *The Jackdaw* into second place. Jack[1.13], incidentally, gives a different range of dates (1641–1651), but that matters little because the pub was probably not actually built until at least 1650 and the first written record of it being called the *Eagle and Child* is not until 1684. I have not been able to find out what the link is between the Eagle and child legend in Lancashire (Chapter 2) and most of the pubs of that name in the same county, and this one in Oxford.

The *Stork Hotel* (which is also variously named the *Stork Inn* and just plain *The Stork*) in Condor Green near Lancaster dates from the 1660s. Tragically it burned down in a major fire in 2020 and as far as I am aware has not reopened. We will explore Stork pubs further in Chapter 4; some of them also appear to be old, but exactly how old I have not been able to discover.

There are two pubs in London called *The George and Vulture*. The one in Pitfield Street just north of Tottenham Court Road is of uncertain age, but certainly not old enough to be included here. Its sign depicts a be-wigged King George I (which appears to have been copied from a portrait in the National Portrait Gallery) and a Vulture; the Vulture is one of the smaller species, probably an African Hooded Vulture. The second, much older pub is in Castle Court, Cornhill in the heart of the City and has a fascinating history. A notice outside the pub says "established 1600", but it was not then called *The George and Vulture*. It was originally called *The George* and in 1598 was described by John Stow, the great historian of London, as "a common hostelry for travellers". When the Great Fire of 1666 swept through London it left *The George* as a burned-out shell. A wine merchant of George Yard (whose sign had been a tethered live Vulture – history does not record of which species) also lost his home and his livelihood and after the tavern was rebuilt he negotiated with the landlord for part use of it. Unhappy with the idea of having a live bird squawking around the door he agreed to

The George and Vulture, Pitfield Street, London

George and Vulture, Cornhill, London

change the name to *The George and Vulture.* Exactly when this happened is uncertain, but it must have been some time after the 1666 fire. If rebuilding proceeded apace, the renamed (and possibly relocated) pub could well have reopened by 1670. And who was "George"? Well, not George I, who did not ascend the throne until 1714. The inn sign for *The George and Vulture* in Castle Court is a highly stylised, double-headed heraldic spread Eagle (Chapter 2) overlying the red cross of Saint George. I take the depiction of the Vulture as a spread Eagle to be a bit of taxonomic and artistic licence.

A suite of at least five old pub birds are Pelicans, which I again discuss in more detail in Chapter 4. The name probably has religious connotations, explicitly reflected in the *Pelican in Her Piety* in Ogmore by Sea in Wales, which dates from about 1750. A Pelican in her piety is an allegoric early-Christian reference to the death of Jesus. The oldest Pelican pub is *The Pelican Inn* in Gloucester, a Grade II listed building dating from 1679. It's current splendid sign forms the frontispiece for this book. For some hard-to-fathom reason, given this long history, it was briefly renamed the boring and nondescript *College Arms* between 1995 and 1999, after which it reverted to being *The Pelican Inn.* The *Ship and Pelican* (the oldest pub in Heavitree near Exeter) dates from at least 1740, when it was originally simply *The Ship.* And just making it on to the list are *The Pelican Inn* in Froxfield (Wiltshire), marked on a road map from 1773, and the *Pelican* in Stapleford near Salisbury which is "18th century" and originally named after a ship of that name. I suspect that some other Pelican pubs are also old but have not been able to clearly establish a date for them.

The Hood Arms in Kilve, overlooking Bridgewater Bay in Somerset, is an old coaching inn and smugglers' pub that dates from 1689. It used to be called *The Chough and Anchor,* but the name was changed in 1832, although the inn sign still has a Chough and an anchor on it. Choughs are without question my favourite member of the Crow family, with their striking red, curved bills and red legs and their joyous bouncing flight and onomatopoeic "chuff" calls. In the late 17th century Choughs may still have bred somewhere in the vicinity on the coast or just inland from Kilve in the Quantock Hills, but they were extinct in the county by

1875–1900 (although populations survived further west on the coast of Cornwall and the north coast of Devon)[3.5]. From the mid-16th century onwards, the birds were often referred to as Cornish Choughs[1.15] to distinguish them from their continental cousins, Alpine Choughs, which have never been recorded in the UK. Although formerly abundant in Cornwall, Choughs finally became extinct there in 1952[3.6] and didn't recolonise until 2001[2.25]. Changes in agriculture appear to be the main drivers of the Chough's declining population and range. In the UK they are now limited to regions with very mild winters, suitable nesting cavities in caves and abandoned buildings and closely grazed winter pastures with patches of rocky and bare ground, a combination of requirements mainly (but not entirely) confined to western coastal fringes warmed by the Gulf Stream[2.25]. Choughs feed by probing and digging with that long, curved, red bill for insect larvae in cattle dung, particularly in winter, and for ants in the summer. The reinstatement of traditional farm management practices by the voluntary conservation sector (particularly outdoor wintering cattle on closely grazed coastal fields above sea cliffs) has allowed Choughs to recolonise some of their historic coastal range in western Britain.

So, was the original *Chough and Anchor* named after a bird that bred locally? I thought it might be, but the answer is "no", at least not directly. Cornish Choughs feature prominently in heraldry – they are depicted accurately as black birds with red bills and legs on the coats of arms of Cornwall County Council, the Dutchy of Cornwall, Thomas Cromwell, and many others. A Chough and an anchor are the crest of the Acland-Hood family, local landowners from St Audries, which lies nearly three miles west of Kilve along the A39. Heraldry, not habitats, give us this particular pub bird.

In another reference to a member of the Crow family the *Crowtrees Inn* at Tosside near Skipton in West Yorkshire claims (both on its website and on the sign over the pub door) to be a 17th-century pub, and it is certainly old. But I am unable to find out just how old. "Crowtrees" could refer to Carrion Crows, but since they nest solitarily why "trees"? It seems possible that "Crowtrees" is a reference to a rookery, which could have been a significant local landmark. But as with so many pub names, its origin seems lost in the mists of time.

Crowtrees Inn, Tosside

Lion and Pheasant, Shrewsbury

The Dog and Duck, Soho

The Crane, Wandsworth

As we move into the 18th century, dating doesn't necessarily get any easier. The earliest records of the *Lion and Pheasant* in Shrewsbury[3.7] are from letters, the first dated 27 February 1707, to be left "with Mr. Benbow at ye Lyon and Pheasant" and the second dated 5 April 1714, which was "to be left at ye Lyon and Pheasant on ye Wile Cop". The first official record of the inn does not appear until 1804, a gap of nearly 100 years between when we know it existed and official recognition, re-enforcing the difficulties of being certain about the age of a pub.

Also surviving from the early 18th century (the exact date doesn't seem to have been recorded) is *The Dove* by the River Thames in Hammersmith, which has a lovely sign (p. 54) of the white dove of peace carrying an olive branch in front of a rainbow; Noah is missing from the picture. It was originally *The Dove Inn* then a coffee house (also called *The Dove)* and reverted to being *The Dove* pub once more, although I don't have any dates for the changes. We met the pub in Chapter 1 and will meet it again in Chapter 5.

The original *Dog and Duck* on Bateman Street in Soho was built in 1734 and replaced on the same spot by the present building in 1897. Information in the pub itself says that "so-ho" was a "Royal hunting call", and the area was a royal hunting ground, possibly involving dogs (the sign has a King Charles Spaniel and a Mallard on it). In the 16th century this part of what is now Central London was indeed a hunting ground, but sources on Google make it more likely (but by no means certain) that the dogs were harriers[1.19], the hunted were Hares not Ducks, and "so-ho" was used to call the dogs off, not encourage them to act as decoys for Ducks as depicted on the sign.

The Crane in the London Borough of Wandsworth has a complicated pedigree. It dates from "at least 1748"[3.8] and was called by its current name before becoming *The Armoury* (date unspecified – the pub is on Armoury Road) and reverting to *The Crane* in 2016. But the bird on the current sign and on its website isn't a Common Crane because it has a small crest on its nape and lacks the striking, dishevelled tail-like bustle (formed from the tertial wing feathers) at the rear of an adult Crane. The image is just a white silhouette and might possibly be taken from a picture of a Grey Heron. Etymologically speaking, such a 'mistake' would be reasonable, because when 'real' Cranes became extinct in England in the 16th century (see later) "the name was transferred to the Heron"[1.15]. However, on the pub website is an older inn sign that shows what is undoubtedly a Common Crane, perched (wait for it) on the gantry of a giant red crane. We will encounter this play on words again in the next section. The information displayed outside the front door of the pub is coy[3.8]: "It is not known whether the pub is named after a crane, the bird, or the old-fashioned lifting device. This part of the [River] Wandle was busy with industry at one time."

At last, for what is clearly not the oldest pub in England, and not even close to being the oldest pub bird, we finally get to *Ye Olde Fighting Cocks* in St Albans. The building is described by Historic England as being of 16th-century appearance, and was originally known as "The Round House" but there is no record of it being licensed as a public house under that name. The first known reference to it being an alehouse is in 1756 when it appears to have been trading as the *Three Pigeons*. Around 1800 its name changed to the *Fighting Cocks*. The prefix *Ye Olde* is a late-Victorian affectation.

Described in Chapter 2, the nursery rhyme *Pop! Goes the Weasel* immortalises *The Eagle* on the corner of City Road and Shepherdess Way in London. The meaning of the nonsense verse has been much debated, but from our perspective the important thing is that it clearly names *The Eagle*, and given that the rhyme may have originated in the 18th century (but did not become popular until Victorian times) the pub must also date from sometime during that century. But when is unclear. We do know that it closed as a pub in 1825 and did not reopen until 1901.

Last but not least *The Bird in Hand* in Ironbridge in Shropshire opened in 1774, five years before the famous iron bridge itself was completed in 1779 (it opened to traffic in 1781). The bridge, the world's first cast iron bridge, spans a spectacular gorge above the River Severn with as dramatic a sense of place as one could hope for. The pub does not have a sign, just a name, so we cannot be sure what bird it might be (Chapter 2). I was not alone in believing that the bridge was the brainchild of two giants of the Industrial Revolution, Thomas Telford and Isambard Kingdom Brunel, perhaps in part because the village (also now called Ironbridge) lies just south of the small market town of Telford, and Thomas Telford did build bridges (the Menai Bridge in North Wales being the most famous). But they had nothing to do with it. The bridge was the brainchild of Shrewsbury architect Thomas Pritchard. He worked with ironmaster Abraham Darby, who discovered a way to make the production of cast iron financially viable.

Birds Out of Place

A significant number of pub birds occur in locations in which we might reasonably expect to find their wild, living namesakes. I will come to them next. But a few appear to be in the wrong place, in the sense that (excluding birds escaping from captivity) the species would only occur there, if at all, as a vagrant, miles away from where it should be. It is these vagrant real birds that set twitchers' pulses racing and make them willing to travel, sometimes hundreds of miles, to see a new species they can add to their life list. (One supposed derivation of the word "twitcher", which only entered birders' vocabulary in the 1950s, is the nervous twitching of rarity hunters as they search frantically for a sight of the bird.) On balance, I think that at least three of the four pub birds apparently in the wrong place and discussed next may have distinctly non-birdy origins and not be 'lost' at all.

Storm Petrel was the last regular British breeding species to go on my (real-bird) life list. Breeding populations of this tiny seabird are confined to "remote, small, rat-free offshore islands on the Atlantic fringes of north and west Britain and Ireland from Shetland to the Channel Islands"[2.25], and I had never had the opportunity to be in the right place at the right time to see one. It wasn't until the end of June and early July 2001, 50 years after I started seriously birding, that I finally caught up with it on Skomer off the coast of Pembroke, where Dot and I were guests of Chris and Mary Perrins[3.9]. Chris caught a bird in a mist-net as it came into its nest site in a rockface below the warden's house in the dark, and we could see in our torchlights the white rumps of others swirling about like moths. We could also smell them – they had a pleasant, musty odour. (Can you 'tick' a scent if you haven't actually seen them? Now there's an interesting question for a twitcher: if you can tick a bird from its call, why not its scent?) Of course, you can see Storm Petrels out to sea during sea-watching sessions from land as they pass close to the coast, or from a boat. I just never encountered one. They also occur extremely rarely inland as storm-driven vagrants. In my local bird-club's recording area around York (The York Ornithological Club) there has been just one recorded vagrant (on 1 November 2000) in the last 25 years – a bird flying over floodwater on what is now the Lower Derwent Valley National Nature Reserve. It wasn't me who saw it.

All of which makes *The Stormy Petrel* on Tern Hill in Market Drayton, about 50 miles from the Irish Sea in landlocked Staffordshire, a very rare bird indeed. Unfortunately the pub was demolished in 2017 and the one surviving sign (apart from the name) on the web appears to show a bird head-on with raised wings. But I can't be sure. The name in any case may originally have had its origins not in a vagrant seabird but from the description of a person who was "fond of strife" or a "harbinger of trouble"[3.10] and subsequently transformed into the bird by a previous owner or signwrite. We may never know.

Marsh Harriers are wonderful birds of prey, one of three species of Harrier that nest in the UK, each in different habitats and in this case (as the name implies) in marshland. Like so many other large raptors, they were persecuted to extinction as breeding birds in the UK by gamekeepers, the last pair breeding in Norfolk in 1899. A halting recolonisation started in 1911, and the species has bred annually since 1927[3.5]; by 2016 there were somewhere between 590 and 695 pairs[2.13]. Numbers are still increasing. I saw my first Marsh Harrier at Leighton Moss in Lancashire (now an RSPB reserve) in August 1958, when they were still incredibly scarce birds, and my second not until September 1965 at Wicken Fen in Cambridgeshire, where they may have bred the previous year. Both were the right (real) birds in the right places. In my database there are three pubs called the *Marsh Harrier*, one in Norwich (close to the Norfolk Broads, one of the bird's last strongholds and a site of initial recolonisation, so very appropriate) and a second in Oxford. The latter is on Marsh Road, and according to the taxi driver who took me to photograph it in 2012 it was originally called *The Bullington* and changed its name "about 20 years ago"[3.11]. That was about 30 years

The Marsh Harrier, Oxford

ago now, and back then there were no Marsh Harriers anywhere near Oxford. I guess being on Marsh Road was sufficient. It has a lovely sign of a pair of Harriers. The third *Marsh Harrier* is in St Ives in Cornwall. It's a modern pub and as far as I know these Harriers have not bred in Cornwall in the last 200 years.

Terns are predominantly seabirds although one species (Common Tern) also breeds extensively inland, particularly in England on lakes, reservoirs and flooded gravel workings, either on islands or on specially provided floating Tern rafts. But there are no confirmed breeding records[2.25] near *The Tern Inn* in Chipping Sodbury (South Gloucestershire) and even though all sea Terns do turn up inland on migration from time to time (Common Terns much more often than the four other regular UK breeding species) if the name does refer to a bird passing through the area it would be unique among pub birds. But it is even more complicated than that. The pub is currently closed[3.12] but the sign on its website shows probably the least likely sea Tern of all to appear inland – a Little Tern, in flight, with its characteristic yellow bill, black cap and white forehead. Little Terns in England are confined as a breeding species to sandy beaches in three main areas (the Humber and Lincolnshire, East Anglia, and the Solent). There are none anywhere near the Bristol Channel – the nearest bit of coastline[2.25]. In all likelihood this is probably another example of the signwriter being given a picture from a bird book and being told to "paint that". But why a Tern at all? Possibly *The Tern Inn* is a deliberate pun by a landlord keen to have you turn in as you drive, cycle or walk by.

At the top of Parliament Street in York is a pub, the *Three Cranes*, which has one of the most unusual and beautiful sign of a pub bird anywhere. On it, three Cranes are depicted above the front door and window on 18 large ceramic tiles, one large adult and two smaller birds presumably supposed to be young ones. The sign is so striking that it feels churlish to point out that young Cranes are dull sandy-grey-brown in colour and lack the black-and-white head and neck pattern of the adult. More interestingly, why three Cranes? The pub is quite old. It features in Cooper's book published in 1897[1.12] but with no indication of the pub's age, and he is clearly being wildly optimistic when he says "On the sign are painted three birds, representing the migratory fowl often seen in the marshy districts of England." Prior to quite recent recolonisation commencing in 1979, the last recorded breeding record by Cranes in England was in Norfolk in 1542[3.13]. The pub certainly didn't exist back then. I asked the landlord when I first started on this journey in 2010 if he knew the origin of the pub's name and sign, and got a withering look that implied "Why would anybody want to know that?" But whenever the pub was established, Cranes would have been anything but "often seen" anywhere around York.

Three Cranes, York

Cranes disappeared as a breeding species in the UK not primarily because of the drainage of most of their fenland habitat (as is commonly assumed) but because they were killed in unsustainable numbers for food and 'sport'. Eggs, young birds and adults were all taken. The numbers are staggering[3.13]. King John, flying Gyrfalcons in pursuit of Cranes, is reported to have killed seven adults in Cambridgeshire in December 1212 and nine in Lincolnshire in February 1213. It isn't clear whether some or all of these ended up on the banquet table, but others certainly did. The Christmas feast of Henry III in York in 1251 included 115 Cranes (plus the 351 Mute Swans mentioned in Chapter 2[2.3]). A later banquet also in my home city (in 1465) to celebrate the enthronement of a new archbishop is reported to have included 204 Cranes. They really knew how to party.

If there were no surviving Cranes anywhere near York for several hundred years, why was *Three Cranes* selected as the name for a pub in the centre of the city? The answer (as you may have guessed) is that the three cranes were not birds at all. According to Cooper[1.12]: "It is probable that the sign…originated in the circumstances of a like number of cranes being placed in the lane adjoining, for raising and lowering goods in the warehouses which stood there." Waymarking.com repeats the story that the name probably originally referred to three narrow lifting cranes used to haul goods up into higher stories of buildings in an adjacent narrow alley called Three Cranes Lane. The lane no longer exists. An inn sign depicting three lifting cranes does not strike me as being very attractive. Depicting them as these magnificent birds was a marketing ploy. But by whom and when is a mystery.

The Right Birds in the Right Places

We have already encountered several pub birds in the 'right place'. *The George* with a Brent Goose on its sign in Cley next the Sea; several pubs called *Eagle and Child* in Lancashire, the county where the legend is supposed to have originated; *The Falcon* at Arncliffe in the Yorkshire Dales, close to one of the Peregrine Falcon's traditional breeding cliffs; two pubs called *The Harnser* (Norfolk dialect for Grey Heron in a county where Herons abound); the *Old Swan Uppers* on the Thames at Maidenhead; and two called *The Seabirds* on the Yorkshire Coast. There are plenty more pub birds like them in, or close to, places and habitats where their living namesakes occur. But I am going to start with a pub bird that is currently ubiquitous in lowland habitats throughout the country and yet its single representative is arguably in an appropriate place.

Invaders from the East

It could have been anywhere in England but turned out to be Cromer on the Norfolk coast. The invasion[3.14] started in far off Turkey shortly after 1900 when Collared Doves (for reasons unknown) began to spread from their Turkish stronghold into the Balkans, where they remained until 1928, after which a push north-west across Europe started in earnest. The invasion reached England in 1955, when the first pair nested in Cromer on the north Norfolk coast. The arrival was to be expected. The Doves had reached the North Sea coasts of Germany and the Netherlands by 1949. For birders (or as they were known at the time, birdwatchers) the event was nevertheless exciting and terribly secret[3.15]. Collared Doves are now found throughout virtually the whole of England, most of Wales and all of lowland Scotland[2.25]. *The Dove* in Poringland on the south-east edge of Norwich and about 25 miles inland from Cromer has a Collared Dove on its sign. The pub itself dates from at least 1786[3.16] when it was called *The Dove* but of course if it had a sign back then it couldn't possibly have been a Collared Dove and there is nothing I can find on the web to suggest when the current sign was painted. The building had become decrepit enough to be condemned as unsafe in 1968 but was fortunately spared and restored.

I like to think but cannot prove that it acquired its sign in the rebuilding and that the landlord deliberately picked a Collared Dove to celebrate this remarkable bird's invasion of England from a bridgehead just up the coast. On the other hand, it may just be a total coincidence.

The Dove, Poringland

Uplands, Moors and Mountains

Britain's uplands, moors and mountains support a highly distinct set of birds[3.17], although rather few of them make it as a pub bird in these habitats. Of the Golden Eagles, Peregrine Falcons and Ravens discussed in Chapter 2, (as I have already mentioned) only *The Falcon* in Arncliffe, Wharfedale, with a Peregrine on its sign, is in the 'right' sort of place; none of the rest are likely to occur naturally except as vagrants in the vicinity of the pub, and none appear to have been named with a sense of place in mind, but rather for other reasons (for example heraldry, falconry, local legend or to impress potential customers). Only four or possibly five pub birds inhabiting British uplands feature the right bird in the right place. They are Red Grouse, Black Grouse, Dotterel and Common Sandpiper, and, pushing it a bit, Golden Plover.

The Falcon, Arncliffe

Chapter 2 discussed the illegal persecution of Eagles and other birds of prey on grouse moors. The quarry species being illegally 'protected' is the Red Grouse. As Ian Newton puts it in his book *Uplands and Birds*[3.17]: "No other wild bird species has had so much influence on British upland landscapes or indeed on upper-class life. The annual recess of parliament still coincides with the opening of the grouse hunting season on 12 August (the Glorious Twelfth), and by the end of the day the first grouse of the season have already reached the more exclusive London restaurants." As Ian reminds us, the Red Grouse is "Scotland's national game bird, a former mascot of the Scottish rugby team, the emblem of a famous whisky brand, and the logo of the ornithological journal *British Birds*". Taxonomically,

Moorcock Inn, Wensleydale

it can be viewed as an endemic UK and Irish species, or as a subspecies of the much more widespread Willow Grouse (or Willow Ptarmigan), which has a global distribution across the whole of northern Europe, Asia and North America. When this distinct UK bird evolved is uncertain, but it is now confined to heather moorland, and adults feed primarily on heather shoots. Perhaps after the last ice age Red Grouse may have occurred on heather-dominated lowland heaths, but they have never done so in historical times. And like the birds themselves, all three pubs named after them are in the uplands – two in the Peak District and one in the Yorkshire Dales. Two of the pubs, both called *The Grouse Inn*, are in Birch Vale (on the western edge of the Peak District National Park) and in Longshaw, within the Park itself. The other is at Garsdale Head in Wensleydale, in the Yorkshire Dales National Park. And thereby hangs a tale. This one is called the *Moorcock Inn*.

The bird on the sign of the *Moorcock Inn* is a Red Grouse (and W.B. Alexander gives "Moorcock" as an alternative name for "Grouse" i.e. Red Grouse) but as a pub bird this name is more often associated with its (now) much rarer and certainly more exotic-looking relative, the Black Grouse. As *Birds Britannica*[1.22] explains "Black grouse are regularly depicted on the signs of pubs called *The Moorcock*, despite there being very little evidence that the bird was ever known by this name." In that section of *Birds Britannica* Tim Melling goes on to speculate: "It would be interesting to know if there was an unacknowledged folk tradition of using 'Moorcock' as a name for both grouse species and whether the pub's choice of title reflected the former presence of black grouse themselves." *The Oxford Book of British Bird Names*[1.15] does not record anything about Moorcock being a former name for Black Grouse, giving "Heathcock", "Black game" and just plain "Grous"[sic] as older alternatives.

Black Grouse used to be much more widespread and abundant than they are today. In the last quarter of the 19th century, for example, they occurred throughout Britain's south-west peninsula, a substantial part of Wales, Worcestershire, Staffordshire, the whole of northern England and Scotland[3.5]. As gamebirds we might expect pubs to be named after

The Blackcock Inn, Falstone

The Bonny Moorhen, Stanhope

them as a familiar, but striking bird. Today the picture is very different. Breeding Black Grouse were recorded in just 15% of the UK's National Grid of 10km squares[2.25], and almost all were in northern England and Scotland. The main cause of the decline is habitat loss. Unlike Red Grouse, Black Grouse have demanding requirements. They need a mosaic of habitats over a large area providing a variety of foods[3.17] of which heather is just one. Large areas of the UK are now too tidy and too uniform for them to survive. The three pubs definitely named after them in my main database are in the north of England, in landscapes that still support surviving populations of Black Grouse. But the names of these three pubs open up a can of worms[3.18].

One of the pubs, called *The Blackcock Inn*, in Falstone, just below the Kielder Dam in Northumberland, is simple and straightforward, with a male Black Grouse on the sign. The second is *The Moorcock Inn* at Hill Top near Middleton-in-Teesdale, which has a pair of birds on the sign that are not Red Grouse. It shows a brown-and-black-speckled female Black Grouse hidden behind a showy, glossy-black male with striking red wattle 'eyebrows' and a wonderful lyre-shaped tail.

The third pub is apparently not a Black Grouse at all. It is called *The Bonny Moorhen* and is in Stanhope, Co. Durham. I have nothing against Moorhens. They are remarkably successful and used to be considered one of the most widely naturally distributed species of bird on the planet until the taxonomists got their hands on them and decided that the Common Moorhen of the Old World is not the same species as what is now called the Common Gallinule of the New World (they look essentially identical but have very different calls)[2.10]. But despite their success as one, or two, species nobody (except perhaps another Moorhen) would describe the bird as "bonny". And Stanhope, about 200m up on the edge of the Durham Pennine uplands, is hardly prime Moorhen territory. But it is Black Grouse territory, and the answer seems to be that the bird has changed her identity. The species on the sign used to be a female Black Grouse, with Moorhen being the female equivalent of Moorcock[3.19]; as a female she could be bonny, and being on the edge of the Durham moors she was in an appropriate habitat. Keith Bowey (my correspondent) tells me that the inn sign was repainted sometime around 2005; it appears to be another example of the landlord giving the signwriter a bird book and saying something like "paint one of these" (adding in this case) "it's a proper Moorhen". Just for the record, there is one other Moorhen pub – *The Three Moorhens*, in Hitchin, Hertfordshire. None of the websites I looked at tell us anything about its history (except the first record of somebody living in the building is 1839), and there is no photograph of a sign. Was it a pub in 1839? Why Moorhens and are they really 'proper' Moorhens? And again (as with Doves – Chapter 2) why three? W.B. Alexander[1.2] claims "it is possible" that the name has an heraldic origin, but there the trail goes cold.

Black Grouse and the next species in this section (Dotterel) could not be more different in their breeding strategies. Black Grouse lek – that is, groups of males gather at dawn and before dusk at traditional natural arenas primarily in spring, take up small territories and spar with one another. The territories are advertised and defended with a truly remarkable suite of bizarre calls (the two most frequent described as a "crowing-hiss" and "rookooing" – the latter rendered as a far carrying and ventriloquial "rrooo-OO-rroo-rroo") together with some extremely complex behaviours including showing off their tails, wattles and conspicuous white under-tail coverts. So-called "flutter-jumps" are common – the birds appear to bounce up and down. Encounters between competing males are not all showing off and can lead to physical violence. The whole pantomime-like performance takes up over four large pages of very small print in *The Birds of the Western Palearctic*[3.20]. I remember vividly being dumfounded when I encountered my first lek in Grizedale Forest in the Lake District on a misty dawn morning in early April 1963. It was at one and the same time the most peculiar, spectacular and amusing birding experience I had ever had. But it isn't a pantomime. It is deadly serious. The whole point is to attract a female and mate, a sort of avian disco with sex on the dance floor. Females (bonny Moorhens) come to the leks and watch from the margins. The dominant males occupy territories in the centre of the lek and are approached and solicited by females much more often than the subdominant males around the edges. Females may mate with more than one male, but once she has mated the males take no further part in caring for her or her chicks. He may never see any of his children nor their mum again. The bonny Moorhen does all the work.

Dotterels do it as differently as it is possible to in terms of avian breeding systems. These plovers, relatives of Lapwings, Golden Plovers and Ringed Plovers, breed in the high alpine mountains of Europe. More of that in a moment. Dotterel go in for an even rarer form of breeding system in birds than leking, one in which the males do all the incubation and childcare and the females simply lay the eggs and leave for pastures (or rather mountain-tops) new to mate with another male, lay a second clutch and again abandon him. Some 80–90% of females may mate with one male in Scotland and then, footloose and fancy-free, cross the North Sea to find a second mate in Scandinavia[3.17]. Consistent with this role reversal, unlike most birds, female Dotterel are much more brightly coloured than their rather dowdy (and temporary) male partners.

If the Yorkshire Strickland family knew of the very unladylike behaviour of the females it did not stop them calling their pub at Reighton on the Yorkshire Wolds *The Dotterel*. But the Wolds are hardly alpine; they have a maximum altitude of around 200m; the altitude is only 139m at Beacon Hill just east of Reighton, which is near the coast. The highest pub in the UK (the 17th-century *Tan Hill* also in the Yorkshire Dales) is located at just over 500m; Dotterel don't consider a mountain as a suitable breeding site in the Scottish Highlands unless it is at least 700m high or 500m in the far north-west[2.25], and most nests are well above these altitudes. What is going on here? The Dotterels that breed in the UK winter in the Atlas Mountains of Morocco, and flocks (known as trips) returning in the spring use traditional stopover sites to feed up and rest on their way north, including the Yorkshire Wolds. As the renowned Yorkshire ornithologist Jonny Mather explains[3.21]: "*The Dotterel Inn* was built by one of the Strickland family and designed for the accommodation of gamekeepers, who came from all parts of the neighbourhood for the purpose of shooting Dotterels in the spring." The slaughter of trips of migrating Dotterel throughout the UK was terrible and is almost certainly one of the reasons why they are now

The Dotterel, Reighton

much rarer here than formerly. Mather goes on: "The original inn sign, depicting a Dotterel, was painted by Mrs Strickland. I wonder if it was any better than the one now adorning the front of the building?" The current sign is recognisable as a Dotterel, but it is not one of the best illustrations of a pub bird that I have seen.

Coincidentally, Jonny Mather also provided me with information on another upland pub bird[3.22], Common Sandpiper. You might not associate Sandpipers with the uplands, because the birds sharing the moniker "Sandpiper" are a varied bunch of mainly shorebirds and birds of lowland wetlands. Common Sandpipers are indeed common on migration on lowland marshes, lakes and rivers throughout the UK, when travelling to and from their wintering sites in West Africa. But they breed close to the water on the margins of shingly, stony or rocky upland rivers, where their piping calls and characteristic flight, low over the water with alternate rapid fluttering wingbeats followed by a glide on down-bowed wings are one of the delights of a walk up a river in summer in northern and western Britain. They are common in the Yorkshire Dales, where there is a single pub called *The Sandpiper Inn* in the Market Place in Leyburn, the town in which my adventures with pub birds began. Jonny Mather takes up the story. "When I was in business, one of my companies dealt with pub signs and we did work for…one pub, *The Sandpiper* in Leyburn. My artist was very good and I gave him a Common Sandpiper reference [in a bird book]; it has since been re-done and it is not as good." When I last saw it there was no sign at all, just a name. Leyburn stands just above the River Ure at the entrance to Wensleydale and Common Sandpipers breed along the riverbank close to the town. They are model parents, sharing incubation duties and the care of the chicks.

If you head up the Ure to the high open fells of heather moorland and blanket bog you will find breeding Golden Plovers. You are more likely to hear them first – a wild, evocative, even plaintive whistle, rendered "püü" or "tüü(ü)" in my field guide. They are handsome relatives of Dotterel, with gold-spangled backs and a black face running down the neck in a narrow stripe to black underparts, separated from the upperparts by bold white side-stripes. The only pub named after them isn't in the Yorkshire Dales. The *Golden Plover* is in Sheffield. It is a fairly new pub, so the name owes nothing to history, but it is (just about) a candidate for a pub bird in the right place. From Sheffield you can see the eastern edge of the Peak District National Park, and the open fells where Golden Plover breed – their most southerly regular locality in England[3.23].

Lowland Heaths

Oliver Rackham puts it nicely[2.27]: "Heaths are in dry parts of the country, are subject to periodic droughts, and have mineral soils. Moors are in high-rainfall areas and have more or less peat-covered soil." The most northerly examples of heath lie around York in the Vale of York. Heathland vegetation is dominated by dwarf shrubs (several species of heathers, plus gorse), with areas of bracken and sometimes grasses. "Of the many features of heathlands, bleakness and barrenness…come most easily to mind."[3.24] However, the habitat has a distinctive avifauna, and three of the most charismatic species have made it onto my pub-bird list. They are Dartford Warbler, Nightjar and Woodlark.

The Furze Wren is a modern pub in Broadway Square, Bexleyheath, a part of East London just south of the Thames near Dartford. Inside the pub is some (all too rare) information about how it got its name. A plaque on the wall says:

> *"Less than 200 years ago Bexley Heath was rough open land, unfit for cultivation and frequented by highwaymen. Across the Heath ran the old Roman road, approximately along the line of Broadway/Market Place. In 1773, Doctor John Latham, then living in nearby Dartford, discovered a previously unknown bird on the Heath. The species has since been named the Dartford Warbler, although its old country name was the Furze Wren. The population of this small, dark, long-tailed warbler crashed to a few pairs in the 1960s, but its numbers have since recovered. There is a carefully preserved specimen of the Furze Wren in Dartford Museum, part of the collection bequeathed by John Latham."*

Born in 1740, Latham was a doctor by profession, a natural historian, and one of the leading British ornithologists of his time[3.25]. Whoever decided to call the new pub after this delightful little bird had a real sense of place. The heath is long gone from here, but elsewhere the birds themselves are thriving. They are demanding and need just the right combination of tall gorse (furze) bushes and heather for them to prosper, and unlike all their relatives (in the genus *Sylvia*), which leave Britain for the winter, they stay here. As the plaque indicates, during the very hard winters of 1961/62 and 1962/63 the population was almost exterminated, with no more than a dozen pairs surviving[3.6]. But they hung on and by 2017 there were estimated to be 2,200 pairs[2.13] in England and (relatively recently colonised) Wales, with a conspicuous northward and eastward spread away from their former southern heathland strongholds[2.25]. This conservation success story is due to milder winters (a product of climate change) and to heathland habitat restoration and recreation.

The birds themselves can be very hard to see but are very beautiful, with slate-grey upperparts, wine-red underparts, a red ring around their eyes and long, often cocked, tails. Growing up in the north of England I did not see one until 1970. My wife, two very small children and I were having our first family holiday together and staying in a B&B in Poole on the Dorset coast. I must admit to having ulterior motives in suggesting to Dot that we go to Poole, because I knew the surrounding heaths were (at that time) about the only place in which you could find Dartford Warblers in England. Whilst the family played on the beach I took off to Studland Heath to find my quarry – and failed. After a couple of hours flogging through rough heather and fruitlessly searching gorse bushes, I returned dispiritedly to the family where Dot said: "There's a funny little bird in the bushes by the car park. Is that what you are looking for?" (Dot isn't a birder). It was. Tick. It's strange to feel both elated and very foolish at the same time.

Nightjars are summer visitors to the Dorset heaths but they are also much more widespread as a breeding species in the UK than Dartford Warblers. And they are very strange birds. They are about the size of a Blackbird but are shaped more like a hawk, and when sitting on the ground they are so highly camouflaged (even keeping their eyes closed) they look like a dead branch. The birds stay hidden during the day, only becoming active at twilight when their 'song' (if you can call it that), delivered from a perch, rattles across the landscape like a distant motorbike changing gear. Their prey consists primarily of large night-flying moths and beetles, which they catch on the wing in flight (like a Swallow) or from a perch (like a Flycatcher), aided by an exceptionally wide gape ringed by basket-like rectal bristles (modified feathers) that form a trap for their prey. Gilbert White makes several references to Nightjars in *The Natural History of* Selborne[2.43] , the first detailed comments being in his letter to Thomas Pennant dated 2 July 1769. "There is no bird, I believe, whose manners I have studied more than that of the *caprimulgus* (the goatsucker), as it is a wonderful and curious creature.... [It] utters its jarring note sitting on a bough. This bird is most punctual in beginning its song exactly at the close of day; so exactly that I have known it strike up more than once or twice just at the report of the Portsmouth evening gun...". *Caprimulgus* is still the generic name for Nightjars and is made up of two Latin words, *capri* (goat) and *mulgus* (milker). It has its origins in the folk myth that the birds sucked the teats of nanny goats to obtain milk[1.15] when what they were actually doing was flying around goats at dusk to catch moths and beetles. Other vernacular names include Fern-Owl, Churn-Owl and Wheel Bird.

So where do pubs come into the Nightjar's story? One is definitely the right pub bird in the right place. The website for *The Nightjar* in Ferndown in Dorset explicitly says that it takes its name from a species of bird that lives on the surrounding heathland. *The Nightjar Inn* (in Aylesbeare near Exeter) is close to, if not actually in, Nightjar country and has a picture of the bird in flight on its sign. But think about it. What is a more appropriate name for a pub than a night jar (providing it isn't goat's milk)? Among pub names in general there has been ample scope for both puns and plays on words (Chapter 2). Examples include *The Open Arms* and *The Gnu Inn*. Most bird names don't lend themselves to such happy, clever frivolity, but there are exceptions (including *The Puff Inn* on St Kilda, encountered earlier in this Chapter). *The Nightjar* in Ferndown has it both ways, with a pavement banner on its website advertising it as the Night Jar. The three remaining Nightjar pubs may well also be simple plays on words rather than the right birds in the right place. Two are just plain *The Nightjar* (one in Bransholme outside Hull, the other in Weston-super-Mare in Somerset) and neither are in or close to the right habitats nor do they appear to have a sign. The third is *The Nightjar Bar* in Hebden Bridge, West Yorkshire with its name in neon lights and definitely not to my taste. I do wonder just how many of their clientele know what a Nightjar really is.

Gilbert White[2.43] devoted the entire contents of his (undated) letter number VI to Thomas Pennant[3.26] in the *Natural History of Selborne* to the "forest of Wolmer". Woolmer Forest (as we now spell it) still exists. It is (and was) heathland and a 'Forest' (with a capital F) only in the legal sense of being an area of land subject to special laws as a royal hunting preserve[2.27]. In White's words: "three-fifths perhaps lie in this [i.e. Selborne] parish…and has afforded me much entertainment both as a sportsman and as a naturalist". In his day it was about seven miles long and 2.5 miles wide (roughly 15 square miles) and consisted "entirely of sand covered with heath and fern" (bracken). Today it is still the largest and most diverse area of lowland heath in England outside the New Forest, albeit now much reduced in size and more fragmented by roads, houses and other infrastructure. The surviving remnant is a five square mile Site of Special Scientific Interest and part of the Whealdon Heath Special Protection Area within the South Downs National Park[3.27].

Gilbert White noted that Woolmer used to support Blackcock[3.28], and to this day it still has breeding populations of all three of our special heathland birds (Dartford Warbler, Nightjar, and Woodlark). The first two occur as 'real' birds and the latter both as a 'real' bird and as a pub bird. *The Woodlark* pub is in the village of Bordon, which is about four miles north-east of Selborne at the northern end of Woolmer Forest. From its website the pub looks to be relatively new, and it appears not to have a sign, just a name; and as happens all too often the website is totally silent about how it got its name. But credit where credit is due (as with *The Furze Wren*), whoever chose the name got the sense of place spot on.

Gilbert White clearly loved Woodlarks, and in particular their wonderful song, which he describes in both prose and poetry in several letters to Pennant and to Barrington. He noted that they sing both during the day and at night from a perch or in flight "suspended in mid air", "While high in air, and pois'd upon his wings/Unseen, the soft enamour'd woodlark sings." The song is much slower than that of Skylarks, with sweet rising and falling phrases interspersed with slow melancholy "loo-loo-loo…" notes. Woodlarks stopped breeding in Yorkshire in 1958[3.21] (in line with a general national decline from unknown causes), but they recolonised the county on northerly remnants of southern heathland in the Vale of York in the early 2000s (again for unknown reasons). I never get tired of hearing them.

There is only one other pub featuring a Woodlark on its sign, but not in its name. *The Lamb and Lark* in Limington (near Yeovil) features both a lamb and an unequivocal Woodlark on the inn sign, rather than the more likely Skylark. The name could well be due to the merger of two pubs (Chapter 1), and I can only assume (as with other unusual species) the signwriter copied it from a book, because Woodlarks certainly don't occur on the floodplain of the River Yeo and probably never did, even though historically they were quite an abundant breeding species in that part of North Somerset in more suitable habitats[3.6] (which include rough grassland, downland and young plantations, but not river floodplains).

The Lamb and Lark, Limington

Wetlands, Lakes and Marshes

One of the three pubs called *The Marsh Harrier* (the one in Norwich), as we have already seen, is the right pub bird in the right place. It was originally called *The King of Prussia* in 1840, when the building was a small café, not a pub, and renamed *The George IV* in 1914, and finally transformed again as *The Marsh Harrier* (its website doesn't say when) "to reflect [the] rural surroundings and proximity to the river Yare". Norfolk's extensive wetlands, particularly the Broads, also host large numbers of Grey Herons and (as we have also seen) two pubs both called by their dialect name *The Harnser*. *The Heron* in London W2 is on Norfolk Crescent (p. 143). I'm not sure if that counts. But the *Pike and Heron* in Hornsea, adjacent to Hornsea Mere on the Yorkshire coast definitely does (or rather did). This unique and distinctive name, bringing together a bird and a fish, was apparently not sufficient to persuade some marketing guru to keep it. It now goes by the very undistinguished name of the *New Inn*.

Back in Norfolk, *The Grebe* on the High Street in Stalham on the edge of Sutton Broad is also very much the right bird in the right place. I cannot find out anything about the pub's history, and its name could refer to either of the two species of Grebe (Little or Great Crested) that nest on the Broads along the River Ant to the south of the town, or on Hickling Broad a few miles away. The pub has no sign, but my guess is that the bird is a Great Crested Grebe not a Little Grebe (aka Dabchick). Dabchicks are cute, quite dumpy balls of diving energy but seem an unlikely choice for the name of a pub. Great Crested Grebes have the 'wow factor'. They are quite large, incredibly graceful birds with long necks, a dagger of a bill and (in the breeding season) striking head plumes. And it was the head plumes (known as "tippits") and the skin and feathers on their underparts (known as "grebe fur") that did for them. Their plumage became all the rage for a Victorian fashion industry that turned them into boas and muffs (grebe fur) and adornments for ladies' hats (the tippets). By 1860 one estimate suggests that only between 32 and 72 pairs survived[3.5]. The population in the Broads, close to London, was particularly badly hit, the slaughter made worse by egg collecting. But (probably because of the extent of the Broads) Norfolk was one of the counties (the other was Cheshire) where the Grebes made their last stand. Legal protection turned the tide and by 1890 Great Crested Grebes had returned to breed on almost all the Broads from which the species had been exterminated. In 2016 the UK population had reached an estimated 4,900 breeding pairs[2.13]. It would be interesting to know when *The Grebe* was so named and whether it celebrates their slaughter for the fashion trade or their subsequent recovery on the adjacent Broads.

Great Crested Grebes often share their watery world with Coots, a bird which most birders, myself included, find hard to get excited about. A friend once described them as "big black blobs with funny feet". "Bald as a Coot" comes from the featherless white shield on their forehead, above the white bill. And their feet are indeed rather odd. They are not webbed (like a Duck) or 'normal' like the legs and feet of a Hen or their close relative the Moorhen. Rather, to facilitate swimming and diving Coots have lobe-shaped lateral extensions on both sides of each toe. "Funny feet" is a good description; they also makes them 'walk funny'.

Although Coots are no longer shot for food (or at least not very often) they used to be killed in large numbers and were apparently good eating. The shoot at Hickling Broad dated back to 1825, and over a 62-year period between 1894 and 1956 a total of 55,269 were killed, with "little appreciable effect on coot numbers"[1.22]. Being shot for 'sport' and/

or food may be the reason that Coots make it as a pub bird at *The Coot* in Horsham (West Sussex) and *The Coot on the Tarn* in Great Urswick near Ulverston in Cumbia. *The Coot on the Tarn* is close to Urswick Tarn where there are undoubtedly Coots, and I have seen Coots on Warnham Mill Pond on the north-west corner of Horsham, near the pub.

Coast

We encountered the (now-closed) *Puff Inn* on St Kilda at the start of this Chapter and discussed W.B. Alexander's interests in both pub birds and seabirds in Chapter 1. Chapter 1 suggests that the pubs grouped by Alexander under "Gull or Seagull" could have included *The Gull Inn* in Framlington Pigot (Norfolk), *The Gulls Nest* in Edinburgh and *The Seagull* in Abergele, North Wales. He definitely identified "Kittiwake" (a small Gull) which may well have been *The Kittiwake* in Whitley Bay, Co. Durham. Only *The Seagull* and *The Kittiwake* are on the coast. But I pointed out that he missed *The Stormy Petrel* in Market Drayton, Staffordshire (discussed earlier in this chapter because it is *not* on the coast). He also missed *The Cormorant* (in Portchester, Hampshire, which I will come to in Chapter 5); the delightfully named *Pig and Puffin* near Tenby (this one in south-west Wales, and now also closed); and two *Seabirds,* in Bridlington and Flamborough respectively.

"Seagull" is a popular, non-ornithological term for a group of related species of birds all technically Gulls[3.29], and for the holidaymakers in Scarborough it also includes the Kittiwakes that nest on the cliffs, buildings and bridges of the seaside town. The most likely species to be called seagulls are Herring Gull and the much smaller Black-headed Gull, and both are at least as common inland as on the coast. As an undergraduate at Durham University one of my lecturers was Dr John Coulson, a world expert on Gulls in general and Kittiwakes in particular[3.30]. John was one of an inspirational quartet of lecturers in the botany and zoology departments who taught me ecology, entomology and botany, and to whom I owe my career.

The Kittiwake in Whitley Bay is the only seagull pub on the coast clearly identifiable as a species (although in name only, there is no sign). Kittiwakes are one of the most attractive of all Gulls – quite small, with smart white heads and bodies and grey, black-tipped wings (as if dipped in ink), black legs and a green bill revealing a scarlet gape when it is opened. Their onomatopoeic calls, ringing out from the breeding cliffs, are among the most evocative sounds in the birding world. It was on the cliffs looking out over the North Sea by Whitley Bay, on a field trip with my 12 fellow undergraduates and John Coulson, that I saw my first breeding Kittiwakes, their nests clinging precariously to tiny ledges on the cliff face. We travelled by public transport and on the way back to Durham on the top deck of the bus, with buckets of seawater holding a generous collection of marine life, the driver had to break suddenly, tipping over several of the buckets and confronting the conductor with a small tsunami of crabs, starfish, and seaweed as he came up the steps to check our tickets. I don't remember what happened to our precious collection. I do remember being very embarrassed.

Kittiwakes are also common further south, in the huge seabird colonies on the chalk cliffs at Bempton and Flamborough on the Yorkshire coast. These cliffs are now more or less contiguous RSPB and Yorkshire Wildlife Trust reserves along about six miles of the north face of Flamborough Head as far west as Speeton. In the breeding season the Kittiwakes share the cliffs with thousands of Puffins, Guillemots, Razorbills, Herring Gulls, Fulmars and Gannets. It is one of the great wildlife spectacles of Europe (and a great smell if you are downwind). The birds are now protected but in the past were heavily persecuted in two main ways[3.21]. Birds were shot both from the land and from boats. Kittiwakes in particular were shot in their thousands to supply feathers for the millinery trade. 'Sportsmen' shot any of the species for target practice. Local tenant farmers and their workers concentrated on harvesting Guillemot eggs for food. They were used for the manufacture of patent leather, whilst oologists (egg collectors to you and me) prized the eggs for their beauty and enormous variation in both background colouring and markings. Kittiwake eggs were also taken for food. Jonny Mather[3.21] estimates that between 35,000 and 36,000 Guillemot eggs may have been harvested every year from these cliffs. (Guestimates up to three times higher than this have no basis in fact.) The practice dates to at least the early 1700s. The collectors, known locally as "climmers", were lowered down the cliffs on hemp ropes about 100m long and hanging from iron stakes driven into the cliff top. As well as detailed historical accounts, there are old photographs in Jonny Mather's *Birds of Yorkshire*[3.21]. It looks terrifying. I like to imagine the survivors celebrating in one of the two *Seabirds* in Flamborough village or in

Bridlington (on the southern edge of the headland) but apparently surprisingly few of them were killed or injured. The slaughter of the birds themselves finally stopped with the passing of the Protection of Birds Act in 1953.

The other main group of coastal pub birds, those on flat, sandy, muddy or rocky coasts are often referred to as "waders". Like "seagull" the term embraces several species[3.31], not all of which are coastal (see Common Sandpiper earlier). The right waders in the right place on the coast include several Oystercatchers, a Dunlin, two Curlews, some indeterminate Sandpipers and a Turnstone.

In 1972, a group of birding friends and I established an RSPB members' group in York. Committee members gradually became a focus for enquiries about birds from members of the public, and one evening in April the following year I had a phone call from a local farmer that went something like this:

> "Is that Dr Lawton?"
> "Yes, how can I help you Mr [let's call him Tattersall – I don't remember his name]?"
> "I've got a Puffin nestin' in one of me cereal fields," said Mr Tattersall.
> "Sorry, can you repeat that please? What does it look like?"
> "It's a Puffin. It's black and white and it 'as a brightly coloured beak."
> "Hm. Is the nest down a hole in the ground?" (Puffins nest in holes in sea cliffs and in burrows on more level ground).
> "No, it's on't top. Wi two big, speckled eggs," said Mr Tattersall.

And the penny dropped. "It's an Oystercatcher, Mr Tattersall. They used only to nest on the coast in England but have recently moved inland to nest in – well, fields like yours."

I never met Mr Tattersall and I don't know what happened to his pioneering pair of Oystercatchers. But his puzzlement was understandable. Oystercatchers had long nested inland and on the coast in Scotland, but in the first *Atlas of Breeding Birds in Britain and Ireland*[3.6] for which fieldwork ended in 1972 there was a small number of inland breeding

The Scolt Head, London

Oystercatchers in the uplands of west Yorkshire and coastal breeding pairs on the Humber, but none in the Vale of York. They are now widespread (several pairs nest within a mile or so of my house) and their main prey items are not oysters but earthworms. As Mr Tattersall said, they are striking black-and-white birds with brightly coloured bills. But their bill isn't 'puffin shaped' and striped in bright colours. It is long, stout and orange, and they use it to pull earthworms and other prey out of the ground.

With one exception (heavily urban Chorlton-cum-Hardy inside the M60 in Manchester) all the pubs called *The Oystercatcher* are in the right habitat on the coast, albeit in one case vicariously. They are in Hull on the Humber, Littlehampton just inland from Bognor Regis, Polzeath in Cornwall, Rhosneigr on Anglesey and Tighnabruaich on Lock Fyne (where they might actually take the odd oyster). *The Scolt Head* is on Culford Road in London but the sign has a fine Oystercatcher on it; the real Scolt Head is a National Nature Reserve on the north-west coast of Norfolk, a shingle spit running parallel to the main shoreline on which Oystercatchers abound. I have no idea why *The Scolt Head* pub is so named.

Dunlins are one of the commonest waders in the UK, with a winter population mainly on the coast of about a third to half a million birds, primarily from Iceland, Greenland and Fennoscandia[3.32]. We have a much smaller breeding population numbering less than 10,000 pairs on the boggy uplands of northern and western UK[2.13]. Just one pub bird is a Dunlin and it is called the *Sandpiper* in Cullercoats, North Shields. The sign is an attractive, stylised, small wader with shortish legs and a characteristic long, slightly downcurved bill used to winkle prey items out of mud and sand on wet shorelines.

Curlews are in a bad way. They have gone as breeding birds over large swathes of their former breeding haunts in the wet lowland meadows of England (largely because the meadows have been drained and 'improved' – but obviously not from a Curlew's perspective), and are fast declining as an upland breeding bird in the north and west of the country, again because of land-use changes and predation pressure from increasing populations of foxes, crows and other predators of their eggs and chicks[2.25 & 3.17]. Most Curlews winter on the coast, their numbers swollen by immigrants from Fennoscandia, and there are just two pubs called *The Curlew*, both in areas where Curlews are still familiar wintering birds, one in West Parley (north-east of Poole Harbour on the Dorset Coast), which has a lovely, stylised Curlew on the sign, the other in South Woodham Ferrers on the inner Crouch Estuary in Essex. The Essex pub is on Gandalf's Ride. What a splendid name for a road.

The Curlew, West Parley

A couple of summers ago I was 600m up on Fleet Moss in the Yorkshire Dales looking at peat erosion and restoration. I was with a party of young civil servants from Defra who had travelled up from London specifically to see the restoration work. They were a very intelligent, motivated group, but most of them had never been on a Pennine moor before, so I was taking the opportunity to give them some gentle natural history lessons by showing them plants such as Cotton Grass, Sphagnum Moss and Bog Asphodel. A Raven flew over – exciting. Then a Curlew. "Curlew!" I shouted. "What's a Curlew?" one of them asked. I was shocked. But then if he had lived all his life in London why should he have necessarily known? I would hate the only answer to be "a pub in West Parley" because Curlews are extinct in the UK. But that's a real possibility.

With no inn sign to help, pubs called *The Sandpiper* could be one of many possible species[3.31]. *The Sandpiper* in Melton Park on the north bank of the Humber in East Yorkshire has an indeterminate, long-legged, long-billed wader on its sign that might be a Redshank or something more exotic. Their names aside, I have no other information about two pubs called *The Sandpiper*, one in Christchurch in Dorset (Christchurch Harbour is one of the UK's top spots for seeing waders), the other in Bickerstaff near Ormskirk (which in any case is nearly 12 miles as the wader flies from the Lancashire coast so may not count here anyway). *The Sandpiper Brewers Fayre* is on the south Wales coast in Llanelli, in the right place on the north shore of the Burry Inlet/ Loughor Estuary, another great birding area. It's on Sandpiper Road, of which more next.

Roads and Other Places

There are a few other single species of pub birds in 'the right place' because of the habitat or the location or because they share their names with a street, road or town, all adding to the locality's sense of place.

The *Bustard Inn* in Shrewton near Larkhill on Salisbury Plain is (or was) on Great Bustard Road. It was reported to me by a colleague[3.33] early in my exploration of pub birds, and from its website it now appears to be either a therapy centre or a tea room. As a pub it dated from the 17th century. In 1863 it was the headquarters of the Old Hawking Club, which is now the British Falconers Club, from where the members sallied out over Salisbury Plain to go hawking. In 1863 they would not be hunting Great Bustards, which became extinct in Britain in (or about) 1832 when the last one was reportedly shot[3.34]. They certainly don't make it into *The Historical Atlas*[3.5], which starts in 1875. But the wide and open chalk downland of Salisbury Plain was one of their strongholds in older times. Gilbert White knew them from elsewhere; in letter VII (October 1770) to Daines Barrington[3.26] he says: "There are bustards on the wide downs near Brighthelmstone. No doubt you are acquainted with the Sussex-downs."

Great Bustards are amazing birds and look like super-sized, spangled-brown, grey-and-white Turkeys. The males are huge, weighing in at 7–11kg (but some individuals may reach 16kg); the females are much smaller and lighter at 4–8kg. Male Mute Swans (Chapter 2) tend to be marginally heavier (11–12kg) but the Bustards have a larger wingspan. I have only ever seen Great Bustards once in the wild, in April 1986 in the Kiskunság National Park in Hungary, with birding friend and work colleague Gabor Lövei. We watched from about a mile away, across a vast grassy plain as five males displayed to four females. It is one of the most bizarre displays in the bird world. The huge males literally appear to turn themselves inside out, flashing wings and tail to resemble enormous, ball-like feather dusters. The Great Bustard Group (a UK charity)[3.35] is dedicated to bringing back Great Bustards to Salisbury Plain using eggs taken under licence from healthy populations in Russia. Salisbury Plain is probably the only surviving area of downland in England big and empty enough to provide them with suitable habitat and space. The group was established in 1998 and reached the magic target of 100 free-flying Bustards in 2019. I can't help feeling it would be very appropriate to reopen the *Bustard Inn* as a pub in celebration.

There is one other pub called *The Bustard Inn*, in South Rauceby, Lincolnshire. It has a slightly stylised Great Bustard on its sign. The village lies well away from the chalk of the Lincolnshire Wolds (where they must have occurred historically), but whether they ever occurred on farmland further west I did not know until W.B. Alexander[1.2] enlightened me. He also knew of this pub and commented that "the Lincolnshire Heath regions" were also "former haunts". The heaths have presumably long gone, 'reclaimed' for farmland, and with them the Bustards.

The Bustard Inn, South Rauceby

Three Swallows, Cley

We have already encountered two pub birds in the birding Mecca of Cley next the Sea in Norfolk (*The George* with a Barnacle Goose on its sign, and *The Harnser*, a Grey Heron). At the eastern end of the village, facing away from the sea and overlooking what used to be the harbour, stands the *Three Swallows*, which (when I photographed it in 2011) had three beautifully painted Swallows on its sign. The sign has now been replaced by three equally artistic but stylised Swallows. "Swallow" could of course be a pun, a play on words for the name of a pub, but in this case I think not. Cley, as one of the great birding spots in the UK, is a key ringing station for the study of bird migration. Swallows gather not in threes but in 100s, on the telephone wires in the village prior to setting off on their epic 6,000-mile journey to South Africa, where they spend the winter. What better name for a pub for them to come 'home' to in the spring.

At least one pub celebrates the successful reintroduction of a formerly exterminated bird. *The Golden Lion* in Winlaton Mill, west Gateshead, changed its name to *The Red Kite* after Kites were reintroduced to the Derwent Valley on the south-west edge of Newcastle in a programme started in 2004 by the Northern Kites Project and for a time led by my correspondent Keith Bowey[3.36]. The

Black Swan, North Walsham

Dog and Duck, Beverley

sign (Chapter 1) is in the form of a splendid wooden cut-out Red Kite. Despite the Kite being 'adopted' by local schoolchildren they still suffer illegal persecution, but are managing to slowly increase in number. Keith can watch them from his office window and he tells me that they also fly over the pub.

As well as the *Bustard Inn* on Great Bustard Road and *The Sandpiper Brewers Fayre* on Sandpiper Road, Llanelli, several other pub birds share their names with a place, often a lane, road or town square but also other localities – the village or town itself, for example. When a pub and a road share a name, the consensus seems to be that the pub generally gave its name to the road and not vice versa: "Not infrequently…streets have been called after inns which stood in them"[1.24], although it doesn't always have to be that way round[3.37]. I have not attempted to research a comprehensive list. Examples of 'pub names road' include: The *Black Swan* on Black Swan Loke[3.38] (North Walsham, Norfolk): *The Gull Inn* (in Framingham Pigot), also in Norfolk on the other side of the B1332 from Gull Lane; Kites Nest Lane which is about 100m from *The Kites Nest* in Stroud, Gloucestershire; *The Falcon Inn* on Falcon Road (Clapham Junction, London); and the *Dog and Duck* in Beverley (East Yorkshire) on Dog and Duck Lane.

There are two associated with Carrion Crows: *The Old Crow* is on Crow Lane in Bristol, whilst the *Crow Bar and Kitchen* is on Crowtrees Lane, Rastrick (West Yorkshire). In this latter case I am sure that the pub takes its name from the road and not the other way round. It used to be called *The Greyhound* and according to its website was "recently" renamed. Similarly, *The Wrens Nest* in Telford (Shropshire) is on Wren's Nest Lane. The pub and its general surrounds do not look old and the modern pub probably takes its name from the road. Which came first of *The Royal Dog and Duck* on Dog and Duck Square in Flamborough, Yorkshire and of *The Raven Inn* and Raven Square on which the former is situated in Welshpool, Powys, is reasonably clear. Both pubs are quite old, and I would say the squares get their names from the pub. But *The Raven* on Tower Bridge Road in London takes its name from the Tower's famous tame Ravens.

Other roads possibly or probably derive their names from a local pub. The triple-barrelled *Bush, Blackbird and Thrush* (Chapter 2) is on Bush Lane in Tonbridge, Kent. According to Pigot's Directory of 1828[3.39 & 3.40] the pub used to be called simply *The Bush* (a common name for a pub – see Chapter 2); the pub itself is old (it dates from 1781) and almost certainly gave its name to the road, but how it subsequently acquired two pub birds remains a mystery. There is a lonely, single *Blackbird* on Blackbird Road in Leicester.

There are 43 avenues, closes, lanes, roads, squares, etc. called Nightingale listed in the *London A-Z Street Atlas*, and at least two of them host Nightingales as pub birds. As Richard Fitter explains[1.20]: "It is many years now [1945] since a real Nightingale sang in Berkeley Square, though…in 1703…the Duke of Buckingham...found there a 'little wilderness full of Blackbirds and Nightingales'. " Pubs named after Nightingales may reflect a yearning for a lost, greener London. The *Nightingale* in Balham and *Nightingale on the Green* in Wanstead (in different parts of London) could both have given their names to two different Nightingale Lanes. The first is a major route that runs from Clapham Common at its north-east end to Wandsworth Common in the south-west. It is just possible that Nightingales may have occurred on one or both commons in 1830 (when they were present "between Hyde Park Corner and Kensington gravel pits"[1.20]). I do not know which came first; the road may have given its name to the pub, but the Wanstead Nightingale Lane is a winding former country lane now surrounded by the linear roads of suburbia, and almost certainly the road took its name from the pub before London spread out to surround them both.

I don't know what to make of the road given in the address of *The Coot* in Horsham. It appears to be on the corner of two roads, Merryfield Drive and Cootes Avenue. Is that coincidence a spelling mistake or am I overanalysing things? I probably need to get out more.

Nightingale on the Green, Wanstead, London

Without question the origin of the name of *The Queslett*, on Queslett Road East in Streetly, Sutton Coldfield was one of the most difficult to pin down. "Ques", Wikipedia tells us[3.41], is a 16th-century word for Wood Pigeon, and "lett" is apparently an even older Anglo-Saxon word for a small valley, so "Queslett" translates as "Wood Pigeon valley". How such a strange word survived into 21st-century Sutton Coldfield on the edge of the major Birmingham conurbation remains a mystery, at least to me. Nor is it at all clear which came first, the name of the road or the name of the pub.

The Cat and Canary, Canary Warf, London

Bird in Hand, Wreningham

The Bald Buzzard, Leighton Buzzard

Other pub birds have also definitely taken their name from the place and not the other way round, but typically they refer not to roads but to larger localities, villages and towns. *The Cat and Canary* is (or was, it is now closed) on Fisherman's Walk in Canary Wharf and is part of the redevelopment of the former West India Docks in London's Docklands. Its sign was among the most beautiful of all pub birds, depicting a joyful Canary that had succeeded in locking a predatory cat into a birdcage. The *Stock Dove* (Stock Doves are attractive Doves a bit smaller than a Wood Pigeon) is a modern pub in Stockport (Cheshire). *The Swallow Inn* is in the village of Swallow in Lincolnshire and the *Crow and Gate* is in Crowborough, East Sussex. The latter pub (its website tells us) is over 200 years old and the building was originally owned by the gatekeeper of the Crowborough gate (the guarded entrance to the town). We have already encountered (Table 2) the *Bird in Hand* (one that doesn't refer to a falconer's bird) in the village of Wreningham in Norfolk, which has a Wren perched on the finger of an upstretched hand. *The Three Jays* in Jaywick (Clacton on Sea, Essex) is a similar play on words. The Jays are North American

Blue Jays (Chapter 4) and are yet more birds to come in threes. I do wish I understood why.

Last but not least *The Bald Buzzard* micropub in Leighton Buzzard has a sign depicting a cartoon not of a Buzzard (because real Buzzards are not bald) but of what is obviously a Vulture holding a pint. However, it isn't an Old World Vulture. Turkey Vultures are called "Turkey Buzzards" or just "Buzzards" over large parts of the USA, and, although they superficially resemble Old World Vultures, they are more closely related to Storks than to Eagles, Hawks, 'real' Buzzards and Old World Vultures. The inn sign is one of only a handful of amusing depictions of a pub bird. It reminds me of one of my favourite ornithological cartoons[3.42], which depicts two Turkey Vultures sitting on a cactus in the rain, looking thoroughly miserable. One says to the other: "Oh to hell with being patient, I'm going to kill something."

A New Game

Bob Holt is a long-standing American friend and work colleague with whom I have birded (with great pleasure and considerable intensity) in the US, Cameroon and England. I casually told Bob in an email that I was writing this book and he came back almost immediately with a brilliant idea for a new pub-birding game.

"I can think of a new, hybrid recreational activity: *Ticks and Tipples*. The goal would be to go to a destination, find the real bird shown on the pub sign nearby (the tick), and then go to the pub for a drink (the tipple)...going to the pub first doesn't count, since one can see all manner of improbable things when a touch inebriated!"

There would have to be rules (of course). Pub birders would start outside the pub of their choice and have a time limit on how long they could search for the real bird – for simplicity say within 24 hours of leaving the pub. Some pub birds will be easy. Mute Swans are conspicuous, widespread and abundant and there are (as we have seen) hundreds of pubs all over the country from which to launch a search. Other species will be much more difficult. For example, although there are 44 Eagle pubs (Chapter 2), there are only two (both non-specific – the *Eagle* in Edinburgh and the *Eagle Inn* in Dunbar) in Scotland, where the only wild Golden Eagles in Britain are currently to be found. That may change of course, and as White-tailed Eagles are reintroduced in England, other non-specific Eagle pubs may be plausible ticks, particularly in Norfolk (say, launched from the *Eagle Arms* in Heydon, near Norwich). But if you wanted to be really strict, by not counting non-specific Eagles, you couldn't do it. There are no pubs named after White-tailed Eagles (Chapter 3) and there are no Golden Eagle pubs anywhere near Scotland. Other pub birds would at least require dedicated travel to their sole representatives (for example *The Cormorant* in Portchester, Hampshire, where real Cormorants ought to be easy to find on the Solent or in Portsmouth Harbour). And some involving foreign species (unless there is a zoo with an aviary nearby) would be absolutely impossible.

Taking part would require a good understanding of Britain's birds, and British pubs. It might just catch on.

CHAPTER 4: MYTHICAL BIRDS, ALIENS AND FOREIGNERS

I've grouped mythical birds with foreign species because for many pub patrons and publicans between the 15th century and (to take an arbitrary but reasonable date) the publication of Charles Darwin's *The Origin of Species by Means of Natural Selection* in 1859, mythical birds such as a Phoenix could well have existed 'somewhere' in largely unexplored (to Europeans at least) parts of the world inhabited by vast numbers of poorly known or un-discovered species. You cannot name a pub after an unknown species but choosing an exotic species from a faraway land, or distinctive aliens brought here as pets, food or for other reasons, might make your pub stand out from the crowd. In a few rare instances it can, but in general this happens nowhere near as often as you might have thought. Familiarity may be more important than novelty.

Take Penguins. As the world opened rapidly to European explorers in the 18th century the true wonder, variety, beauty and strangeness of the natural world finally imprinted itself on people from all walks of life. The first Penguins to be named and described by taxonomists were Jackass Penguins from the Cape of Good Hope in 1758. Then in just two or three decades' time another six species were described, including in 1778 the spectacular King Penguin from South Georgia. The even more wonderful Emperor Penguin wasn't discovered in Antarctic seas until 1844[2.10]. But despite their familiarity and current popularity, as far as I am aware not a single pub dating from the 18th century through to today is named after a Penguin. By this measure, Black Swans are a spectacular outlier. They were discovered by Dutch explorers in Australia in the 17th (Chapter 2) century and formally described as a new species by John Latham (of Dartford Warbler fame – Chapter 3) from specimens in 1790, with the first live birds being brought here in

1791. And as we saw in Chapter 2, by this time pubs had already been named after them. But Black Swans are a notable exception. Along with Penguins, many other wonderful, colourful and curious foreign species are notable for their absence as pub birds.

Amusingly, a Penguin does feature in one pub – stuffed inside a glass case alongside memorabilia of Antarctic exploration. It's an Emperor Penguin in *The Birds Nest* in Deptford, London, which is doubly odd because Emperor Penguins don't build nests. Their single egg is incubated on the parent's feet in the depths of the Antarctic winter. They are almost mythical birds.

Mythical Pub Birds

W.B. Alexander, R.S.R. Fitter, Steve Shaw and I all take rather different approaches to recording mythical pub birds[4.1]. Here I am using my own (limited) database and choice of species. Two mythical birds in my database have given their names to pubs, namely Liver Bird and Phoenix. I will also say something about the Firebird, which appears in Steve Shaw's list, and Martlets on pub signs courtesy of heraldry.

The Griffin, Leeds. Bird-like but not a pub bird

You could be forgiven for thinking that the *Crown and Liver* in Ewloe just outside Hawarden on Deeside was some strange amalgam of royalty and a butcher's shop if you didn't know that "Liver" (pronounced Ly-ver) is a mythical bird, not something you eat with onions and gravy. The Liver Bird is the symbol of the city of Liverpool, so quite why a pub in Hawarden, which is about 17 miles south-west of the centre of that city and on the other side of the Mersey has taken this name is not explained in anything I can access. The sign is what it says on the tin – a crown and a Liver Bird. It looks heraldic, but again I cannot find any explanation.

Crown and Liver, Ewloe

The two most famous representations of a Liver Bird are on the twin clock towers of the Royal Liver Building on Liverpool's pier head. The male, Bertie, looks over the city and the female, Bella, looks out to sea. The origins of the mythical bird are contentious[4.2]. It is normally now represented on the city's coat of arms as a Cormorant carrying a piece of seaweed known as laver[4.3] in its beak, supposedly as a pun on the name Liverpool. And, whilst the mythical bird's origin may now have settled on a Cormorant, it probably started life as an Eagle. King John founded the borough of Liverpool by royal charter in 1207. The borough's second charter, granted by Henry III in 1229, gave the townspeople the right to use a seal which depicted a bird with a plant sprig in its bill. The bird was almost certainly intended to be an Eagle, the symbol of John the Evangelist, who was both the namesake and the patron saint of King John. By the 17th century the bird's real identity had been forgotten and it began to be interpreted either as a Cormorant (a common bird on the Mersey) or as a "lever", which has a completely different supposed origin for the "liver" in Liverpool. In his 1688 work *The Academie of Armorie* Randle Holme records the arms of Liverpool as a blue "lever" upon a silver field. Holme takes this word to be an adaptation of the German *loffler* or Dutch *lepler/lefler*, both referring to Spoonbills. So it is possible that these continental words were adopted for the bird in Liverpool's arms as they made a fitting allusion to the name "Liverpool"[4.2]. I never cease to be amazed at what you can glean from Wikipedia, and puzzled by how on earth a non-expert such as myself is supposed to sort out the origins of the strangely named Liver Bird.

The second mythical pub bird is a Phoenix. In my database there are pubs called *The Phoenix* in Bristol, Edinburgh, Sheffield, Sunbury-on-Thames, Twyford, Westminster and York. The possible origins of the myth of the Phoenix are as fascinating, unusual and downright strange as they are contentious. Wikipedia[4.4] and *Birds and People*[1.23] give a succinct account. The Phoenix is a sacred Firebird, found in the mythologies of the Persians, Greeks, Romans, Egyptians and Chinese, with appropriate geographical variation for a widely distributed species in its supposed appearance and biology. Universal characteristics are its brilliant colours and a lifecycle of 500 to 1,000 years. (In one version the maximum lifespan is given very precisely as 7,006 years.) Near the end of its life, it builds a nest of twigs which (spontaneously?) ignites, reducing the bird and nest to ashes from which a new young Phoenix, or a Phoenix egg, arises, reborn to live again. To my mind the strangest thing about myths like this is how

The Phoenix, York

Phoenix Inn, Twyford

on earth anybody came to believe them, and who made them up. And also, what (if any) real species of bird underpins the story?

Originally the Phoenix was identified by the Egyptians as a Stork or Heron-like bird. The Greeks subsequently pictured it as a bird more like a Peacock or an Eagle. One (to my mind at least plausible) explanation for the Egyptian Phoenix is the suggestion that it has its origin in very early encounters between explorers and Flamingos in East Africa. Lesser Flamingos breed in huge colonies in the Rift Valley on salt flats that are too hot for eggs and chicks to survive at 'ground level', so Flamingos build mud-mound nests to lift them into cooler air. Viewed through intense heat haze, the mounds of a colony of pink, breeding Lesser Flamingos shimmer like flames. But there are other attributions including Bateleur Eagles, Purple Herons and Golden Pheasants. The one unifying feature of all the ramifications of the Phoenix myth is the notion of the bird as an expression of eternal life. That would appeal to pub goers. In the past, the story (or myth) of the Phoenix would probably have been more familiar to many customers than almost all 'real' foreign birds, which may explain why this one mythical species is not rare as a pub bird.

Finally, cheating just a little, *The Firebird* in Edgbaston (Birmingham) is on Steve Shaw's list (which is how I encountered it) but it closed in 2008, just before my time period. However, it is such a lovely mythical bird (I had previously never heard of it) that it deserves a brief mention. The Firebird features widely in Slavonic mythology. Wikipedia[4.5] describes it as large, with majestic plumage that glows brightly, emitting red, orange and yellow light like a bonfire. A single plucked feather continues to glow and will light a large room. In later iconography the Firebird is usually depicted as a fire-coloured Falcon, complete with a crest on its head and tail feathers and glowing Peacock-like "eyes". Again, who made this stuff up?

A Digression into Heraldry

The Deramore Arms, Heslington

It is not unusual for pubs to be named after the arms a local family (Chapter 2). *The Deramore Arms* is my local pub in Heslington near York. Its sign is taken from the arms of the Barons Deramore. The 4th (and last) Baron Deramore (George de Yarburgh-Bateson) served as Lord Lieutenant of the East Riding of Yorkshire from 1924 until 1936 and died in 1943[4.5]. The family seat (Heslington Hall) is now the offices of the central administration of the University of York. The family shield and crest on the pub sign is complicated but includes in the supporting surrounds what is unquestionably an Eagle apparently attacking (or at least perched on the back of!) what looks like a Goose (but could be a poorly depicted Swan). And herein lies a problem for a pub-bird lister. Heraldry is a highly specialised subject, with its own, ancient terminology of which I know virtually nothing, so I will undoubtedly have missed numerous pub birds drawn from the tradition. Some are clearly identifiable (such as the Eagle on *The Deramore Arms* – Eagles are the most widely depicted birds in English heraldry[4.5]), some are obscure but 'real' birds (for example the Swan or Goose) and some unidentifiable. Others are mythical, which is why I am including them here, albeit in a way that is far from comprehensive.

Liver Birds clearly have an (admittedly obscure) heraldic origin and "*The Phoenix* has armorial connotations"[1.24], though to which of the several *Phoenix* pubs this refers is unclear. Martlets are a third mythical or semi-mythical bird widely depicted in heraldry and from there portrayed on pub signs[4.5]. They are typically a stylised bird, roughly like a Swift, Swallow or House Martin, with a forked tail. *The Rockingham Arms* near Tadcaster (west of York) has three black Martlets and three crescent moons on its coat of arms. I only found it by accidentally driving past. It is the coat of arms of Charles Watson-Wentworth, the 2nd Marquess of Rockingham, who was born in York and served two terms as Prime Minister)[4.5]. The *St. Vincent Arms* in Sutton upon Derwent, east of York, has on its sign a shield with a single Black Martlet on it, which it shares with a Dragon and a Unicorn[4.6]. From

St Vincent Arms, Sutton upon Derwent

what I can glean from the heraldic literature Martlets are frequently depicted without any legs or feet. That chimes with the scientific name for Swifts (*Apus apus*, "apous" from the Greek "a" – lacking, and "pous" – a foot)[4.7]. But the *St. Vincent Arms* bird has a peculiar, trunk-like, three-toed 'leg' (that Wikepedia[4.5] describes as "three short tufts of feathers"). Whatever, it isn't any bird I can clearly identify. Legend has it that Martlets never landed on the ground, so there was no need for them to have feet.

Several other armorial pub signs feature Martlets, but my list is very incomplete. I do know that the *Golden Martlet* in Hellingley (Sussex) burned down and closed in 2001. W.B. Alexander was more clued up. "*The Three Blackbirds*, a sign of several inns in Hertfordshire, was probably derived from the arms of the Sebright family and should really be three Martlets." (Here we are again with three, in this case possibly with an explanation from heraldry). Two other pubs with the same name, in Blexley (London) and Ditton Green near Newmarket (Cambridgeshire) may also take their names from heraldic Martlets. Three regulars sitting outside *The Three Blackbirds* in Blexley told me that its sign (now gone) used to have a coat of arms with three black birds on it, but of course as well as Martlets they could be heraldic depictions of Choughs, Crows, Ravens or even 'real' Blackbirds. From the poor images on its website *The Blackbird* in Leicester looks like a Crow. As my scientific colleagues are fond of saying: "more research is needed". Pub signs with single Blackbirds (on Earls Court Road in London (p. 143) and on the triple-named *Bush, Blackbird and Thrush* in East Peckham) both refer to 'real' Blackbirds.

So much for mythical species. Let us return to real non-native birds.

Non-native Pub Birds in the Top Baker's Dozen

Chapter 2 lists the 13 most common pub birds in Britain, a mixture of clearly identifiable species and types of birds. Domesticated Red Junglefowls (Cockerels, Hens and Chickens) weigh in at number two, which is to say that 'sport', food and familiarity have been more than enough to outweigh prejudices or suspicions about foreigners. (That is, if people ever even think about Hens as 'foreign'; hardly anybody would.) Black Swans may have proved popular for their 'shock value' (Chapter 2), but I still worry about this explanation as being the only origin for the name and will return to Black Swans in Chapter 5. And again, most people will be totally unaware that the familiar, well-established and good-to-hunt-and-eat (but non-native) Pheasants are foreigners. Most Eagles in the top 13 are non-specific but nine are clearly identifiable native Golden Eagles. Foreign Eagles are rarer: there are five Bald Eagles from North America, a Black Eagle from Africa and a Martial or Harpy Eagle from Africa or South America. Probably the signs were copied from a bird book and to the signwriter and publican one Eagle probably looked pretty much like any other. Being big, bold and fierce carries the day. Peacocks, meanwhile, have dazzle, bling and edibility that few other birds can compete with. After these five, non-native pub birds tend to be lonely individuals. For example there is just one Swan Goose among the numerous domestic deese derived from native Greylag (Chapter 2).

It is also striking that Partridges make it into the final slot in the top 13 most abundant pub birds (Chapter 2) and yet all the Partridges I can identify specifically are native Grey Partridges; none of the birds visible on the inn signs appear to be foreign (i.e. introduced) Red-legged Partridges, *aka* "French Partridges", despite the fact that they are now much more important as a quarry species on lowland agricultural land than Grey Partridges[2.30]. Clearly no right-minded publican was going to invoke a French bird in their search for customers.

Turkeys emphasise the point. The widely held view is that they were first brought to Britain (from North America) by Yorkshireman William Strickland in 1526 (his family coat of arms has a Turkey in its crest)[4.5] and domesticated. We now eat millions of them every year, particularly at Christmas. But unlike Hens, as far as I am aware there is only one pub currently named after them. (Richard Fitter has "*The Turkey Cock* at Norwich" on his list but it no longer appears to exist.) The survivor is the *Turkey Inn* in Laycock, Yorkshire. I did wonder if it had any connection with Strickland but the pub only dates from the 19th century and Laycock is about 60 miles away on the opposite side of the county from his family seat in Boynton. I cannot find out why it is called the *Turkey Inn* and cannot come anywhere near to explaining why Turkeys are not more frequent pub birds. I wonder if it has anything to

Turkey Inn, Laycock

do with "a turkey" being US and Canadian slang for a project that has failed or a rather stupid or incompetent person. Or are Turkeys just rather odd, ugly foreigners? I don't know.

Established Aliens

Unlike the popularity of Pheasants, Black Swans and Peacocks, other alien species that have established self-sustaining or almost-self-sustaining populations in the wild in Britain are rare as pub birds. Ruddy Ducks, Canada Geese and Snow Geese all hail originally from North America, and all three have escaped into the wild in Britain from ornamental wildfowl collections. All are (rare) pub birds.

There are two pubs called the *Ruddy Duck*, one in Peakirk near Peterborough (Cambridgeshire), the other in Wakefield (West Yorkshire). Ruddy Ducks are small, elegant, compact birds, about the size of a Teal but with a saucy cocked tail. The males are very handsome, mainly ruddy brown in colour with a bold white face, black crown and brilliant pale blue bill. In the winter of 1952–53 and subsequently, Ruddy Ducks escaped from the Wildfowl Trust's collection at Slimbridge in Gloucestershire. The first wild broods appeared in 1958–59 at Chew Valley Reservoir in the adjacent county of Somerset further down the Bristol Chanel, and by 1997 about 3,600 pairs were breeding in the wild in Britain[2.7]. When birds from this population reached Spain (which they did in the early 1990s) and started to hybridise with the globally endangered White-headed Duck (a close relative) conservationists became alarmed, resulting in a highly controversial cull of UK Ruddy Ducks, commencing in 2005[2.25]. The birds were shot by expert marksmen. By 2014 only 40 individuals remained and five years later the population was "tiny, perhaps only just into double figures"[4.8]. I do not know whether Ruddy Ducks are now extinct in Britain.

Peakirk is the location of the second of the Wildfowl Trust's collections (now the Wildfowl & Wetlands Trust) and was "an early destination for some of the surplus Ruddy Ducks from Slimbridge. Shortly after transfer the title of the village pub was altered from 'Black Bull' to Ruddy Duck'"[1.22]. I have no idea why the Wakefield pub is also called *The Ruddy Duck*.

Canada Geese, by contrast, have never been subject to a concerted control programme and continue to increase. The diarist John Evelyn describes them as occurring in the collection of Charles II in St James's Park in London in 1665[2.7]. They still occur there. However, by the 19th century they were widely distributed on the estates of the great and good throughout England and lowland Scotland, but it was not until the late 1930s that they began to establish self-sustaining populations in the wild. I saw my first wild birds on the Ribble Marshes in Lancashire in August 1957 (when I was 13), by which time there were probably about 5,000 in Britain[2.7]. At the last count (2013–17) there were 54,500 breeding pairs[2.13] in the UK and numbers continue to increase. But somehow we have never taken these fine birds into our collective psyche. As Stephen Moss puts it[4.9]: "Because they are non-native, and perhaps because they originally hailed from North America, we have an ambivalent attitude towards Canada Geese." They can certainly be a real nuisance. Droppings from large numbers of Geese pollute watercourses and are a human health hazard, and in places the Geese can cause severe damage to crops and to natural vegetation by trampling and grazing. Stephen Moss again: "In their original home Canada Geese are regarded with far greater affection and respect"[4.9]. Quite why there is such a difference in attitude towards them is anybody's guess, but it is indeed probably "because they are non-native"; they can be no less of a nuisance in the US than in the UK. But given this difference in attitude it is probably not surprising that only one pub bird is a Canada Goose, and then not in name. *The Sitting Goose* in Bartle near Preston (Lancashire, close to where I saw my first one) has on its sign a rather nice portrait of a Canada Goose sitting on a nest. It is also a relatively rare reference to a breeding bird. Pub birds don't often have nests (Chapter 6).

Snow Geese are the third species of alien wildfowl to make it as a pub bird, with three pubs. Two of them are *The Snow Goose* in Farnborough, Hampshire and *The Snow Goose* in Stoneyfield, Inverness. Neither place has any obvious association with the species. The birds themselves come in two genetically determined colour forms (morphs) unrelated to age or sex, one white (from which the species gets its name) and the other so-called blue, with a rather messily patterned slate-blue-grey-and-blackish body and a white head and upper neck. Hybrids between the two morphs also exist and have varying amounts of white. The Stoneyfield pub doesn't appear to have a sign but the Farnborough pub

Green Goose, Bow, London

shows the white morph with black primaries in flight. Confusingly the blue morph (or a hybrid morph) is depicted on the sign for the *Green Goose* in Bow (London). How can a Goose be both blue and green? It isn't a riddle. "Green" is the name given to a dead young Goose that has not been hung prior to cooking and which is usually eaten with a sharp green sauce made from either Watercress or Sorrel[4.10], not to the colour of the Goose. And I guess the artist simply copied a picture of any old Goose from a book.

Snow Geese are widely (albeit thinly) recorded, with the exception of a small but apparently self-sustaining wild population on Coll and Mull in the Inner Hebrides[2.7 & 2.25]. This could be about to change, because (according to birding gossip) there is a growing flock of currently about 100 birds established in the vicinity of Farmoor Reservoir in Oxfordshire. Also, a mixed skein of up to 30 birds (both white and blue morphs) regularly pass over my house from a free-flying flock on the University of York campus where they breed unaided, but only within the confines of the campus and not on any of the adjacent more natural wetlands.

It must be a coincidence, but along with *The Sitting* [Canada] *Goose*, another established alien species also has a nest: *The Owls Nest* is in Haycock, Lancashire and is inhabited by a beautifully painted Little Owl sitting outside a tree hole nest site. The sign for *The Little Owl* in Chester depicts another accurate illustration of this charming small Owl, together with an adjacent, striking tree stump carving of an Owl in flight. After several failed attempts commencing in 1842, Little Owls were deliberately and successfully introduced into England from continental Europe when birds were imported from the Netherlands between 1880 and 1890 by the ornithologist Thomas Littleton Powys (the 4th Baron Lilford); others were subsequently released in the early 1900s[2.7]. They are now reasonably widespread throughout England[2.25]. Most non-birders probably don't realise they are not native here. Unlike most Owls they are diurnal and feed mainly on large (often harmful) insects and also small mammals, and as Christopher Lever says [2.7]: "of the 60 or so alien vertebrates naturalized in Britain, the Little Owl is the only one that is actively beneficial to man". Nevertheless, it is celebrated as a pub bird only twice. Owls in general do not feature prominently as pub birds (they are often birds of ill omen – Chapter 5) and Little Owls may simply have been caught up in these prejudices.

The Little Owl, Chester

Carving at The Little Owl, Chester

Failed or Dubiously Successful Deliberate Introductions

There have been two other deliberate attempts to introduce non-native bird species into Britain that have made it onto an inn sign. They are Wood Duck (otherwise known as a Carolina Duck), which has repeatedly failed, and Golden Pheasant, which looked as though it might have been successful but is now struggling to survive.

For no obvious reason other than that they are extremely beautiful a pair of Wood Ducks adorn the sign for the *Riverside* pub on the River Avon just west of Bath (Chapter 1). Wood Ducks are primarily natives of the eastern half of North America and the Pacific Coast, where they nest in holes in trees. The males are one of the world's most beautiful Ducks, sporting a bushy mane and a head and body patterned in glossy greens, bronzes, gold, black and white, and a red ring around their eyes and a red base to their bill. They look like the depiction of a Duck drawn by a child armed with a set of coloured crayons. The females are drab olive-grey with a hint of a crest. Repeated attempts to introduce them into the UK from 1870 onwards have failed[2.25], which is odd because their close relative from China (in the same genus – *Aix*) the Mandarin Duck is now firmly established in the UK (but doesn't yet have a pub named after it). Several reasons have been proposed for the Wood Duck's failure to establish[2.25 & 4.11] – their ducklings take longer to reach maturity then Mandarin ducklings, for example, making them more vulnerable to predators. I find this rather unconvincing, but I don't think anybody knows for certain.

We are in something of a beauty contest here. To my mind, male Mandarin Ducks just pip male Wood Ducks into first place for the world's most gorgeous Duck. But in a competition for the world's most beautiful bird both must compete with Golden Pheasants. And in my eyes Golden Pheasants win hands down. The males are a crazy combination of golds, fiery-bronzes, blues and black, with a judge's wig-like gold-barred mane and a spectacularly long tail. The first introduction into this country from their home in China was apparently as early as 1725[2.25]. Attempts to introduce them into Scotland started in the 1880s and continued in England and Scotland well into the middle of the 20th century. I have seen birds in one of the naturalised populations on Tresco in the Scilly Isles, where they were originally released in 1975[2.8]. Steve Shaw[1.5] lists five *Golden Pheasants*, specifying one in Plumley, Cheshire, that still exists and has a lovely depiction of a Golden Pheasant as its sign. However not all pubs bearing this name necessarily refer to 'real' Golden Pheasants and may well be the equivalent of the *Golden Hind, Golden Egg* or *Golden Martlet* as pub names, with origins in, for example, heraldry or mythology. I know of one other genuine article, *The Golden Pheasant Inn* in Burford (Oxfordshire). There are other pubs of this name but their signs either depict a golden 'ordinary' Pheasant (Anchinlock, Dundee), a Common Pheasant (Farringdon in Oxfordshire) or have no obvious sign (Biggleswade in Bedfordshire and Elton near Peterborough), and so could be either. Even for such a spectacular gamebird, being foreign seems to have restricted the popularity of Golden Pheasants as pub birds.

The Golden Pheasant Inn, Burford

This may be prophetic because the bird is struggling to maintain a presence in Britain. For a time in the second half of the 20th century there appears to have been self-sustaining populations in the wild in England in Breckland, north-west Norfolk and on the South Downs in Hampshire and West Sussex, plus populations on Anglesey in Wales and in Dumfries and Galloway in Scotland[2.25]. But by the 2007–11 *Atlas*, however, only the Brecklands and another area of north-west Norfolk remained as strongholds, with local extinctions on the South Downs, in Dumfries and Galloway and on Anglesey. The most recent estimate (2010–14) puts the UK breeding population at just 15 males[2.13] and an unknown number of the difficult-to-see brown ('Pheasant-coloured') females. The reasons for this decline are unknown. It matters, because in their native China the species is under severe threat and the UK population offered a lifeboat on another continent. Seemingly not any more. I do not know if the birds on Tresco are self-sustaining, but I ticked them nonetheless.

Cage Birds and 'Pets'

You might have thought that (as with Peacocks) other exotic foreign birds popular as cage birds or free-flying pets would feature prominently as pub birds. They do not. Their numbers are strictly limited. Canaries must rival Budgerigars as pets, but no pub is named after Australian Budgies. There are two Canaries, however. *The Cat and Canary* in Canary Wharf, London had a Canary on its sign (Chapter 3). *The Canary and Linnet* in Little Fransham in Norfolk has no sign but both birds come from the nicknames of two rival football teams, the Canaries (Norwich FC) and the Linnets (Kings Lynn FC); the publican was clearly hedging their bets because Dereham is situated roughly halfway between the two. The Canaries play in yellow shirts and most domestic Canaries are yellow. Kings Lynne FC was declared bankrupt and closed in 2009. When it was first founded in 1899 players wore red jerseys with blue shorts. The club adopted gold shirts and royal blue shorts in 1909[4.12]. Neither sets of kit remotely resemble the plumage of a Linnet. The official website says "The nickname 'The Linnet' seems to have been around for some time" but does not say why. Wikipedia is no more helpful.

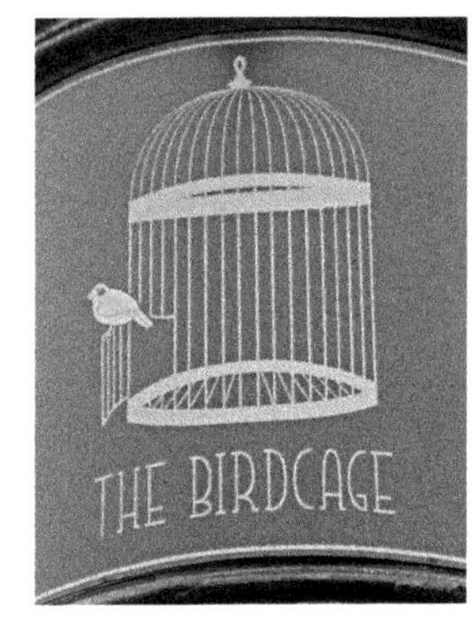

The Birdcage, Lincoln with Red-cheeked Cordonbleu

One other small, Finch-like cage bird features as a pub bird. A Red-cheeked Cordonbleu appears outside its cage in Lincoln at a pub called *The Birdcage*. It is one of three species of Cordonbleu in Africa and its range extends across the whole of Africa south of the Sahara and north of the lowland forest, where there are drier grassy and bushy habitats, roadsides and villages and where there is farmland. They are small, slim Finches related to Waxbills, with sky-blue faces and underparts, brown backs and a brilliant red patch on each cheek; the signwriter has cheated slightly and given the

Lincoln bird a blue back. It is "one of the most popular exotic finches" among aviculturalists[4.5] but I have no idea how or why it appears on the sign of a pub in Lincoln.

Parrots are much more familiar pets, but even these striking, intelligent and beautiful creatures only make it as pub birds on eight pubs with just two clearly identifiable species, one Cockatoo and five unspecified "Parrots". The unspecified Parrots are *The Parrot* in Cheltenham (Gloucestershire), the *Parrot Inn* in Drury near Buckley (Denbighshire), two pubs called the *Dog and Parrot* (in Newcastle upon Tyne and Nottingham) and (surely a marketing executive's choice) *The Frog and Parrot* in Sheffield. *The Hook and Parrot* in Bridlington (p. 147) on the Yorkshire coast has a cartoon-like sign depicting a pirate and a Cockatoo (which has a distinctive upward-curling crest and is most likely an Australian Sulphur-crested Cockatoo). The two clearly identifiable species are on a sign depicting the head of a Scarlet Macaw (the *Bird in Hand*, Hayle, Cornwall) and a Yellow-headed Amazon (the *Magpie and Parrot*, Shinfield in Berkshire). Some, but not all the names of these pubs "may have been the choice of a retired seaman" taking up a landlubber's role as a landlord[1.24], which may explain the origin of the name for the *Magpie and Parrot*. However, this is not the explanation for the unexpected Scarlet Macaw on the sign for the *Bird in Hand* in Hayle. The pub was established alongside a bird garden in the 1970s by the father of the current licensee Nick Reynolds, and the sign refers to one of the garden's inhabitants[4.13]. This and the second identifiable Parrot are natives of Central and South America (Scarlet Macaw) and Mexico and Belize (Yellow-headed Amazon), and both are (or were) popular cagebirds and pets. Yellow-headed Amazons are reputedly "one of the most sought-after Neotropical Parrots in captivity [and] reputedly the best talkers"[4.14]. Sulphur-crested Cockatoos are Australian, and again are popular cagebirds.

The Parrot, Cheltenham

Bird in Hand, Hayle (Scarlet Macaw)

The only other captive birds are Vultures, with two pubs called *The George and Vulture* in London (discussed in Chapter 3) and possibly *The Toucan* on Carlisle Street in Soho (also London). The bird is a Toco Toucan, a native primarily of Brazil, Bolivia and Paraguay, and is sometimes kept as a cagebird. But this one depicts the bird made famous by Guinness sitting on the edge of a pint of one of my favourite drinks, and the thought of what "two can do" for me.

The Toucan, Soho, London

Pelicans

Vagrants (birds that turn up lost but unaided in this country, far from where they really belong) set twitchers' hearts racing (Chapter 3). Several species of pub birds have occurred as vagrants to Britain, but the pubs were almost certainly not so named because they were vagrants, but for more prosaic reasons. The simplest (which I have repeatedly suggested) is that somebody copied their picture from a bird book without realising that it was not a native British bird. However, this first example (Pelicans) is very much an exception both to the generalisation that foreign species are not popular as pub birds and to the unintentional copying of a picture from a bird book. Pelicans are probably popular because they have strong and ancient religious overtones.

There are eight species of Pelican in the world, of which six are predominantly white with black primaries and secondaries[2.10]. Pub Pelicans could be any of these, but most of the identifiable birds on pub signs bear a closer resemblance to White Pelicans than any of the others. Two (Dalmatian Pelican and White Pelican) occur naturally in Europe and Dalmatian Pelican has been recorded once as a vagrant to Britain[4.15]. These two and the other four species also range across Africa, Asia, Australia and North America. Intriguingly (if you are a birder), although Dalmatian Pelican is now rare in Europe (where it is confined to a few large, mainly protected wetlands from Montenegro to Greece and the Russian Federation[4.16]), its bones have been excavated from fenland peats in England of Neolithic, Bronze and Iron Ages some 5000 to 2500 years before the present day[2.6]. Some of the bones were from young birds, so they were clearly breeding here.

The Pelican, Salisbury

The orginal old sign for The Fox and Pelican, Grayshot

There are 26 pubs called *The Pelican* on Steve Shaw's list and they rank 14th in W.B. Alexander's (almost making it into his top dozen – Table 1, Chapter 2). As usual, many of these pubs no longer exist, or have been renamed, but a significant number are still open for business, including two pubs (*The Fox and Pelican* in Grayshott, Hampshire and *The Ship and Pelican* in Heavitree in Devon) from Shaw's list. In addition to these two I have 11 other pubs called either *The Pelican* or *Pelican Inn* on my list[4.17]. Virtually all of these are white Pelicans of some kind bar one Brown Pelican from North America, which is shown in flight on the sign for *The Pelican Inn* (or *Tafarn y Pelican*) in Newcastle Emlyn in Carmarthenshire. (This is again probably the result of the signwriter unwittingly copying a picture of a foreign species.) A significant number, but not all, Pelican pubs look (or are definitely) old[4.17] (see Chapter 3), and herein may lie the explanation for their unusually large numbers for a foreign bird.

Pelicans have a rich and at times bizarre mythology associated with them, with strong religious overtones[1.23]. The Pelican in her piety – a female reviving and feeding her young with blood from her own breast – was a common Christian symbol for centuries and was used as a pictorial analogue of the death of Jesus. The story persisted into the 17th century. In *Birds and People*[1.23] Mark Cocker (quoting Isabelle Charmantier) wrote: "For some early modern naturalists the pelican did indeed pierce its chest in order to revive its chicks, just as they believed in the existence of the phoenix." Cocker prefaces these remarks with: "Another aspect of the myth was its reinvention…as writers applied new layers of fantasy to the original claim, presumably without one of them going anywhere near a genuine pelican." If the folk memory of the Pelican in her piety persisted into the 18th or 19th centuries (even if most people no longer bought into the fable) it may explain the popularity of Pelicans as pub birds. *The Fox and Pelican* in Grayshott was established in 1899, and the original sign (by the artist and designer Walter Crane) shows a Pelican piercing her breast to feed three small chicks and a Fox sneaking past below the nest. It was apparently put in a skip and lost when the pub was sold in 1913 but reappeared in Wales following enquires by Grayshott resident Richard Peskett and was sold at auction in April 2010. The pub's current sign is a much simpler heraldic affair showing a Pelican on the right facing a fox on the left, separated by a sword[4.18]. According to Hyde-Parker[1.4] the Grayshott pub takes its name from the coat of arms of Bishop Richard Fox (or Foxe) who was Bishop of Winchester (in Hampshire). He died in 1528. His coat of arms bore a Pelican in her piety.

There is also a pub explicitly called *The Pelican in Her Piety* in Ogmore by Sea, near Bridgend in Wales (Chapter 3). It too is old. An entry on the pub's website says it has been serving customers "for almost 300 years", which takes us back roughly to 1750. Many of the images on the website have no indication of an inn sign, just the name, but one depicts a coat of arms with a Pelican piecing her breast to feed her chicks[4.18].

Not all old Pelican pubs have this possible religious origin for their names. *The Pelican* in Stapleford in Wilshire is an 18th-century pub with a lovely modern sign depicting the silhouettes of one white and one black Pelican in flight. It reputedly takes its name from a galleon called "The Pelican", which (renamed) became Sir Francis Drake's *Golden Hind*. The tale has a further twist. *The Pelican Inn* in Gloucester (the frontispiece for this book) is the oldest of the Pelican pubs (dating from 1679) and it reputedly has beams that were recycled from the *Golden Hind*, presumably when she was broken up. Somehow the dates of these two stories don't add up.

And to finish these Pelican tales, *The Prospect of Whitby* on the Thames at Wapping in London is one of Britain's most famous old pubs. It would seem to have nothing to do with pub birds, but it has. In its first incarnation it too was called *The Pelican*, and later the much more sinister *Devil's Tavern*. After a fire in the early 19th century it was rebuilt and renamed *The Prospect of Whitby* after a coal-carrying ship from Tyneside that docked nearby. All that remains of the earlier pub is the 400-year-old stone floor[4.19].

Ostriches

Neither Steve Shaw nor W.B. Alexander have an *Ostrich* on their lists, even though the much shorter article by Richard Fitter has no less than four.

The first *Ostrich Inn* I encountered when assembling my main database was in Bristol on the harbour. It dates from 1745[4.20] and was frequented by sailors and harbour workers during the height of the slave trade. It is named after a sailing ship, not a bird (Chapter 1). But there are some genuine Ostriches. We have already encountered the very old *Ostrich Inn* in Colnbrook (Buckinghamshire) in Chapter 3 (one of Fitter's four), and there are other *Ostrich Inns* in Castle Acre (Norfolk) and Newland near Monmouth. Both the latter take their names from Ostriches on the coats of arms of local families: the Coke family from adjacent Holkham Hall in Norfolk and the Probyns in Newland. Ostriches are such exotic and unusual birds that they would have been familiar to many people who had never actually seen the living bird. At one time there were no less than ten *Ostrich* pubs in Norfolk alone[4.21].

Vagrants, Foreign Species and two that are not Pub Birds

The Bald Buzzard micropub in Leighton Buzzard aside (Chapter 3), two further North American species are pub birds at just one pub each. Two other species that have never been recorded here in the wild also have single pubs bearing their image, and there are two other North American species that might have been, but are not, pub birds.

The sign for *The Cuckoo* in Alwalton, Cambridgeshire is highly unexpected. It isn't 'our' Cuckoo (which has several pubs named after it) but is a Jacobin Cuckoo, which is widespread across sub-Saharan Africa and India. The species has never occurred in the wild in Britain. They are highly distinctive black-and-white Cuckoos with a ragged crest. In Africa, in true Cuckoo fashion, they mainly parasitise Common Bulbuls (a host that is about the same size and shape as a Song Thrush).

I saw just a single Jacobin Cuckoo when I worked at the University of Legon in Ghana in 1982. As an introduction to African birding it couldn't have been better because I had no transport and the university campus and farm were not too overwhelming for a novice Africa birder. Back then the bird books were not great, and there are some things I saw that I just couldn't identify, but not this striking and quite large Cuckoo. Feeling quite nostalgic whilst writing this section I stopped to look at an illustration of a Jacobin Cuckoo in one of the modern Helm identification guides[4.22] and I swear that bird 6a on plate 55 is the one the signwriter copied for the inn sign. It's identical. The book was published in 2001, and because the pub is old (17th century) and used to be called *The Wheatsheaf*[4.23] I would put money on the prediction that it changed its name and sign sometime after 2001.

By sheer coincidence I definitely know the source of the image copied by the signwriter for another bird that has occurred several times as a vagrant to Britain and elsewhere in Europe. It's a North American Whistling (sometimes called Tundra) Swan. We do have the same species as a regular winter visitor here – the Bewick's Swan – but it is a different subspecies, the main difference being the amount of yellow on the mostly black bills of the adults. It is the extent of this yellow that identifies the bird currently depicted on the sign of *The White Swan* in Walsham, Norfolk as a Whistling Swan. Bewick's Swans have a large yellow area at the base of the upper mandible and these yellow patches join on the bird's forehead; Whistling Swans just have short yellow lines in front of each eye, which don't meet. The depiction of a Swan as a Whistling Swan is surprising enough; what is even more surprising is that when I first saw the pub in 2015 the bird on it was a highly stylised, but still recognisable, Mute Swan. In 2019 it had been transformed into a Whistling Swan. The image had been clearly taken from a painting by the pioneering North American ornithologist John James Audubon (1785–1851)[3.25] in his monumental work *Birds of America*. On the inn sign the image of the Swan's head and upper neck among bullrushes is reversed to face to the right; Audubon painted the whole Swan among water lilies and facing left. But the birds' posture, plumages and bill markings are identical. How the signwriter or publican found the illustration I may never know.

The White Swan, North Walsham

Audubon's Whistling Swan (John James Audubon Centre, Audubon PA)

The White Swan, North Walsham, (before sign changed to Whistling Swan)

The penultimate foreign bird in this section is also from North America, a rare vagrant to Britain and Europe and yet another species that changed identity. The bird on the sign for *The Kestrel* just outside Harrogate in North Yorkshire in 2012 (p. 48) was a native 'Common' Kestrel, the familiar small Falcon with an appropriate string of vernacular names in different parts of the UK[1.15], coined because of its ability to hover into the wind, head stationary, as it scans the ground for prey. They include Wind Bibber (Sussex and Kent), Wind Cuffer (Orkney), Wind Fanner (Sussex and Surrey), Windhover (southern and western counties), Wind Sucker (also Kent) and (spare your blushes) Wind Fucker and Fuckwind ("northern term")[4.24]. By 2019 the bird had metamorphosed into its diminutive North American cousin (p. 48). The American Kestrel is smaller than 'ours' and has a characteristic boldly patterned 'moustache and sideburns' head pattern. This one is depicted sitting on a falconer's gauntlet (Chapter 2). It too hunts by hovering. Again, I can only assume that the signwriter simply copied the picture from a book without realising exactly what they were painting. For the record, there is one other pub called *The Kestrel Inn*, just outside Crickhowell in Wales. It doesn't appear to have a sign but is surely named after a Common Kestrel.

There may have been a third change of identity during the period covered by the book but because I don't know when, or even if, it happened I have reserved *The Redstart* in Barming, Kent for Chapter 7.

As far as I know there are no pub birds that can be attributed to Eurasian Jays, despite 'our' Jays being one of the most handsome and colourful of British birds. They are (or were) hated by gamekeepers and some bird lovers because of their penchant for eating eggs, nestlings and even adult birds, and are heavily persecuted accordingly. Somehow, as we have seen, 'noble' birds of prey (Eagles and Falcons), which are entirely carnivorous, are popular as pub birds. Jays are omnivorous and eat large numbers of insects, seeds and fruits as well as killing things, and play a particularly important ecological role by stashing acorns in autumn, to be recovered and eaten over the winter. Many of these acorns are missed and become Oak trees yet Jays get no credit as a pub bird.

It is possible that the only Jay pub, *The Three Jays* in (appropriately) Jaywick in Essex was intended to be named after our Jay, but once again the signwriter was given the wrong illustration to copy – the sign depicts three Blue Jays, common North American relatives of ours and never recorded in the wild in Europe. The birds on the sign are stylised (one green, one white and one black – no blue!) but with the crest and characteristic markings of Blue Jays. They are common east of the

Mississippi. Awoken at 5am by their piercing "*jay-jay-jay*" calls, they were the first birds I ticked on my first visit to the US, whilst jetlagged in Florida in August 1976.

Two other North American birds that have never made it as vagrants to Britain (or anywhere in Europe) seemed promising candidates as pub birds until I checked them out. *The Bluebird Inn* (in Mellor Brook, Lancashire) is named after Donald Campbell's jet-powered speed boat, not an Eastern Bluebird (nor have Bluebirds ever flown "over the White Cliffs of Dover" despite what Vera Lynn sang). Campbell was killed attempting the world water-speed record on Coniston Water in 1967. The hull of the boat was built by Salmesbury Engineering and the inn sign is a picture of the boat. *The Meadow Lark* in Dudley (West Midlands) was an even longer shot. It's a modern pub with not a bird in sight and seems extremely unlikely to have been named after an American Eastern Meadowlark; it's on my list as an unspecified Lark, probably a Skylark.

Storks and Dodos

These unlikely foreign bedfellows are linked because they illustrate very clearly how 'being foreign and strange' limits the appeal of potential pub birds, whilst 'familiarity and feelgood' can enhance it. Both species have a rich folk and literary history, and yet one (the Dodo) has only one pub named after it. The other (White Stork) has at least seven.

The Dodo in Hanwell (London) is a modern micropub opened in 2017. Why the pub is so named is unclear[4.25]. Dodos have, of course, the dubious distinction of being the poster boys and girls of extinct species. "More has been written about the Dodo...than any other extinct bird species. But in reality, virtually nothing is known about it in life"[4.26]. Even the date upon which it disappeared for ever (variously recorded as 1662 to 1693) is unclear. It was found only on the island of Mauritius (in the Mascarine Islands east of Madagascar), but apparently a live specimen was brought to London in 1638. It is possible that the head and foot of a Dodo in the Oxford University Museum of Natural History belonged to this bird. I've seen them but not ticked it; indeed, I know of no birders who ticks museum specimens. The sheer strangeness and unfamiliarity of the Dodo may account for the fact that only one (modern) pub is named after it, despite it featuring in Lewis Carroll's *Alice's Adventures in Wonderland*[4.27].

The Dodo, Hanwell

What sort of bird is (or was) the Dodo? Answer – a very unusual Pigeon[4.26]. Along with the closely related Rodrigues Solitaire from Rodrigues (also in the Mascarines and also extinct) DNA evidence shows that both evolved from an ancestor of the extant Nicobar Pigeon (still widespread on islands along the eastern side of the Indian Ocean). I tried to find a convincing story to link *The Dodo* in Hanwell with *The Dead Pigeon* in Rochester but failed miserably.

In continental Europe White Storks have been "an emblem of spring and fertility for thousands of years", and "frequently encountered in literature and other media…as the bearer of human babies"[1.22]. *Birds and People*[1.23] devotes three full pages to the mythology surrounding these charismatic birds. As well as delivering babies, they have served as symbols of religious and political prejudice. For instance, Storks only breed in republics, not in countries ruled by a monarch, and in the Ottoman Empire they only nest on Muslim and Turkish buildings, not Christian roofs. Neither of course is true, although if you really want to torture the evidence you could point out that it is generally believed that Storks have not bred in Britain in more than 600 years of rule by a monarch. Archaeological remains of White Storks are rare in Britain[2.6], with occasional remains from Bronze and Iron Ages, and rare Roman, Saxon and medieval finds. Clearly they were never common, "the famed nesting in Edinburgh in 1416 being perhaps the last, even only nesting"[2.6]. However, some place names strongly hint at the presence of Storks in Saxon Britain[4.28] (but there is also the potential for confusion with other long-necked, long-legged birds, loosely called "Storks", not least Grey Herons) and it seems likely that the majority of the inhabitants of these islands over a timespan that is longer than any extant pub may never have set eyes on a living Stork. And yet at least seven pub birds are White Storks, and Steve Shaw lists 13 (including one already closed)[1.5 & 4.29].

I think the explanation is simple. Although the living birds could have been unfamiliar to most people, the mythology and folklore spilled easily across the Channel. People knew what a Stork was, even though they had never actually seen one. Such a striking, large, black-and-white bird with a red beak and legs that delivered babies was familiar through writing, pictures and storytelling and made a great inn sign.

The *Stork Hotel* in Simonstone, Lancashire has on its sign a White Stork attending a baby in a nest-like crib on a chimney pot[4.30]. There are two things to note about this pub. First, it is clearly quite old, as are several other Stork pubs. How old has been impossible to pin down but it must have been named before most customers would have seen a real Stork. And second it is just one of five (or six – depending on when you count them) called *The Stork Hotel.* No other pub bird in my database has the epithet "Hotel" more frequently than this (Mute Swans only four times in total, from many more pubs). Some are also unusually flexible in alternatively being an "Inn" or dropping the epithet all together. I have no idea why. The others are in Birkenhead (Liverpool), Rowrah (Cumbria), Billinge (Lancashire, also known as *The Stork Inn*) and Condor Green near Lancaster (also known as *The Stork Inn* and plain *The Stork*). *The Stork* in Handsworthy (Birmingham; also known as *The Stork Hotel* and *The Stork Inn)* submitted a licence application in 1869. It is now closed. The pub in Billinge was originally a farmhouse dating from 1718, and the one in Condor Green dates from the 1660s. Both the latter are also now closed, the one in Condor Green after a disastrous fire in 2020. *The Stork Tavern* in Bolton, Lancashire is still open for business and is also an old pub, being first registered as an alehouse in 1789. The present Grade II listed building dates from 1850 and used to be called *The Fox and Stork* until at least 2011.

Stork Hotel, Simonstone

Dodos are globally extinct, and White Storks appear to have been extinct in Britain as a breeding species since 1416 (or possibly at some unspecified time later), although they have long been regular but rare visitors from continental Europe without attempting to breed. In 2020 that dramatically changed when a female from a captive but free-flying flock on the Knepp Estate in West Sussex attracted a passing wild male and, in a nest built in the top of an old Oak tree, the pair reared the first two young Storks in the wild in England for hundreds of years. In 2021 the number of breeding pairs at Knepp soared to at least six and it looks like White Storks are about to become regular breeding birds in the country[4.31]. Knepp is only about six miles from Storrington[4.28], the Saxon "village of Storks". How wonderfully appropriate.

Rare Birds are Rare

There is an expression in birding circles that "rare birds are rare", meaning that any birders not living at a birding hotspot or able to visit one regularly (such as Fair Isle), and who report lots of rare birds, are either delusional or deliberately fraudulent. Deliberate fraud is now very rare among modern birders but it was not always so. The saga of the Hastings Rarities still reverberates through the UK birding community[4.32]. The distinguished statistician J.A. Nelder did a spectacular hatchet job on a host of records of rare birds in the Hastings area (East Sussex and West Kent) between 1894 and 1924. He showed that very many of those records were statistically extremely unlikely to be genuine, based on their number, specific nature, seasonal distribution and very odd things such as pairs (a male and a female of the same rare species) or even flocks apparently appearing together (but never seen alive, always shot). The motivation it turns out was money, and the leading suspect was George Bristow, a taxidermist and gunmaker who stood to gain financially by selling his unlikely rarities to well-to-do collectors, who in turn sought prestige from having specimens that rival collectors lacked. It was basically 'listing' on steroids. The species involved were predominantly from the Mediterranean, North Africa, south-east Europe and even southern Asia. (We now know that some birds from these areas do make it to Britain, but not often.) Exactly how Bristow obtained them is unknown, but they were certainly not shot in the Hastings area by local 'gunners' (many of those credited by Bristow with obtaining them cannot be traced and most of the shot specimens have no named collector). The general conclusion is that they were shot abroad and either prepared as museum skins locally (to be remounted by Bristow) or more often brought to Bristow by ship as chilled or refrigerated corpses. There is a section in Nicholson and Ferguson-Lees's paper[4.32] that exposed the saga entitled "Possibilities of cool deception".

Only one of the Hastings Rarities definitely features as a pub bird[4.33], namely three Goshawks. In 1904 and 1905 (when they were reportedly collected) they were exceptionally rare birds in that part of the world. Even today you are very unlikely to encounter one in the area. *The Goshawk* in Mouldsworth (Cheshire) was a former 19th-century coaching inn close to Delamere Forest, where with a bit of luck you might just find one if you were playing Ticks and Tipples.

In Summary

We have seen that birds that are very rare or unknown in the wild in the UK, and even some foreign species popular in captivity, are generally (with a few notable exceptions) scarce as pub birds. That is, there are surprisingly few species, and individual species tend to be represented by a single or small handful of individual pubs. To put some rough numbers on that argument, between 13 and 17 foreign pub birds (depending on what I include) make up a total of just over 30 pubs[4.34]. Unusually abundant (non-domestic) foreign pub birds number just three species (Black Swan, Pelican and White Stork – four if you include Pheasants, five with Peacocks) for reasons I have already discussed. It matters little exactly what this number is because it is tiny compared with the number of native British species of pub birds.

Of course, it is impossible to say with any precision how many species of bird are native to Britain. The total 'British List' curated by the British Ornithologists Union as I write stands at 626[4.35], but the majority of these are anything from scarce or irregular visitors to rare or very rare vagrants. The consensus is that there are about 200 regular breeding species plus about 50 regular winter visitors. About 80 of them are pub birds[4.36]. That means that about one-third of the entire regular British avifauna makes an appearance as a pub bird. Contrast that with the 13–17 foreign pub birds, from a potential world list of over 11,000 (Chapter 1). Foreigners are not popular. They are even less so once you recall that many of these pubs are not deliberately named after non-native species. A significant number of foreign pub birds appear to be accidental, where the signwriter has innocently copied an illustration from a foreign bird book rather than there being a deliberate choice of name.

Nor is it the case that there used to be many more in the past. Steve Shaw has *Albatross* (2) and *Flamingo* (4) on his list (six pubs comprising two additional foreign species). None remain. Shaw also has two other possibles. One is a mysterious pub bird called a *Hopops* in Bideford (Devon). There is still a pub called *The Hoops* in Horns Cross just outside Bideford, which is surely the same pub. And "Hoop" is "an obsolete name for a Hoopoe"[1.15]. "Hopops" is the perfect description of the bird's call. I cannot find any reference that confirms that Hoopoes were ever called Hopops, but they must have been. They are pink with a conspicuous crest, a long, slightly downcurved beak, bold black-and-

The sign for The Hoops, Horns Cross, depicts a Goldfinch

white wings and tail and a floppy flight, exotic-looking and scarce-but-regular visitors to the UK. They turn up particularly in spring when they 'overshoot' on migration from mainland Europe, and they have occasionally both bred and wintered here. Their scientific name (Appendix 1) is *Upupa epos*, again reflecting the species' call. Sadly the current sign for *The Hoops* does not have a Hoopoe on it (if it ever did). It shows a Goldfinch perched among some hoop-like objects that appear to be some kind of leaded glass. Why is a mystery.

The second possible (but less likely) addition on Shaw's list is the *Sociable Plover* at Cosham in Hampshire. It is another pub that has closed although a very limited website still exists, but it is impossible to see what was on the inn sign. *Sociable Plover* could be a simple play on words, implying a friendly pub named after a Northern or Common Lapwing for example. Or it could be a reference to (in twitchers' parlance) a 'mega' Sociable Plover (otherwise known as a Sociable Lapwing), a rare vagrant to this country from Asia[4.37]. The former seems much more likely than the latter, and I have not included Sociable Plover on my pub-bird life list.

Richard Fitter alerted me to Ostriches as genuine pub birds (see above) but there are no additional foreign species on his list. And W.B. Alexander adds *Condor* towards the end of his ranked list, so it was perhaps just a single pub. It too no longer exists[4.38]. So, I do not think I am missing many, if any, other foreign species. In Bristow's day, bird collectors coveted extreme rarities, as do modern twitchers armed just with cameras and a great deal of skill. But as pub birds, funny exotic foreigners mostly don't cut it.

CHAPTER 5: ART, MUSIC, LITERATURE AND LEGEND

The Owl and Hitchhiker on the Holloway Road in London ticks three of these boxes: art, music and literature. The inn sign is brilliant – a modern, slightly cartoony work of art, amusing and puzzling at the same time, until you discover the origin of its name. The sign depicts a small Owl (of indeterminate species) perched on the thumb of a human hand. When I started this journey in 2010 it was called the *Edward Lear* and not a pub bird at all. But that name is part of the clue. Lear[5.1] was an artist, musician, author and poet who was born in 1812 in Holloway, within easy walking distance of where the pub now stands. He was the 20th of this parents' 21 children (!) and grew up to be (among other things) an accomplished musician; he is now most famous for his limericks. In 1871 he published *Nonsense Songs, Stories, Botany and Alphabets*, which he wrote for the children of his patron Edward Stanley, the 13th Earl of Derby, and included *The Owl and the Pussy-cat*, which he set to music. There can be few readers who don't know the first verse:

"The Owl and the Pussy-cat went to sea
In a beautiful pea-green boat.
They took some honey, and plenty of money,
Wrapped up in a five-pound note."

So that's the Owl bit. How does a hitchhiker get in on the act? Douglas Adams[5.1] was born 140 years after Lear in the East End of London but moved as an adult to Upper Street in Islington and then to Duncan Terrace nearby in the late 1980s. Both are within easy walking distance of the pub. By now most readers will have got it. Adams originally wrote *The Hitchhiker's Guide to the Galaxy* as a BBC radio comedy in 1978, before it was published as a 'trilogy' of five

The Owl and Hitchhiker, Holloway Road, London

The Owl and Pussycat, Shoreditch, London

books (Adams had a wicked sense of humour). *The Owl and Hitchhiker* celebrates these two local literary giants.

At least three pubs celebrate *The Owl and Pussy-cat* (one in Leicester and two in London – in Northfields and Shoreditch). The first two don't appear to have inn signs but the Shoreditch pub has a lovely sign featuring a white cat with her front paw around the shoulder of a horned (or 'eared') Owl[5.2], in a pea-green boat full of money bags and lit by the light of the moon; art and literature beautifully combined. It is one of the (relatively) few pubs I have been into after photographing the sign, having spent a whole day tramping and tubing around London photographing pub birds for this book. Exhausted and needing a drink, I mentioned to the young barman what a lovely sign it was. He looked at me as if I was a creature from another planet. I suppose, compared with most of his punters, I was.

Without forcing things too much there are also two other logical connections with pub birds involving Edward Lear and Douglas Adams. There is at least one pub in the *Hitchhiker* series, although it doesn't feature a bird[5.3]. *The Horse and Groom* was the pub in which Arthur Dent and Ford Prefect topped up on protein restoratives (aka peanuts) and muscle relaxants (alcohol) before their journey through hyperspace to the Vogan spaceship on which they hitchhiked using an electronic thumb. Douglas Adams himself apparently loved pubs, and was an ardent wildlife conservationist; he would have been appalled by the continuing illegal slaughter of Eagles and other birds of prey (Chapter 2).

The second link is through another of Lear's famous limericks, which goes:

"There was an old man with a beard,
Who said: 'It is just as I feared!–
Two owls and a hen, four larks and a wren
have all built their nests in my beard'."

All four species are, appropriately, pub birds.

A Confession

The arts, literature and music are not my strong suits. Which means that this chapter is quite short. A colleague who was one of my contemporaries as a graduate student at Durham in the late 1960s went on to work as a young lecturer in botany in another university. Soon after he wrote a review of a botanical ecology text by one of the UK's most senior professors in the field at the time. My colleague didn't like the book at all (a position that was entirely justified in my view). His most memorable phrase was: "This book creates a much-needed gap." This chapter probably does the same, and hopefully will inspire somebody to fill it.

What is Included and What is Not?

Mythical birds are dealt with in Chapter 4. In the current chapter I briefly discuss the possibility that some *Black Swan* pubs were named after a mythical bird and explore how folktales, myths and legends have played a part in naming other pubs after birds.

'Real' birds that have given their names to pubs also crop up with varying frequency (depending on the species) throughout English literature. But unless I can be reasonably sure that the pub derives its name from the bird's appearance in a literary work, I have not included it. An example: Shakespeare frequently included a reference to birds in his plays. *Birds Britannica*[1.22] provides an authoritative, succinct summary for ten of his plays, which name 15 or possibly 16 species of bird, all but two of which are also pub birds[5.4]. But as far as I know not a single pub has been named after one of these birds because it is mentioned in one of Shakespeare's plays. So they do not appear here. He does give a name to several pubs in the plays themselves but it seems that only one of these (*The Three Pigeons* in *The Merry Wives of Windsor*) is a pub bird[5.5]. After that, the *Swan at the Globe* on the Embankment in London next to the Globe Theatre is the nearest we come to him.

Swan at the Globe, Embankment, London

On my list are a small number of pubs named after birds that feature in other works of literature or in films (with one tenuous exception I have nothing from television). They either feature as the real thing or thinly disguised with an alias. Works of literature

Three Swans, Selby

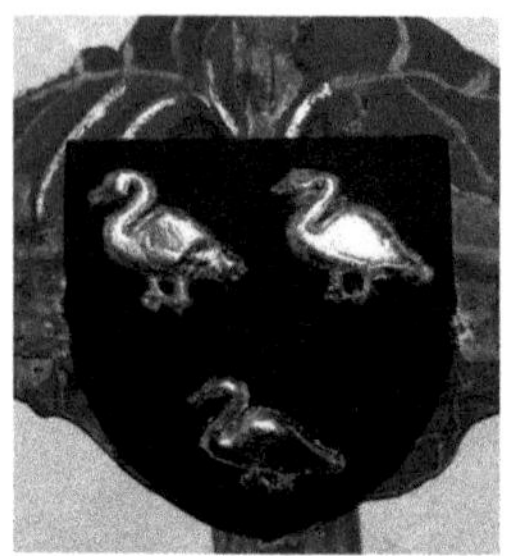

Three Swans, the crest of Selby Abbey

with birds in the title also appear to have been the inspiration for some pub-bird names. And great literary figures have frequented others. There are probably many more of all these that I should know about but do not.

Inn signs as art get a section to themselves.

Swans (again)

The Kalevala is an epic poem from Karelian and Finnish oral folklore and mythology. It tells the story of the creation of the Earth, with a Black Swan floating on the river that separates the worlds of the living and the dead[5.6]. The myth could provide an explanation for W.B. Alexander's assertion (Chapter 2) that *Black Swan* pubs existed before the bird's discovery in Australia. But if so, as Chris Perrins pointed out to me, "they shouldn't have white wings". Some of the birds on extant signs do have white wings but I haven't checked them all. A genuine all-black *Black Swan* may have its origin in *The Kalevala*. The strange pair of black Swans on one of the signs for *The Swan with Two Necks* in Bristol (on display in the Art Gallery later in this chapter) is one possibility.

Selby Abbey in Yorkshire was founded by Benedict of Auxerre in 1069. The story goes[5.7] that Benedict, a French monk, was visited in a dream by Saint Germain and instructed to go to Selabie. He did as he was told and sailed up the River Ouse (carrying a conveniently preserved finger of the saint), when three Swans landed on the water. Taking this as an auspicious sign Benedict founded an Abbey there. The crest of the Abbey bears three Mute Swans and next door to it now is the *Three Swans* pub, which is possibly Victorian and certainly nowhere near as old as the Abbey.

The *Golden Swan* in Wilcot, a lovely thatched inn in Wiltshire, could take its name from several folktales. My favourite is an Indian story from the *Jakata Tales*[5.8], in which a poor mother and her two daughters are helped by a golden Swan which moults golden feathers, one at a time, for the mother to sell. Eventually the greedy mother tries to capture the Swan and pluck all its feathers. They turn to ordinary feathers and the Swan escapes, never to help the family again. The moral? Excess greed brings nothing. It's a good story, but whether this pub derives its name from the tale is unclear. Currently the sign shows a Mute Swan wearing a golden crown as a neck ring, an image it shares with the wonderfully carved 15th-century sign of *The Swan Inn* in Clare, Suffolk[1.22]. Known as Bohun Swans, they were the heraldic badge of the medieval de Bohun family, which was later adopted by Lancastrian kings (Chapter 2). The folk story underpinning the Bohun Swan is almost as good as the *Jakata Tales*. It has its origin in a collection of works known as *Le Roman du Chevalier au Cygne* from about 1268 which "centres on the tale of seven children, six girls and a boy, born to a European royal family"[5.9]. I do not fully follow the details but basically each child was born with a chain around their neck. When the chains were removed, they turned into Swans. One of the sisters retained her chain and remained a Swan, whilst five brothers turned back to men. At least I think that's what happened. But what was the fate of the sixth brother? Who made up stories like these, and did anybody actually believe them?

The moral of the Indian version of the story of the golden Swan is essentially the same as Aesop's fable of *The Goose that Laid the Golden Eggs*. This version is taken from the archives of the US Library of Congress[5.10].

> "There was once a Countryman who possessed the most wonderful Goose you can imagine, for every day…[it] laid a beautiful, glittering, golden egg. [He] took the eggs to market and soon began to get rich. But…he grew impatient with the Goose because…he was not getting rich fast enough. Then one day…the idea came to him that he could get all the golden eggs at once by killing the Goose and cutting it open. But when the deed was done, not a single golden egg did he find."

Moral: Those who have plenty want more and so lose all they have, from which we get the expression "Don't kill the goose that lays the golden egg". But somebody did. *The Golden Egg* on Kilburn High Road in London is now closed.

The Golden Egg, Maida Vale

The signs for *The Goose* in Walthamstow and *The Goose on the Broadway* (both in London) used to be identical, carved golden Geese (they presumably belonged to the same chain), but neither made any link with golden eggs. In any case, the website for *The Goose* in Walthamstow now has a stylised white Goose in flight on a black background and can no longer claim any links to folk tales about gold, and when I visited again in October 2021 that too had disappeared and all that remained was the name.

The Goose, Walthamstow

Other Folk Tales, Myths and Legends

Positive Tales: Wrens, Robins and the Goddess Minerva

White Storks deliver babies (or so we are told) and some pubs reflect this folk tale (Chapter 4), whilst Magpies are probably pub birds partly because they feature in various versions of the rhyme "One for sorrow, Two for joy, Three for a girl, Four for a boy", etc. (Chapter 2). Other species may be pub birds because of similar positive publicity in myth and legend. Others apparently suffer from evil imagery. The positive tales first.

Wrens are the ultimate 'small brown birds' and not obviously the sort of species to make an appearance as a pub bird. Small and brown they may be but they have a very loud, highly distinctive song, are "amongst the most widespread [birds] in Britain"[2.25] and have an interesting folk history[1.22], so they make it as a pub bird. Steve Shaw has five on his list and Alexander ranks them 22nd from the end of his list (between Rook and Brent Goose). There are no less than eight in my database. They feature on the sign of the *Bird in Hand* in Wreningham, Norfolk (Table 2, Chapter 2); there are three called the *Jenny Wren* – in Beal (Lincolnshire), Calne (Wiltshire) and Sittingbourne (Kent); *The Jenny Wren Inn* is in Susworth in Lincolnshire; and the other three are *The Wrens* (plural) in Leeds, the *Whistling Wren* in Leigh (Greater Manchester) and *The Wrens Nest* in Telford (Shropshire), on Wren's Nest Lane (Chapter 3).

That four of these are *Jenny Wrens* is telling. Wrens are but one of a handful of birds with "personalised nicknames"[5.11], implying that they have a special place in folk memories. For the Wren, myths circulate around ritual hunting ('wrenning') that survived until recently in parts of western Ireland and the Isle of Man and that once included large parts Scotland, Ireland and southern England. According to *Birds Britannica* the birds were either captured and caged or killed and nailed to a pole. Claims have been made that the ritual is very old, with a pre-Christian, possibly Celtic or Bronze Age origin. *Birds Britannica* (p.332)[1.22] debunks the myths. "There is absolutely no evidence for it prior to the late seventeenth century", where it was first recorded in Pembrokeshire. But this is old enough for it to have influenced pub names from the 18th century onwards. Whether the *Bird in Hand* in Wreningham has anything to do with this barbaric practice is unclear. There are no clues on any of the websites that refer to the pub.

Wrens also enter folk mythology in another curious but much less violent way. It was a long-held belief that male Robins paired with female Wrens. As David Lack points out[5.12]: "Cock and hen robin look alike, despite the popular belief, not extinct even now [at least in 1965 when he first published this] that the robin's wife is the wren." Lack cites William Blake's *Popular Rhymes*[5.13]:

"The Robin and the Wren
Are God Almighty's Cock and Hen,
Him that harries their nest
Never shall his soul have rest".

It is a nice story and may have helped both species to become pub birds. There are just four (possibly a few more) definite Robins on Steve Shaw's list, but they are well up in Alexander's ranking (at 26, well ahead of Wrens). I now only have two: *The Robin* in Hull on the Humber Estuary and the *Robin's Nest* in Edinburgh. Given the endearing behaviour of Robins, and their popularity of symbols of Christmas, even if I am missing a few I am surprised that they do not feature more often as pub birds, and neither of the two I have seen has a picture of the bird.

You need to concentrate to follow the next mythological trail. The inn sign of *The Minerva* in Hull Marina shows the head of a large, stylised horned Owl, probably an Eagle Owl. The pub was opened in

1829 and named after HMS *Minerva*. The ship's prow consisted of an Owl's body with a woman's head – the Roman goddess Minerva. There is an old pub sign high up on the front showing the goddess as a woman. Minerva was the Roman goddess of wisdom, who from the 2nd century onwards was equated with the Greek goddess Athena. Athena herself is often depicted with her sacred Owl of Minerva (or Athena), a symbol of her association with wisdom and knowledge but also in some accounts the goddess of war[5.14]. Just to complicate matters further *Athene* is the generic name for Little Owl. I have no idea how this transformed itself into an Eagle Owl. And if you follow this you definitely haven't had one too many.

Halcyon

In Ancient Greek mythology, Halcyon (or Alcyon), a Kingfisher, built its nest on the surface of the sea. I have nine pubs called the *Kingfisher*, and one each of *The Kingfisher (Inn)* in Cockermouth, Cumbria and *Kingfisher Tavern* (Kirkham, Lancashire) and just one called the *Halcyon* in Peterborough (Cambridgeshire). Most, including the *Halcyon*, are modern pubs. Why an Ancient Greek mythological bird was chosen for the name of a pub is unclear. But the myth (like so many) is intriguing in its elaborate, highly implausible detail[1.23]. It involves two lovers, Halcyon, the daughter of Aeolus, the god of the wind, and Ceyx, the son of the Morning Star. The lovers managed to annoy Zeus, who summoned up a storm that wrecked their ship and drowned them, whereupon a repentant Zeus turned the doomed pair into Kingfishers. Every year thereafter Halcyon and Ceyx proceeded to build their nest on the surface of the sea and Aeolus then stilled the wind for two weeks to allow them to rear their young. There are periods of calm in the Mediterranean during midwinter (not where or when real Kingfishers nest!) which we refer to as halcyon days.

The Kingfisher, Cockermouth

Kingfishers actually nest in a burrow they dig into a riverbank in spring. Discovering a Kingfisher's nest is one of my most enduring memories from my time as a young birder. My nature diary for 20 April 1960 records that in the morning I found a hole in the bank of a small tributary of the River Lostock in Worden Park, Leyland that looked "interesting". That evening I returned with a torch and, peering into the hole (paddling bare feet in the river), I was greeted with the stunning spectacle of a Kingfisher on its nest less than half a metre away at the end of the hole and staring straight at the light. I was overwhelmed with excitement. On 29 May five youngsters fledged, my notes tell me. I have never seen another Kingfisher on its nest in 70 years of birding, although what I did then would now be illegal under the Wildlife and Countryside Act 1981. Kingfishers are "Schedule 1 Birds", which means that it is a crime to deliberately disturb them at the nest without a permit – even a little bit.

Negative Tales: Owls and Cormorants

Folk myths and legends can also work against some species becoming popular pub birds, not least Owls. Compare Owls with Eagles and Falcons. In my database there are 44 Eagle pubs and 26 Falcons but at best only 15 Owls[5.15]. Yet Eagles, Falcons and Owls are formidable hunters, with (compared with us) phenomenal eyesight; many Owls have hunting skills far superior to those of Eagles and Falcons[5.16] – they can see in near total darkness and can detect, locate and capture prey without being able to see at all, simply by using the sounds the prey makes. Some Owls will break through snow or soft ground to catch invisible mice or voles. This almost miraculous ability rests on their wonderful, semi-human 'faces', which are technically a facial disc[5.2] and which act like a parabolic reflector to focus sounds on the birds' real but hidden *asymmetrical* ears (one is higher than the other); one hypothesis is that because of the asymmetry sounds arrive at fractionally different times to each ear, allowing the Owl to pinpoint the exact location of the prey. They are truly remarkable birds. Eagles and Falcons live in a daylight world and epitomise powers that we can both envy and comprehend. Owls live in a world of darkness, beyond our comprehension. Owls are spooky, particularly when (like Barn Owls) they inhabit ruins and churchyards and hiss and scream in the dark. They scared the living daylights out of me as a nine-year-old trespassing in the ruins of Worden Hall in Leyland where I

Old sign for The Owl at Hambleton

first encountered them one summer evening. (The same Worden Park where I found that Kingfisher's nest eight years later; I spent a lot of time there.) "Owls carry upon their backs the whole weight of English folklore"[1.22], which is why, I think, they are so much less popular as pub birds than Eagles and Falcons[5.17].

There is only one pub called *The Cormorant* (in Portchester, Hampshire), although it is also one of the possible sources of the Liver Bird myth (Chapter 4). Cormorants are big, impressive birds, not much smaller than the equally black, but much more popular, Black Swan. And they are adept hunters, with the ability to dive underwater to catch fish in near pitch darkness. But their deathly appearance, and a detestation of any species that competes with us for food, has doomed them in the popularity stakes. To quote *Birds Britannica*[1.22], the bird has "an ancient status as a creature of ill omen...holding out their drying wings like an openly draped black coat".

My own bad encounter with Cormorants happened in the summer of 1964 when I was one of the National Trust's wardens on the Farne Islands in Northumberland and living in an ancient stone tower on Inner Farne. The Farnes are a fabulous seabird city. As well as keeping an eye on the visitors I was doing my own undergraduate research on (since you didn't ask) when and how young Arctic Tern chicks acquire their fleas. (Answer: within two or three days of hatching and largely from Mum and Dad.) With several of the other wardens and scientists living on the islands that summer I was also ringing as many young birds as possible to learn more about their behaviour and biology. The only place Cormorants nested was on a small rocky outcrop known as the Megstone, some three miles north-west of Inner Farne and a short Zodiac ride away. As we approached in the boat the stench was almost overwhelming. Fishy faeces and rotting uneaten fish do not make for a fragrant experience. During the ringing (which was very tricky on the steep rocky outcrop) I slipped shin deep into a gulley full of liquid Cormorant excrement (guano). On the trip back I was banished to the back of the small boat. The smell was so bad I had to peg my shoes in a rockpool for several days after scrubbing them for ages, and still had to throw them away. I have never really liked the birds since.

Richard King[5.18] explores the natural history and mythology of Cormorants worldwide in the appropriately titled *The Devil's Cormorant*, from which I can quote Steinbeck[5.19], writing about the Gulf of

California (aka the Sea of Cortez):

> "Several men were shooting black cormorants; and it developed that everyone in Cape San Lucas hates cormorants. They are the flies in a perfect ecological ointment…They dive and catch fish, but also they drive schools away from the pier out of easy reach of the baitmen. They are considered interlopers, radicals, subversive forces against the perfect and God-set balance on Cape San Lucas. And they are rightly slaughtered, as all radicals should be."

Literature

A small number of pub birds, definitely or in some cases possibly, owe their existence to the title of a work of literature or associated film, or to a character in a novel. Others appear explicitly, as an alias or as an entirely fictitious pub bird in various works of literature.

Jackdaw

The first pub bird named after a work of literature (as we saw in Chapter 3) is *The Jackdaw* (sometimes *The Jackdaw Inn*) in Denton in Kent. It started its long life as *The Red Lion* but was renamed in the 1960s after *The Jackdaw of Rheims*, one of *The Ingoldsby Legends* written by the Reverend Richard Barham who lived in the village. *The Ingoldsby Legends, or Mirth and Marvels*, to give them their full title, are a collection of humorous and macabre stories in prose and verse written by 'Thomas Ingoldsby of Tappington Manor', Barham's nom de plume. They first appeared in 1837 and were compiled as three books between 1840 and 1847[5.20]. The best-known poem in the collection is *The Jackdaw of Rheims*, in which a Jackdaw steals a cardinal's ring. It opens:

"THE JACKDAW sat on the Cardinal's chair!
Bishop and abbot and prior were there;
Many a monk, and many a friar,
Many a knight, and many a squire,
With a great many more of lesser degree,–
In sooth, a goodly company."

Later in the tale the cardinal takes off his ring:

"From his finger he draws
His costly turquoise;
And, not thinking at all about little Jackdaws,
Deposits it straight
By the side of his plate,
While the nice little boys [a dubious reference to choirboys] on his
Eminence wait;
Till, when nobody's dreaming of any such thing,
The little Jackdaw hops off with the ring!"

You will have to read the poem to get the rest of the plot (it's great fun), but when the Jackdaw eventually died:

"The Conclave determin'd to make him a Saint;...
So they canoniz'd him by the name of Jem Crow."

The story has inspired numerous works of art of varying ornithological rigour. One entitled "A Saint, from the Jackdaw of Rheims"[5.21] is undoubtedly a Carrion Crow perched on a pile of red, leather-bound books on a cathedral windowsill and not a Jackdaw at all.

If all this was not enough *The Jackdaw* has one last claim to fame. It makes a brief appearance in the *Battle of Britain*, a film released in 1969 and set in 1940 as the Luftwaffe attempted to bomb Britain into submission (the real battle was indeed fought in the skies above the pub)[5.22]. In the film, Squadron Leader Colin Harvey (Christopher Plummer) and his wife Maggie (Susannah York) are pub patrons. As far as I know it is the only real pub named after a bird to appear in a film.

The Jackdaw, Tadcaster

For completeness (and at the other end of the interest scale) there is at least one other pub called *The Jackdaw* in Tadcaster, Yorkshire. It's a modern pub, and I have no idea why it is so called.

Skylark

The Skylark in Croydon (south London) is a very beautiful Art Deco building, which more than makes up for the fact that it only has a name, not a sign[5.23]. The pub is named after one of Gerald Manley Hopkins's most famous sonnets *The Sea and the Skylark*, written in 1877[5.24]. The second verse is:

> *"Left hand, off land, I hear the lark ascent,*
> *His rash-fresh re-winded new skeinèd score*
> *In crisps of curl off wild winch whirl, and pour*
> *And pelt music, till none's to spill nor spend."*

The rhythm catches the song of a Skylark brilliantly. But why Croydon? Hopkins's grandparents lived in Croydon and he spent time with them. Whoever decided to call the pub *The Skylark* did their homework.

Cuckoo, Snow Goose and Snowy Owl

There are only two pub birds possibly derived from book titles and one from a famous character in a very famous story, but I cannot be certain about any of them.

The Cuckoo's Nest in Chorley (Lancashire) is a mystery. You don't have to be a birder to know that ('our') Cuckoos don't build nests. It just had a name and no sign and closed permanently during the Covid-19 outbreak in 2020. It would have been interesting to see how a Cuckoo's nest could be depicted by a creative signwriter. However, it is at least plausible that the pub did not take its name from 'our' Cuckoo at all, but from Ken Kesey's American novel *One Flew Over the Cuckoo's Nest*[5.25] or its much-celebrated 1975 film adaptation starring Jack Nicholson. Nevertheless, a book or film about a psychiatric hospital in Oregon is a strange name to pick for a pub. If this is its origin it has an ornithological twist. As Charles Darwin well knew "the American cuckoo....makes her own nest".[5.26] Darwin does not specify which "American Cuckoo" he had in mind, but Yellow-billed is most likely because his correspondent, a Dr Merrell, lived in Iowa where the species is common (and it has the specific scientific name *americanus*). Darwin was interested in Cuckoos as an example of how not just morphology but also behaviour evolved: "Now let us suppose that the ancient progenitor of our European cuckoo had the habits of the American cuckoo, and that she occasionally laid an egg in another bird's nest" (as, he pointed out, many species of birds, including

American Cuckoos, occasionally did). Over time he argued, favoured and amplified by natural selection, "the strange instinct of our cuckoo has been generated".

In Chapter 4 I puzzled over why two pubs, one in Farnborough and one in Inverness, were called *The Snow Goose*, because "neither place has any obvious association with the species", which in any case is a (barely established) alien here. Perhaps the origin of one (or both) of the names lies in Paul Gallico's much-loved children's story about a Snow Goose, set in the Essex marshes and the years running up to the evacuation of Dunkirk in the Secon World War[1.22]. It is churlish to point out that a Snow Goose is an unlikely bird to find anywhere near Essex or Dunkirk.

Similar thoughts suggest there could also be a literary connection for the *Snowy Owl* in Cramlington (Northumberland), again not a bird you would expect to find in that part of the world. Hedwig was Harry Potter's pet Snowy Owl in J.K. Rowling's epic Harry Potter novels. Among other things it delivered Harry's mail.

Pelican, Dove and Pigeons

Erik Linklater was a Welsh-born Scottish poet and writer. His *Poet's Pub* was published in 1929 as one of the very early Penguin Classics[5.27]. The pub (in the fictitious village of Downish) was originally called, according to the tale, *The Downish Helicon.* Helicon is a mountain in Greece, believed by the Ancient Greeks to be the source of poetic inspiration and home of the Muses. Linklater elaborates:

> "The inn sign grew battered, and the villagers thought nothing of so strange a name and could never learn to pronounce it. So when the eighteenth century nearly finished a new landlord had the sign re-painted and lettered with what he took to be its proper name, The Downy Pelican. And that's what it's called to-day."

The Water Gypsies (a novel by A.P. Herbert published in 1930) is a romantic comedy set along England's rivers and canals. It features a pub called *The Pigeons*, which turns out to be a thinly disguised real pub that we met in Chapters 2 and 3 – *The Dove* on Upper Mall in Hammersmith, where Herbert lived. The story was subsequently turned into a film (1932) and a stage musical (1955), although I have seen neither and do not know if they feature the pub. The 'real' pub has one final literary, poetic twist. We are told on the pub's website[5.28] that James Thompson wrote the words for *Rule Britannia!* there in 1740.

Several fictitious pubs in stage plays are called *The Three Pigeons*[5.5], a name that Charles Dickens used in his final novel, published in 1865, *Our Mutual Friend*. It is a long, very complicated and in my view boring story that I have not been able to stick with long enough to find the reference to the pub[5.29].

Poetic Links

Aside from *Pop Goes the Weasel*, *The Owl and the Pussy-cat* and *The Jackdaw of Rheims* I know of only two other poetic links to a pub bird.

The Swan Hotel in Grasmere in the English Lake District still exists. Its inn sign was celebrated in a poem by William Wordsworth, the English Romantic poet who died in 1850. I do not know when he wrote this (frankly poor) doggerel[1.24]:

"Who does not know the famous Swan,
Object uncouth and yet our boast
For it [the inn sign] was painted by the host?
His own conceit, the figure planned,
'Twas coloured all by his own hand."

Yes, quite. The present sign was clearly not painted by the landlord. Amusingly, one of the least attractive pub signs I have ever seen used to grace (if that's the correct word) *The Cygnet* in York.

The only other poetic link I know of is cheating because the pub no longer exists. Alfred, Lord Tennyson put *The Cock* in Temple Bar in London into a poem[1.24]:

"Oh plump head waiter at The Cock
To which I must resort,
How goes the time? 'Tis five o'clock.
Go fetch a pint of port."

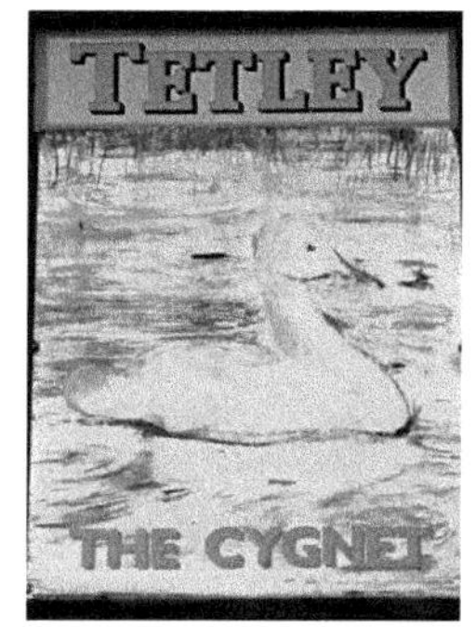

The Cygnet, York

Whoever managed to drink a pint of port? Perhaps he meant or wanted to imply "porter" (a kind of dark beer made from brown malt) which unfortunately doesn't rhyme with "resort".

Music

Additional musical links are also scarce, and the first is more tenuous than the second.

When I first encountered it early in my research I assumed that *The Linnet and Lark* in Hull in Yorkshire might have been the result of a merger of two pubs (Chapter 2) or possibly an old bird catcher's pub. But it doesn't owe its name to either; it is a modern pub on a road (Princes Avenue) that didn't have any pubs on it prior to 1994[5.30]. I thought I had found a possible source[5.31] in an 'Ode on the Death of Henry Purcell', written by John Dryden (1631–1700) and set to music by John Blow (1649–1708) with the opening lines:

"Mark how the lark and linnet sing:
With rival notes.
They strain their warbling throats
To welcome in the spring."

However, the two birds appear in the wrong order, and it doesn't seem, well, quite Hull, which I thought of as having a reputation for being gritty and proud rather than as an arty city until I remembered that it was the UK's city of culture in 2017. But even then, I'm not convinced.

I have considered one other possible origin, based on a letter to the Royal Society of London from the Honourable Danes Barrington in 1773[5.32]. In the letter Barrington is discussing how young male birds learn to sing. He describes one complicated chain of events involving a captive Robin that sang like a "skylark-linnet", that is, a Linnet raised in captivity by a Skylark, which thus sang like a Skylark and which then raised the Robin which in turn learned its song from the aberrant Linnet. (There must have been some bird catchers involved here!) But I can see no way anybody in the pub trade in Hull in the late 1990s is likely to have known about Skylark-Linnets.

In the end I must admit that I have been overthinking the name of this particular pub. In any case, it's now called *The Bowey* – the legendary singer, I thought. But his name was David Bowie, not Bowey. I give up.

But there is a pub bird named after a singer. *The Nightingale* in Sutton (in the London Borough of Croydon) used to be called *The Jenny Lind*[5.33] after an opera singer known as "the Swedish Nightingale". Johanna Maria Lind was one of the most highly regarded singers of the 19th century and a member of the Swedish Academy of Music from 1840. After a dazzling early career she settled in London in 1855, and in 1882 became Professor of Singing at the Royal College of Music in South Kensington. I cannot find out whether she had any special connection with Sutton or Croydon. The pub presumably used to have her portrait as a sign, but it now has a Nightingale.

Art

Most of what I know about works of art I learned between 2007 and 2018 when I was a trustee then chairman of the York Museums Trust (YMT), which, as well as two museums and a public garden, also has an art gallery in its portfolio. York Art Gallery (YAG) was a whole new ball game for me. I essentially knew nothing worth saying about art, and YAG's wonderful collection of paintings, ceramics and sculptures, spanning the great sweep of European art from the 15th century to the some very modern works, taught me a great deal, most of it highly enjoyable and very positive. But I also discovered what I did not (and still do not) like, which I will refer to politely as the pretentious nonsense of some modern art, particularly the stuff made from bits of old carpet, string and cardboard, or involving blurry videos and neon lights. I find the need for some modern artists to 'explain' what their work means quite irritating. Worse, more often than not the 'explanation' is usually incomprehensible. By contrast, the wonderful thing about the art on pub signs is that it needs no explanation, other than how the name arose or was chosen and its symbolism – which is most of this book. In other words, my role is that of a (very amateur) art historian, or an art critic of pub and inn signs. Other than that, the sign must speak for itself and convey something about the pub. A picture, if it's a good one, is worth a thousand words. A picture that draws customers in and makes the pub stand out from the crowd is what it is all about (Chapter 2).

Inn-Signia and the Inn Sign Society

"Today, [inn and pub] sign painting is a specialised branch of the work of a professional artist. In the past it was often combined with the professional trade of coach painting.... Country landlords, however, had to rely on local talent or the visit of an itinerant painter." (Bodge it yourself could be disappointing, as Wordsworth saw only too well.) *Inn-Signia* is not only the title of the book (published by Whitbread in 1948) from which this quote is taken and to which I have referred repeatedly[1.24], it is also (as "insignia") a collective name for inn and pub signs and names, according to the website of the Inn Sign Society[1.25], although more generally it simply means a badge or emblem, or a distinguishing sign or mark. The society has a membership of about 300 and it is "run by members for their own enjoyment". It's aims include bringing together people with an interest in inn and pub signs, to encourage research into the signs themselves and the origins of pub names. "If the Inn Sign Society doesn't bother, perhaps no else will." As I confess in Chapter 1, I am not a member, because pub birds make up only a tiny fraction of great pubs and their signs. But I certainly appreciate what the society does. Its magazine, *At the Sign of...*, appears four times a year and has featured some lovely pub birds on its cover. The two most recent are those of the *Jenny Wren* in Calne, Wiltshire (volume 127, Summer 2021) and of *The Pheasant Inn* in Keswick, Cumbria (Volume 119, Summer 2019), the first of which we have already encountered. It gives an annual award to the sign of the year. The winner in 2017 was the sign for *The House Martin* in Barton on Sea, Hampshire. All these images are pub signs of the highest quality, beautifully executed and immediately attractive, and clearly the work of skilled professional artists.

Art Detective

Chapter 4 described how the stylised Mute Swan on the sign of *The White Swan* in Walsingham transformed into a North American Whistling Swan taken from an illustration in John James Audubon's *Birds of America*. As we have seen, the images of several other unusual pub birds have also most likely been innocently copied by signwriters from illustrations in bird books, but I do not usually know the exact sources. They include *The Bonny Moorhen* in Stanhope (which now shows a Moorhen but used to be a female Black Grouse – Chapter 3), *The Cuckoo* in Alwalton (an African Jacobin Cuckoo), *The Three Jays* in Jaywick (North American Blue Jays) and *The Kestrel* in Harrogate (an American Kestrel, which used to be a Common Kestrel).

The Black Swan Hotel, Leyburn

Two of the *Black Swan Hotel* pubs (in Leyburn and Middleham) that sparked my interest in pub-bird signs have (or at least had) identical signs, featuring an adult bird with a fluffy cygnet in identical poses. Presumably both were painted by the same artist from the same unknown source (or less likely one was copied from the other).

Eagle and Sun, Droitwich

I do know the source for the spectacular painting on the sign for the *Eagle and Sun* in Droitwich, which I took to be a Harris's Hawk but which turned out to be a Golden Eagle (as explained in Chapter 2). There is also one other very beautiful sign where the sources (plural) seem very clear after a bit of detective work. The sign for *The Kites Nest* in Stroud showed two Red Kites, an adult looking directly at the viewer and a youngster. The pub is now closed and converted into houses but I sincerely hope the sign has survived. It is a mash up of illustrations of an Osprey (with a youngster) and a Red Kite by the great bird artist Archibald Thorburn in T.A. Coward's *The Birds of the British Isles and their Eggs*[5.34]. The Osprey forms the frontispiece of the book and the Kite is plate 147. (Both illustrations are on the next page.) Thorburn's style is at the 'heroic' Monarch of the Glen end of the spectrum of bird illustrators and now seems rather dated. But the signwriter for *The Kites Nest* captured it exactly.

The Kites Nest, Stroud

What has occurred to me whilst writing this book is that I know essentially nothing about the names or histories of the artists (I've referred to them as "signwriters") who produced this staggering body of work, with two exceptions, bizarrely both again involving Pelicans.

Osprey from
T.A. Coward[5.34]

Red Kite from
T.A. Coward[5.34]

The frontispiece to this book is by bird artist Ian Coleman; this is his first excursion into inn signs[5.35]. The other is the original sign for *The Fox and Pelican* in Grayshott[4.18], discussed in Chapter 4. The sign, which is the property of Grayshott Heritage, is by Walter Crane (1845–1915), who was "considered to be the most influential, and among the most prolific, children's book illustrator of his generation" and who produced "an array of paintings, illustrations, children's books, ceramic tiles, wallpaper and other decorative art" as well as "a number of iconic images associated with the international Socialist movement". There is no mention of this lovely sign in this extensive quote from Wikipedia and nor does it appear in a gallery of his illustrations[5.36]. There is a whole new world to explore here.

Art Gallery

The most effective way to illustrate literally the richness of the signs depicting pub birds is to showcase some of my favourite examples, as well as several other good pictures and pub birds that we have not yet had chance to see. I am not going to produce meaningless commentaries on each of them but instead have provided some broad contexts, grouping them into images that are:

- accurate (or reasonably accurate)
- recognisable species, but stylised or abstract depictions of pub birds
- humorous and cartoons, which are suprisingly rare

I have not been able to obtain pictures of every species or kind of pub bird. If I had tried to do that the book would have taken another year at least to finish. But I particularly regret not being able to obtain a picture of the Bohun Swan[2.8], depicted in the carved wooden sign for *The Swan Inn* in Clare, Suffolk, which is reputed to be the oldest carved inn sign in Britain (it is illustrated on page 64 of *Birds*

Accurate, or reasonably accurate portraits. From top left to bottom right: The Blackbird, Edgeware Road, London. Cock and Bottle, Skipton. The Cock Tavern, Maida Vale, London. The Eagle, Eaglescliff. Spread Eagle, York. The Heron, Norfolk Crescent, London. Kingfisher, Holme-on-Spalding Moor. The Kite, Oxford. The Magpie, New Street, London.

Britannica[1.22]). Apparently, it did not start life as an inn sign but as an early 15th-century corbel to an oriel window in the nearby manor house.

There are many examples of accurate or reasonably accurate depictions of pub birds throughout the book. Those in the Gallery are additional ones we have not yet encountered. Not all of them are great works of art. I can't quite put my finger on what's wrong with the Bald Eagle on the sign for *The Eagle* in Egglescliffe.

At least three of the stylised pub birds in the Gallery are Black Swans. The fourth, *The Swan with Two Necks* in Bristol is doubly odd; I touched on it briefly in Chapter 2. The sign has two Mute Swans on one side (I was unable to photograph this side because at the time it had scaffolding obscuring it) and two Black Swans (or simply stylised black Mute Swans) on the other. Just possibly it may have its origins in *The Kalevala* discussed earlier in this chapter and may also have mixed up "two nicks" with "two necks". It is one of the most complicated signs for a pub bird I've seen.

Cartoons or other forms of amusement are rare on the signs of pub birds, whatever Paul Nash might have said pub signs in general should be (Chapter 6). I have included five.

Recogniseable, but stylised or abstract pub birds (i). Old White Swan, York. Swan with Two Necks, Bristol. Black Swan, Leeds. Black Swan, Ravenstonedale. The Dog and Duck, Walkinton. Dog and Duck, Walthamstow. The Eagle at Barrow. Spread Eagle, Sawley.

Recogniseable, but stylised or abstract pub birds (ii). White Swan, Crediton. The Swan Hotel, Arundel. The White Swan, Middleham. The Pheasant Inn, Welland Malvern. The Pelican, Hull. The Swans Nest, Exminster. The Merlin, Billingham. Phoenix, Bristol.

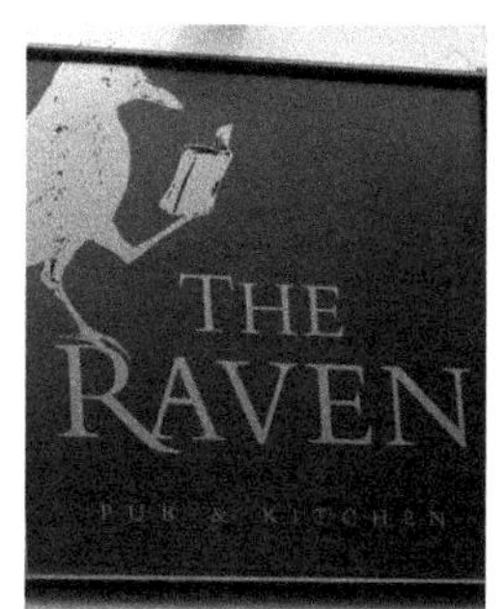

Humorous and cartoon pub birds. The Greedy Goose, Chastleton. Hook and Parrot, Bridlington. The Raven, Bath. New sign for The Owl, Hambleton. Oystercatcher, Hull. The Raven pub and kitchen, Hammersmith

And that brings the Art Gallery to a close.

CHAPTER 6: NESTS, BABIES, FEATHERS AND BIRD PARAPHERNALIA

I wanted to start this chapter by discussing eggs, with the intention of making a feeble joke about eggs coming before chickens. But there is (or was) only one pub that I am aware of with "egg" in its name – *The Golden Egg* in London discussed in Chapter 5 – and that is now closed. In any case, it involved a Goose.

This is a short chapter, bringing together all the pubs with bird-related things that I can find associated with pub birds. Some (most nests for example) have an identifiable species of pub bird either on the sign or in the name. Others have no specific bird associated with them but involve birdcages, dovecotes, henhouses and Duck decoys, examples of miscellaneous things and equipment to do with birds. There are short sections (because very few pubs are involved) on baby birds and feathers. Overall, this is a chapter that would undoubtedly repay further research.

Nests

Paul Nash (who *Inn-Signia*[1.24] described in 1948 as "the well-known modern painter"[6.1]) had strong views about the function of an inn sign, stating that it should be "amusing in a come-hither sort of way, with an invitation intimate, humorous, strange or even sinister; but *it should not be respectable*". Nash's First World War paintings are some of the most haunting and striking I saw during my time as chairman of the YMT but I am not sure how he arrived at his generalisations about inn signs. They do not ring particularly true for pub birds. As we have seen, for example, there are surprisingly few humorous signs, whilst intimate implies something that is private, secret, warm and cosy. That sounds like many birds' nests to me, yet there are very few pubs with "nest" in their name or depicting a nest on the sign. In my database only 19 involve nests, from just 16 specific or generic pub birds[6.2] (although some of these are inconsistent with Nash because they are anything but intimate, though I doubt Nash would have realised). We can run through all of them quite quickly because we have already encountered many. I discussed *The Cuckoo's Nest* in Chapter 5 and, as with that strange name for a pub, even for commoner birds the nest itself is rarely illustrated on the sign.

Perhaps inevitably, given their total number, Mute Swans feature in the list, but only once, at *The Swans Nest* on Station Road in Exminster (Devon); the sign is an attractive stained-glass window depicting a pair of nesting Swans (p.146).

There is one pub simply called *The Birds Nest* in Deptford, London. It has no sign, just a name, and we discussed its stuffed King Penguin in Chapter 4. It's an artists' and musicians' pub and is clearly an incredibly lively establishment. I cannot find out how it got its name.

The Sitting Goose in Bartle near Preston (Lancashire), which we have also encountered in Chapter 4) doesn't explicitly have "nest" in its name, but the sign is of a Canada Goose sitting on its nest.

The Woodcocks (plural) in Burton Waters (Lincoln) doesn't have "nest" in its name either but has a beautifully rendered single Woodcock sitting on a nest, with two eggs implausibly in full view against its breast. Signwriters are allowed a bit of artistic licence. Woodcocks are one of my favourite birds. They are waders[3.31], but very unusual ones because they are found primarily in damp woodland as breeding birds, with a patchy distribution throughout the UK[2.25]. They are so brilliantly camouflaged by their beautifully barred and chequered brown, russet, cream and black plumage (resembling a pile of dead leaves) that the incubating bird is almost invisible against the woodland floor. As a teenager I once spent an entire holiday looking for a nest in a wood close to Worden Park. I failed to find it. I thought they were breeding because the males have a bizarre display flight known as roding, in which they fly with a strange jerky motion low over and through the wood at dusk, with a call that can only be described as a pig-like grunt followed by a loud hiss. As with all waders, Woodcock chicks are up and about within a few hours of hatching. Remarkably, Woodcocks can carry their small chicks away from danger by flying off with them, either carried in their long bill or tucked between the adult's feet[6.3]. Gilbert White[2.43] (in letter XXXI to Thomas Pennant on 14 September 1770) drew attention to this possibility quoting from "Scopolis new work [on] the birds of Tirol and Carniola" and saying cautiously that "candour forbids me to say absolutely that any fact is false". Woodcocks are very hard to study, but we now know that they can and do carry their young from danger mainly tucked under the adult's legs.

There is a *Gulls Nest* in Burnmouth near Edinburgh, an *Eagles Nest* (now closed) with a pair of Golden Eagles on its sign in Kidderminster, a *Falcons Nest* in Gosforth Park, Newcastle and *The Kites Nest* discussed in Chapter 5, all nests of species (to a human observer at least) that tend to become rather smelly, unpleasant and hardly intimate as their charges grow up, whilst the remains of prey accumulate and putrefy. But beauty and intimacy are presumably in the eye (or at least the nose) of the beholder.

We also encountered *The Owls Nest* in Haydock, St Helens in Chapter 4, which has on its sign an established but introduced Little Owl sitting outside its nest site (a hole in a tree). Little Owls are predators like all Owls, but their prey is primarily made up of small vertebrates (mostly mammals and birds) and larger insects and earthworms, and their nests don't seem to become as littered with smelly bones and other bits as do the nests of larger predators. Being inside a tree or similar hole also makes them quite cosy. I vividly remember at the age of about 14 finding my first Little Owl's nest in a hole in the side of a low-growing Oak tree on an island in the middle of Worden Park lake. I had seen a Little Owl on the island and when the water level in the lake was low I managed to get to the site. I had a torch and remember the sheer thrill of seeing the wonderful yellow eyes of the incubating bird staring back at me from the depths of the hole. Unlike my adventures in the same park with Kingfishers, shining a light into a Little Owl's nest wasn't and still isn't illegal; they are not Schedule 1 species in England.

The specific identity of the Lark in *The Larks Nest* in Nuthall, Nottingham is unclear from the sign. I assume it's a Skylark. Skylark nests are well hidden, and when the feathered young are hunkered down out of sight they look cosy and intimate to the human observer. The same may be said of *The Swallows Nest* in Romsley in the West Midlands. Swallows build a mud nest assembled from small, wet pellets collected from the edges of ponds and puddles and built up like bricks and lined cosily with feathers. A brood of young Swallows peeping out over the rim of the nest is a touching and intimate thing to see.

The Wrens Nest in Telford is another (fairly modern) pub on a road of the same name (Chapter 3). Wren's nests are the ultimate cosy, intimate place to bring up a brood. The nest is a neatly domed, closed sphere or oval of variable size (larger than a tennis ball but smaller than a rugby ball) woven out of dead leaves, moss, grass or fern fronds – whatever vegetation is abundant locally. There is a small entrance hole about 2cm in diameter on one side. The nest site varies widely but it is often hidden in a bank or the upturned roots of a tree, in ivy on trees, in the old nests of other birds, or cracks and crevasses in walls, buildings or cliffs. The male builds several nests (called "cock's nests") and the female chooses one to line with feathers to make it nice and cosy. This miracle of miniature avian engineering can hold at least five nestlings packed into a tiny space. Only the most crowded pub could compete in the close-contact stakes.

Robins build one of the most secret and cosy nests. David Lack in *The Life of the Robin*[5.12] describes them as among "the hardest of all British bird's nests to find" deliberately, adding, however, that "The bird is so common that one can hardly help stumbling on at least one nest during the breeding season." Well, if you were David Lack this was probably true. For mere mortals it isn't. Maybe that's why there is only one *Robin's Nest,* on the Glimerton Road in Edinburgh.

Strangely, there are (or were) no fewer than four pubs called the *Throstles Nest* (in Bingley, West Yorkshire, Everton in Liverpool, Stretford in Manchester (which closed in 2010) and Wigton in Scotland). "Throstle" is a traditional name for a Song Thrush[1.15]. I have absolutely no idea why there should be four Song Thrush nests. What is more, their nests are hardly cosy or intimate, lined as they are with a bare layer of mud or sometimes dung, wet rotten wood, or peat, cemented with saliva and moulded by the female's breast. The lining of the nest sets like concrete it is the only British bird to do this. One possible evolutionary advantage of such a hard, smooth substrate is that it makes it impossible for Cuckoos to parasitise Song Thrushes; experiments show that a newly hatched Cuckoo chick is unable to gain sufficient purchase on the surface to eject the Thrush's own eggs[6.4]. But that cannot be the reason for calling four very different pubs *Throstles Nest.*

As explained in Chapter 1, I have not included any *Crows Nests* in the list but there is a single pub named after the Crow's close relative the Rook: *The Rooks Nest* in Hammersmith, London used to be called

Flynn's, an Irish pub. It is now closed. Rooks' nests sway in the tops of tall trees in high winds so must be strong and provide a secure, safe place for the eggs. Rooks nest colonially in large, comfortingly noisy rookeries, so a pub called *Rookery Wood Farm* in Crew (Cheshire) is an indirect reference to their nests.

Equally cosy is a Chaffinch's nest (*The Spink's Nest*, Chapter 1), which must be the most intimate, secure and cosy place in which to rear a family. It is a masterpiece of construction, being made from mosses and grasses, decorated with lichen, held together with spiders' webs and lined with hair and feathers.

Baby Birds

If nests are rare, baby birds on pub signs are even rarer. I might have expected more, given that young birds are often wonderfully attractive to look at, or at least once the positively ugly and reptilian, blind and featherless nidicolous[6.5] young of many species grow their first feathers and become cute. The bright-eyed fluffy balls that are wader chicks and other nidifugous[6.5] species, which leave the nest within hours of hatching, are cute almost from the word go. So maybe Nash is right here. Most baby birds are just too respectable and nice for an inn sign.

There are four Mute Swan cygnets (ugly ducklings): *The Cygnet* on Cygnet Street in York, two called the *Swan and Cygnet* (in North Ferryby, Hull and in Durkar, Wakefield) and one called *The Swan and Three Cygnets* on Elvet Bridge in Durham. I may have been into this one as an undergraduate but it was long before I got into pub birds. Two of the pubs that sparked my interest, *The Black Swan Hotel* in Middleham and *The Black Swan Hotel* in Leyburn, have lovely, identical signs (clearly copied from the same but unknown source by the same unknown artist – Chapter 5) showing an adult Black Swan and a cygnet.

The Eagle, Arundel

Perhaps because Eagles are viewed as bold, fierce birds, references to their nests and babies may be slightly more acceptable than they appear to be for other pub birds. So, as with the *Eagles Nest* in Kidderminster, the sign for *The Eagle* in Arundel (West Sussex) is a Golden Eagle about to feed two chicks. The food looks suspiciously like a worm but is perhaps meant to be a snake.

The outside of *The Eaglet* on Seven Sisters Road in London is covered in attractive deep-red ceramic tiles but unfortunately the pub has no sign. Young Eagles are not the most attractive of baby birds – all beak, large legs and feet, and a messy coat of down and emerging brown feathers, so having no sign may be wiser than a sign with just an eaglet on it. In contrast there are two *Hen and Chickens* (one in Highbury, London and one in Sheffield), both of which have attractive mother Hens and fluffy chicks on them.

And that's it.

Hen and Chickens, Highbury

Architectural detail on the Hen and Chickens, Highbury

Feathers

Although we think of any living creature with feathers as a bird, and hence something quite different from a furry mammal or a scaly lizard, fossil records show that this was not always so. Birds are basically dinosaurs, and, after the discovery of a series of stunning fossils primarily from China[6.6] dating from the Cretaceous and Jurassic periods[6.7], we now know that many dinosaurs had feathers. The discoveries have come thick and fast, each one changing the evolutionary picture somewhat. Modern birds are derived from dinosaurs with names such as Troodontids, Dromaeosaurids and Oviraptorosaurids. These dinosaurs had feathers and we know from fossils that some, including *Oviraptor*, laid eggs in nests and incubated them. *Microraptor* had four feathered wings on its front and hind limbs. I am still looking for the oldest pub in the world called *The Troodontid Arms.*

Feathers have a special place in the ceremonies, badges and clothing of many cultures all over the world. Alice Roberts[6.8] gives several examples ranging from images of people in the Bronze Age wearing feathers on their heads to the obvious native Americans and the much less obvious Hungarian foot soldiers who added a feather to their caps every time they killed an enemy. More generally, the expression "put a feather in your cap" signifies reward for success at almost anything, not just killing enemies[6.9]. It is perhaps not surprising that symbolic feathers feature in pub signs.

Prince of Wales Feathers, Warren Street, London

Prince of Wales, Hanwell, London

The Hat and Feathers, Clerkenwell, London

By far the commonest feathers are various depictions of three white Ostrich plumes derived from the heraldic badge of the Prince of Wales – three feathers encircled around their shafts by a gold coronet. The symbol can be traced back to the badge of the Black Prince, the eldest son of Edward III of England, who lived in the 14th century. Edward himself and other members of the royal family also used Ostrich feather badges in the 14th and 15th centuries[6.9]. As Wikipedia explains: "Many pubs in the UK are named *The Prince of Wales's Feathers, The Prince's Feathers* or simply *The Feathers*, particularly in areas associated with royal estates." My list is far from comprehensive but there is at least a dozen on it that are, or probably are, a reference to the Prince of Wales. The sign for *The Prince of Wales* in Hanwell in the London Borough of Ealing depicts the classical three-feathered badge. It makes a curious pairing with *The Dodo* almost immediately next door. Others include three plain *Feathers* (in Aylsham and North Walsham, both in Norfolk, and Helmsley, North Yorkshire) and two *Plume of Feathers* (in Malvern, Worcestershire, and Park Vista in London). The sign for *The Feathers* on Warren Street in London depicts a single plume, so both sides must be counted to make it plural. There is also *The Old Feathers* (in Framlington Pigot, Norfolk, close to *The Gull Inn*), a *Hat and Feathers* (Clerkenwell, London) and a *Three Feathers* (in Darnell, Sheffield)[6.10], as well as *The Feathers Inn* in Hedley on the Hill (Northumberland).

There are two pubs called *The Fur and Feathers.* One is inside Woodforde's Brewery in Norwich and doesn't appear to have a sign, which means that I cannot be sure how it got its name. The other, in Herriard near Basingstoke (Berkshire), does not derive its name from the Prince of Wales's badge. It has been a pub since about 1850 and was originally *The New Inn*, but changed its name (the pub's website doesn't say when) and the sign is now a wonderfully executed image of a fox surrounded by a large, stylised flock of white Cockerels with red wattles. I should, of course, have included this in Chapter 2, but it was easier to explain the story here.

The Fur and Feathers, Herriard

Many birders may not really be interested in feathers at all, particularly if they are Ostrich plumes. But the study of the pattern and timing of moulting, which all birds must do to renew and replace worn and damaged plumage, is a serious science and often critical for the correct identification and ageing of a bird. The most unusual bird book in my collection is devoted entirely to life-size photographs of the feathers of Japanese birds[6.11], laid out across whole pages (or for larger birds on a folded folio sheet). It is strangely beautiful, but nothing really to do with pub birds, except that it was given to me as a gift by its author (one of my Japanese hosts) in a bar in Tokyo whilst we were drinking sake. I am certain that the bar wasn't named after a bird.

The cover for a book on *The Feathers of Japanese Birds*

Paraphernalia

We have already encountered *The Birdcage* in Lincoln, depicting a Red-cheeked Cordonbleu outside its cage, and *The Cat and Canary* in Canary Warf where a triumphant Canary has managed to lock a tabby cat into a birdcage. I know of just two other birdcage pubs – the *Birdcage* on Columbia Road in London is just a name without a sign and *The Bird Cage* in Norwich had a real birdcage (with ivy growing in it) hanging as its sign, as many of the earliest pubs must have done with familiar objects to

The Bird Cage, Norwich

Birdcage, Clumbia Road, London

advertise their presence (Chapter 1). (Most 'paraphernalia pubs' are just a name without a sign, because they do not really lend themselves to an attractive illustration.)

Dovecotes – the artificial nesting places constructed by humans for Feral Pigeons are ancient. *Birds and People*[1.23] provides a succinct account. Their primary purpose was to provide a reliable supply of meat (from full-grown squabs) and eggs by taking advantage of the birds' colonial nesting habits and a willingness to breed in artificial ledges and holes that mimic the breeding caves of their wild, Rock Dove ancestors. Some of the earliest dovecotes date from Egypt (ca 330BC) and the Romans constructed Pigeon houses known as *columbaria* throughout their empire. Dovecotes were also mainstream in medieval Europe, including Britain. At one time there may have been 26,000 dovecotes in this country, some housing as many as several thousand pairs of birds. They were big business.

Their importance, and the fact that smaller dovecotes housed ornamental white Doves for pleasure, means that using the name for a pub is not surprising. I have eight on my list, from all over the country. One is the *Doocot* in Edinburgh (Chapter 1). The seven others are largely of unknown age but are not old, except possibly *The Dovecote Inn* in Laxton near Newark in Nottinghamshire. Laxton village is mentioned in the Doomsday Book and retains the last surviving, working open fields in the UK[6.9]. Open fields are divided into strips worked communally by local landowners. The pub's website is silent about its history but it looks relatively old compared with the other *Dovecotes*. Its sign is a miniature four-hole, white, slate-roofed model dovecote.

A second *Dovecote Inn* in Capel (Kent) has a stylised white Dove on its sign. The remaining *Dovecote* pubs are in Chingford (London), Long Ashton (Bristol; now renamed *The Ashton*), Narborough (Leicestershire) and Wednesbury (West Bromwich); *The Dovecot* – an alternative spelling – is in Middlesbrough (North Yorkshire). I cannot discover the history of any of them.

The only pub I am aware of that is named after a Duck decoy, *The Decoy Tavern* in Fritton, Great Yarmouth, is discussed in Chapter 2.

Hen houses, in contrast, lack the pleasant connotations of dovecotes and the brutal hunting success of a Duck decoy, and you need to avoid them on hot days. There is only one pub (the *Hen Hoose* in Aberdeen, Scotland) to take the name. I haven't been inside.

The Hen Hoose, Aberdeen

CHAPTER 7: TAIL ENDERS

I could have called this chapter "The Last Big Twitch", which is when birders try to add as many new species as possible to their year list, holiday list or what have you. It is partly that; 18 pub birds have not yet found their way into the book. But it is also about a few species that have already made a brief appearance. For these, either the birds or their pubs deserve more. Most birders have species on their list that they have seen only once or twice and which they would like to see again.

New Species to Add to the List

All 18 new pub birds (species and not specifically identified kinds of birds) are generally rare, represented mostly by one or two pubs (Woodpeckers are an exception). Many of these are relatively new pubs, with a name that appears to have been chosen because the bird is attractive or striking in some way, rather than being linked (as in Chapter 3) to a sense of place. There is only a little to say about most of them. They are listed roughly alphabetically, because the order in which birds appear in modern field guides, scientific papers and annual bird reports is constantly being rearranged as we discover more about the taxonomic relationships of living birds. For an old birder like me this is infuriating because I have to search backwards and forwards to find them. Listing these new species alphabetically keeps it simple.

Two of the species included here cannot be identified with certainty, and two others may not be birds at all. I have included all four of them to be on the safe side.

Bittern

Bitterns are wonderful birds. They are medium-sized, secretive brown Herons. The males have a spectacular booming call best described as a hiccup followed by a foghorn. Under favourable conditions it can be heard several miles away from their dense, reedbed haunts. Formerly they were widespread as a breeding species throughout the UK but the relentless draining of fens, bogs and marshes drove them to extinction by 1868; their plight was exacerbated by hunting for food and as their rarity increased they were also shot, stuffed and displayed in glass cases[3.5]. Their recolonisation started in Norfolk in about 1900 and breeding was proved in 1911[3.6]. There are now over 200 booming males (censused by hearing them as they hide in the reeds). A single pub called *The Bittern* is in Southampton (Hampshire) and as far as I know there are no breeding Bitterns nearby.

As a teenage birder growing in Lancashire I didn't think there were Bitterns anywhere near my home. I was wrong. My family discovered Silverdale (on the edge of Morecombe Bay), an area that was and still is a naturalist's paradise. Among its many special habitats was Leighton Moss, which is now an RSPB reserve but in 1957 was in private hands and primarily used for wildfowling. The area used to be potato fields but when the pumps failed during the First World War the valley flooded and turned into a large reedbed with open pools and crossed by a causeway. On the causeway in April 1957 I heard my first Bittern boom. It was so loud and close that it made me jump. Later that day I saw one fly over the reeds. It turned out that they were breeding there. In 1957 that was a closely guarded secret; the birds were hundreds of miles from what had been their only English toehold, in East Anglia. They still occur in the Silverdale area but for a time stopped breeding at Leighton Moss. They are fussy birds and as the reedbeds aged they became less suitable for Bitterns. Dedicated work by the RSPB has restored the site and you can hear their remarkable booming calls once again (the latest count in 2021 was six booming males – possibly with a Lancashire accent).

Finches

A Goldfinch features as a pub bird on the sign of *The Bird in Hand* in Blidworth near Mansfield (Nottinghamshire), which was briefly encountered in Table 2. A Goldfinch also now graces the sign for the *Hoops Inn* near Bidiford (Chapter 4). I am surprised that there are apparently no pubs simply called *The Goldfinch*, because these birds are without doubt our most beautiful Finch. They are associated with religious iconography, have a rich folk history and were once popular as a cagebird (they very beautiful to look at and also have a pleasing, tinkling song)[1.22]. Males and females are identical. It is said that they acquired their red 'faces' from Christ's blood on the cross. I have not been able to trace the history of the Goldfinch on the sign of the Blidworth *Bird in Hand*, but it is probably linked to the birds being captured to become cage birds.

Two new pub birds are also Finches[7.1], the *Greenfinch* in West Didsbury (in Greater Manchester, now closed) and *The Bullfinch* in Riverhead, Kent. The former didn't appear to have any sign; the latter shows a black-and-white, stylised, all-purpose small bird, which I think misses a trick, because male Bullfinches are striking birds that remind me of small parrots because of their large stubby bills, black caps and bright pinkish-red underparts. They would make a great inn sign. Bullfinches appear to pair for life, stay close together and often duet with soft, single fluted call notes in which one of the birds calls "phew" to be immediately followed by the second bird on a slightly different pitch. I have never been able to discover which goes first. The bird's natural song is quiet, hesitant and unremarkable, but bizarrely they can be taught to sing folk song tunes: "their ability to perfect a tune [is] unparalleled", an ability that made trained birds extremely popular as pets in the 18th and 19th centuries[7.2].

Kinglets

Kinglets are tiny, warbler-like birds in the family Regulidae. There are two species in the US and a total of seven species in the northern hemisphere. In the UK we have two of them – Goldcrests and Firecrests; they have one pub each.

The Goldcrest in Hull (East Yorkshire) is a modern pub with a lovely sign. Goldcrests are widespread and common and there is nothing to link the bird to this particular place. The Firecrest – with a pub of the same name in Wendover (Buckinghamshire) – is a close but much rarer relative. The pub is also in a more relevant location. Both species are tiny, attractive bundles of energy. They are smaller and lighter than a Wren (which is often incorrectly credited with being the smallest British bird). Firecrests are unquestionably the more beautiful. Goldcrests are olive-green overall and sport an orange-yellow (male) or golden (female) stripe down the centre of their crown (which can be raised as a crest). Firecrests have similar headgear but also have a bold white eyebrow and a lovely coppery patch on their shoulders. Firecrests used to be scarce migrants and winter visitors to this country; the first proven breeding was in 1962[2.25], but they are now quite widespread in south-east and eastern England and are spreading north. I suspected that a pub in Buckinghamshire called the *Firecrest*, on the northern edge of the Chiltern Hills, was not a coincidence and that these lovely little birds bred nearby. My correspondent David Gantzel has confirmed it, saying: "Firecrests breed nearby in Wendover Woods. First found breeding in 1971.... This in turn led to parties being taken around the woods [to see them] at that time. Subsequently the pub was renamed [to reflect this wonderful addition to the local avifauna]." The pub dates from 1827 according to its website and used to be called the *Halfway House*. It became the *Firecrest* in 1998. The pub should have featured in Chapter 3 but I decided to save such a special little bird for this one last twitch.

Firecrest, Wendover

[Mistle Thrush]

The heading here is deliberately in square brackets, because it is a convention widely used in regional bird reports to signify a sighting of a species that is likely, even very likely, but not proven or "nailed down". Mistle Thrushes are the bigger, bolder relatives of Song Thrushes. The sign of the *Bird in Bush* in the tiny village of Elsdon in Northumberland looks much more like a Mistle Thrush than a Song Thrush and is depicted singing from a branch surrounded by hop fruits. Like other unexpected pub birds this one may have been copied from a bird book without the artist distinguishing it from the Song Thrush. Mistle Thrushes are fine birds. I love their wild song, which is often given from a high and exposed perch in late winter and early spring, earning them the popular name of storm cock[1.15]. The pub itself dates from the 18th century (whether with this name is unclear) and has The First and Last Brewery on site[7.3].

Bird in Bush, Elsdon

Nuthatch

Nuthatches are the only British birds that regularly climb head first down tree trunks like an upside down Woodpecker. They are yet another extremely cute little bird – short tailed with a dagger-like beak, blue-grey upperparts, rusty-buff underparts and with a conspicuous black line from the beak to the eye and neck. *The Nuthatch* in Middlesbrough has a Nuthatch in flight on a small sign above the door, and may be more of a cocktail bar than a pub. I've been lenient because I love Nuthatches. I decided to go to Durham University to read zoology (rather than wait another year at school to take Oxford and Cambridge entrance exams) on the strength of seeing my first Nuthatches on the banks of the River Wear below Durham Cathedral on my way to be interviewed for a place in University College. My headmaster thought I was in Durham for "a practice interview" and he was not pleased (to put it mildly) when I told him otherwise. In 1962 Nuthatches didn't occur in Lancashire. I was enchanted by the birds and saw them as a good omen. I loved Durham and have always been very grateful to these little birds for my choice of university.

Osprey

The Osprey is another bird that has played an important role in my life, but more of that in a moment. It is at least odd that there is (or was) only one Osprey pub, the *Seahawk* in Old Trafford, Manchester; it closed in 2015. I may even be being too lenient. Sea Hawk (two words) is a vernacular name in the USA for an Osprey, but the Seattle Seahawks (one word) are an NFL football team[7.4]. If the pub was named after an American football team it would be even more remarkable that there are not any actual Ospreys as pub birds, given the prominence of other birds of prey, particularly Eagles and Falcons (Chapter 2).

Ospreys are cosmopolitan, fish-eating birds of prey, catching fish just below the surface of lakes, rivers and the sea in a spectacular feet-first dive. The bird's middle toes each have a ball of prominent spine-like scales behind the long, curved claws that enable them to grasp a slimy, wriggling fish with ease[7.5]. Like so many raptors, the birds were persecuted mercilessly in this country because they were seen by sports fishermen as competitors. And as they became rarer the egg collectors and trophy hunters moved in. They were exterminated as a breeding species in 1916. Natural recolonisation started in Scotland in 1954[3.5] but it didn't go well. The pioneering pairs suffered repeatedly from egg collectors (yes, the loonies were still at it) and at least one bird was shot. In 1958 the RSPB decided to guard the only breeding pair (at Loch Garton on Speyside), but the birds were again robbed under cover of darkness. The following year saw a breakthrough: under 24-hour guard the pair reared three chicks and the same year the RSPB took the bold decision to open a public viewing hide at a safe distance from the nest. In July 1960 I visited the site with my parents and saw my first Ospreys. Five years later I spent two weeks as a warden on the nightshift[7.6]. It was a life-transforming experience; it turned me from being just a birder to a birder who became passionate about the work of the RSPB.

Through natural spread and reintroduction programmes in England and Wales Ospreys are now firmly re-established as a breeding species in Britain. The bulk of the population nests in Scotland but there are several pairs in Cumbria, Northumberland and North Wales. There is also a major hotspot around Rutland Water (the site of the Bird Fair – Chapter 1), where my birding contacts tell me there are now at least ten breeding pairs.

There really should be some pubs called *The Osprey* to celebrate this success.

[Pintail]

Pintails are Ducks, and this is another one for square brackets. They males in particular are slim and elegant, have a beautiful brown-and-white head and neck, and long, pin-like central tail feathers. The females are a slim, long-necked version of a female Mallard, with a long, pointed tail that lacks the male's 'pins'. The inn sign for the *Ducks Inn* at Aberlady in East Lothian depicts the silhouette of a Duck that isn't a Mallard. It is way too slim and has a long neck and long tail. It looks like a Pintail to me, but with no plumage details to go on I can't prove it (or 'nail it' as a birder would say). So, it stays in square brackets on my list[7.7].

Redstart

The Redstart (sometimes *Inn*) in Barming in Kent isn't completely nailed down either. Common Redstarts are summer visitors to Britain related to Robins but with an orange-red tail that is the first thing you see as the

The Redstart, Barming (American Redstart)

bird flies away – hence the name. We now tend to think of Redstarts as birds of the wooded uplands of Wales, Northern England and parts of Scotland. They used to nest in Kent but no longer do so. The original *Redstart* on the site dated from the 1870s; at some time that building was demolished to build the current pub. I cannot find anything on any of the websites[7,8] to explain why the bird was chosen, but given the age of the pub assumed it referred to a native British bird. However, David Gantzel kindly photographed the sign for me in October 2021 and to my great surprise it depicts a male American Redstart. This alien isn't even in the same family of birds as 'our' Redstart but is one of the wonderfully colourful North American Wood Warblers. Like ours, the male flashes brilliant orange-red sides to its tail as it flies away (females flash yellow). I have watched them flycatching in the eastern US woodlands but they are very rare vagrants to Europe and I have never seen one here. I could have included this bird in Chapter 4, where two other pub birds changed their identity from a familiar UK species to a North American species, but for both of these the swap happened between 2010 and 2021. I have no idea when *The Redstart* took a US passport, but once again the most likely explanation for this unexpected discovery is that the signwriter used a North American bird book.

Sand Martin

We have already encountered the two common relatives of Sand Martins (Swallows and House Martins), both of which build mud nests in or on our houses and outbuildings. Sand Martins are also summer visitors to Britain (and often among the first summer migrants to arrive, in March) but unlike the other two nest in holes they dig in sandy banks, or in sand-filled holes in artificially constructed 'Sand Martin hotels' provided by birders, none of which provides any clues as to why there are pubs called the *Sand Martin* in Cardiff or the *Sandmartin* in Grays, Essex. Neither has a sign. Just a name.

Shelduck

Sheldducks are unusual because the males and females look largely identical. (The males of most Ducks we have encountered, such as

Mallards, Pintails, Ruddy Ducks and Wood Ducks, have showy breeding plumage whilst the females sport dull browns and greys; it is typically the males that appear on inn signs.) The usual explanation for the dowdier females is that as it is they that incubate the eggs and care for offspring, so their inconspicuous plumage could help avoid predators. But Shelducks nest in holes in the ground – commonly rabbit holes, where a big, white, strikingly patterned Duck with a bright lipstick-red bill, green head and orange breastband is invisible to most potential predators[3.39]. Whatever the explanation, that's what Shelducks do.

It is disappointing that so handsome a bird is so poorly represented as a pub bird. There is (or was) just one pub called *The Sheldrake,* a name dating from ca 1352[1.15]. It was in Clacton on Sea in Essex (Shelducks are predominantly coastal Ducks). I have to say that from its appearance the pub didn't do this lovely Duck any favours. The roof was blown off in a gale in 2018 and it is now closed.

Snipe and Jack Snipe

Snipe breed in Britain, with numbers augmented in winter by birds from the continent; their diminutive and in my view much more attractive relative (Jack Snipe) is a winter visitor. Both occur primarily in marshes and boggy areas. There are four pubs named after the larger Common Snipe: two plain *The Snipe* (in Audenshaw, Manchester and Sutton-in-Ashfield, Nottinghamshire), one the *Snipe Inn* (in Oldham, Lancashire) and one *The Drumming Snipe* in Mayford near Woking in Surrey. It is unclear why any of them are so named, but (as with several other pub birds) they are popularly shot for 'sport'. Once firearms were used for hunting the challenge was mainly target practice because when flushed at close range by a hunter or their dog they rise with a rapid jinking flight that is a challenge even for a crack shot. A single bird provides only a morsel of food. *Birds Britannica*[1.22] as always puts it nicely: "The plucked carcass weighs just a few ounces, but snipe were probably a common table item for nearly a thousand years…taken in nets or in a horsehair snare. In the late thirteenth century, the birds were priced at four a penny."

The Drumming Snipe captures the most interesting thing about them. No, they don't play the drums but the males in spring have a spectacular display flight in which they dive steeply from a height to produce a loud drumming (often described in bird books as a bleating or throbbing) sound from their two stiffened outer tail feathers, which vibrate as the air passes over them. How this remarkable sound is produced was long a mystery, and it fell to a man called P.H. Bahr to demonstrate to fellow British ornithologists, at the British Ornithologists Club in 1912, that it was a physical not vocal phenomenon. Bahr stuck two outer tail feathers from a Snipe into a cork at just the right angle and whirled the cork around his head to reproduce the sound. Apparently he did it in a restaurant called Pagani's[1.22]. Heaven knows what the waiters thought.

There is only one pub called *The Jack Snipe.* "Jack" as a descriptor has many meanings but in this case it probably reflects the bird's diminutive size compared with 'ordinary' Snipe. But why a pub in Cumbernauld (Glasgow) was christened *The Jack Snipe* I have no idea.

Sparrowhawk

There are three pubs named after Sparrowhawks, two plain *The Sparrowhawk* (in Formby, Liverpool and Upper Norwood, London) and one called *Ye Old Sparrowhawk* in Fence, Lancashire. I have not been able to find out anything particularly interesting about the first two, but at some point recently *Ye Old Sparrowhawk* seems to have restored the name it used to have in about 1890, having been *The Sparrowhawk* in between. The building is a lovely black-and-white, half-timbered structure dating (as a farmhouse) from the 17th century[7.9], but when it became a pub is unclear. It should perhaps be among the oldies in Chapter 3. The pub's current website has photographs of two different inn signs. The larger and more prominent (and hence more recent?) depicts a perched Sparrowhawk, but this was no longer evident when I visited in August 2021. The only existing sign is of a hovering more generic bird of prey which also features in a beautiful stained-glass dome inside the pub. Sparrowhawks do not hover. Kestrels do, so there is some poor birding going on here. The two birds have entire monographs devoted to them[7.10].

The Sparrowhawk, Fence

Just down the road this lovely old pub shares the village with the *White Swan*. Fence is on the southern edge of the Forest of Pendle below Pendle Hill. Extended visits to both on the same evening might just result in seeing the ghost of a Pendle witch[7.11]. Twelve people, accused of murdering ten fellow citizens by witchcraft lived around the hill in the 17th century (and may well have known the farm building that is now *Ye Old Sparrowhawk*). They were tried in 1612 in a series of witch trials and ten were hanged. It is all a bit spooky, and is commemorated (if that's the right word) on the sign of *The Pendle Inn* in the village of Barley a few miles away, whose sign depicts a witch on a flying broomstick. It has not escaped my notice that witches are flying, bipedal creatures, like birds, but neither W.B. Alexander nor Richard Fitter thought to include them on their lists[4.1], even though Fitter included angels as "honorary birds" (Chapter 1).

Starling

When I was a child growing up in Lancashire my young birding friends and I referred to Starlings as "Dustbin Warblers". I have no idea why, except it reflected a certain contempt for a very common, noisy, even boisterous urban bird. They are now much less common, which means that one of the most breathtaking sights in the birding world is rarer and less dramatic than formerly – but it can still be pretty good. A murmuration of Starlings involves thousands, sometimes tens of thousands, of the birds gathering to roost during the winter when they perform spectacular aerial displays of precision flying that from a distance look like billowing smoke, before dropping dramatically into the roost site in the gathering gloom. *The Starling Cloud* in Aberystwyth has a lovely sign showing a single Starling in the foreground and a murmuration in the background; there's a 3D wall sculpture of a murmuration on the pub itself. As far as I know, along with *The Drumming Snipe* (above), these two illustrations of bird behaviour are unique among pub birds. There is even a second reference to a murmuration. *The Starling* in Harrogate (North Yorkshire) has no sign but its website says: "On the face of it a drab little bird just like any other. But to see them flying together in a flock inches from each other's wings more intricately and aerobatically than the Red Arrows and you are blown away by the awesome capabilities of this little bird." I have nothing to add to that.

Unidentified Raptors

There are three unidentified (and probably unidentifiable) birds of prey among the tailend pub birds. *The Cross Keys* (another Lancashire pub,

The Cross Keys new sign, Skipton

Beer Hawk, Leeds

in Skipton, not far from Fence) used to have a pair of crossed keys as a sign, but when it was taken over by Skipton's Greyhawk Brewery some time around 2015 or 2016 a new sign was added with the brewery's brand image, which is of the fierce, beautifully painted, face of a large bird of prey. I have no idea what it is, except that it isn't a Grey Hawk from Central and South America, and there are no other Grey Hawks of any kind in *Raptors of the World*[7.12].

The *Beer Hawk* in Leeds (West Yorkshire) has a generic Eagle-like Hawk's head on its sign. *The Red Hawk* in St. Ives (Cornwall) may not even refer to a bird. But at least (contrary to W.B. Alexander's generalisation in Chapter 1) it's red.

Warbler

As I write, *The Warbler on the Wharf* in Milton Keynes (Buckinghamshire) is still being built[7.13]. It lies alongside the Grand Union Canal and its website has a photograph of a pair of Reed Warblers (taken by a member of the Milton Keynes Natural History Society). They are the ultimate little brown birds, so it will be interesting to see what is on the new pub's sign.

Woodpeckers

Unlike Nuthatches which can belt up and particularly down tree trunks just by gripping with their feet, Woodpeckers only climb upwards using three points of contact – two feet and a tail that acts as a prop. We have already encountered *The Woodpecker Inn* in Newbury (Chapter 2) which has a Green Woodpecker on its sign but a Great Spotted Woodpecker on its website and menus. There is a second Green Woodpecker on the sign for the *Woodpecker* in Wash Water (Berkshire). Without a sign to go on, it isn't possible to say what species is involved in two other pubs called the *The Woodpecker*, in Turves Green Birmingham and Derby), nor the *Woodpecker, Cookhouse and Pub* in Northwich (Cheshire) or the equally long-winded *Woodpecker, Bar and Kitchen* in Ilfracombe (Devon). None of them seems to have a picture of the bird on their menus or websites. But at least Woodpecker pub birds have companions all over the country.

There is one more *Woodpecker* (in Todmorden, Lancashire) that is impossible to identify because the bird appears to be Woody Woodpecker, a famous (and highly amusing) animated cartoon character and the official mascot of Universal Studios[7.14]. The bird is based on a North American Pileated Woodpecker, from which it gets its scarlet quiff and, in the cartoons, somewhat demented laughing call. But in some versions of the cartoon the bird's upperparts are black (correct) or blue (wrong) and it has white underparts (also wrong). It matters little. It's a fun image and another rare example of an amusing pub sign.

Odd Couples

As explained in Chapter 1, and encountered throughout this book, many pubs have double-barrelled names, often, but not always as a result of mergers between two separate establishments. Some of these can be "odd" in two ways. The pairings themselves can be strange, and second (and much less obvious) the distribution of double-barrelled names across species of pub birds is distinctly odd.

The 13 commonest pub birds in Chapter 2 have a curious distribution of double-barrelled names that lack an obvious explanation. Some common pub birds pair up with enthusiasm, others lead a lonely, solitary existence. They are treated here in descending order, from almost all of them paired up, to never paired with anything.

Partridges

The birds most often paired up are Partridges as *Dog and Partridge* pubs, for example the amusing sign for *The Dog and Partridge* in Tosside on the border between North Yorkshire and Lancashire. As explained earlier[2.59] there are at least 36 pubs with that name, compared with just two plain *The Partridge* (in Bromley, London and Stretton, Rutland) and a *Partridge Inn* (in Singleton, West Sussex). I must surely have missed other single Partridges but nothing like 33 to even the score. In addition to the pairing with Dogs there is a *Pear and Partridge* (obviously)[7.15] in Perton near Wolverhampton (West Midlands), a *Plum and Partridge* (much less obviously)[7.16] in Husthwaite near York, and a *Poacher and Partridge* in Tudley, Kent. Partridges clearly don't like going it alone.

The Dog and Partridge, Tosside

Geese and Hens

Half (nine) of the pubs named after Geese (unspecified or Greylags and their domestic descendants) have the bird paired up with either a Fox (7) or a Cuckoo (2). The two Welsh pubs called the *Goose and Cuckoo* are discussed in Chapter 2. *Fox and Goose* pubs are to be found in Ealing (London), Hebden Bridge (Yorkshire), Greywell (Hampshire – a 16th-century pub touched on in Chapter 3), Illston on the Hill (Leicestershire), Lancaster (Lancashire), Parracombe (Devon) and Weavering, Kent. Foxes of course kill Geese, but they also kill Hens (many more than Geese) and despite their being many more 'Hen' pubs (40) than 'Goose' pubs (18) only one Hen is paired with a Fox and then only pictorially on its sign, not its name (*The Fur and Feathers* in Herriard, Hampshire) where the sign is a fox surrounded by white Cockerels – Chapter 6).

Magpies and Mallards

In my database Magpies (four out of 11 pubs) and Mallards and their domestic descendants (eight of 23 pubs) share about one-third of their pub with another animal or bird. But here the database is misleading. For Ducks (as with Partridges) these are nearly all Dogs[7.17] except for one *Fox and Duck* in Petersham, Surrey, which has a sign showing a Fox eyeing up an (escaping?) male Mallard in flight. However, at least five more *Fox and Duck* pubs show up in a Google search[7.17] but only one additional *Dog and Duck*, in Mansfield (Nottinghamshire). So, Mallards actually pair up with foxes and dogs roughly equally, reflecting both themes for pub names – hunting for 'sport' and a grudging recognition of animals with which we compete for food or 'sport' (and so hunt as vermin).

Harte and Magpies, Coleshill

Harte and Magpies, Coleshill

Magpies in contrast are more catholic in their choice of partners, namely two Cockerels, a Parrot and a Deer (Chapter 2). All four could be the result of two pubs merging, but none as far as I know with any certainty. The most unusual is the *Harte and Magpies* (note the plural) in Coleshill,

Buckinghamshire, which is almost certainly not the result a of a merger between two hostelries. It started life as simply *The Magpies* in 1816, and like other older pubs (Chapter 3) it gave its name to Magpie Lane on which it stands[7.18]. The original name was changed to *The Mulberry Bush* at some point, before it was re-christened again as *The Harte and Magpies* in 2009, but I am unable to find out why. Almost (but not quite) uniquely it has two different signs, both of which look heraldic. The apparently more recent sign shows a white Hart (the correct modern spelling for a stag) carrying the flag of St George and flanked by two flying, black-and-white, vaguely Magpie-like birds on either side of the Deer, the rump of which hides a small coat of arms. The older-looking sign has two white stags either side of a coat of arms, surmounted by a helmet and above that a golden lion. The Magpies provide a supporting cast above. The Coleshill website describes the pub as being "in the Rental manor of Amersham", which suggests manorial arms, but I've found nothing to clarify this.

Cockerels, Hens and Pheasants

About one-quarter of Cockerels and Hens (ten in 40) and a sixth of Pheasants (five in 29) are twinned with something, and in both cases no longer with just another animal or bird. Cockerels are joined by two Magpies and a Fox (see above) and by more unusual creatures including a Greyhound (at the *Cock and Greyhound* in Whitchurch, Shropshire), a Dragon (*The Cock and Dragon* in Barnet, London, apparently now renamed the *Cock Inn*) and even (uniquely among pubs as far as I know) a Mole (*The Mole and Chicken* in Easington, Buckinghamshire). For the first time in this section, they are also joined by inanimate objects: bottles (as in three pubs called *Cock and Bottle* in Skipton, Yorkshire, and York itself – see Chapters 1 and 2) plus one in Wavertree in Liverpool, reputed to have the smallest house in England, squeezed into a passage down the side of the pub in the mid-19th century[7.19]. There is a *Cock and Crown* in Crofton, Wakefield and a *Cock and Woolpack* in Cornhill, London.

The Mole and Chicken, Easington

The Cock and Woolpack (which has no sign, just a name) is a delightful small pub on Finch

Cock and Woolpack, Cornhill

The Moor and Pheasant, Dalton

Lane (which is a good start) in the heart of the City. It used to be called simply *The Woolpack* and was renamed "in the last couple of decades"[7.20]. It has a lovely link with another *Woolpack* pub, which Wikipedia tells us we must not confuse with "Woolsack", the seat of the speaker of the House of Lords. *The Woolpack* is also a fictional pub in the long-running TV soap opera Emmerdale[7.21]. When the series first started, the location for the fictional pub was the *Falcon* in Arncliffe in the Yorkshire Dales (Chapter 2).

Not unexpectedly Pheasants share their name with Foxes (for example there are pubs called the *Fox and Pheasant* in Hemingborough near Selby, Yorkshire, and in Chelsea, London). But compared with Partridges there are very few pubs called *The Dog and Pheasant.* (In an auxiliary Google search I can find just six[7.22], even though there are many more pubs named after Pheasants than there are after Partridges.) The *Lion and Pheasant* in Shrewsbury is very old and is discussed in Chapters 2 and 3. *The Moor and Pheasant* in Dalton, North Yorkshire has a fine sign with a cock Pheasant standing on a wall with a wide vista of moorland behind. I know of no other pub twinned with a habitat, unless of course "Moor" was originally a reference to a Muslim inhabitant of North Africa of mixed Arab and Berber descent and no longer deemed acceptable for the name of a pub.

Mute Swan

Despite Mute Swans being the most numerous pub birds, the proportion of Swans sharing the name of a pub with something else is very small – just 8%. We have already encountered most of them but one that we have not yet met has a very strange name – the *Swan and Edgar* in Marylebone (London). The sign depicts (or rather depicted, the pub closed in 2013) the black-and-white heads and shoulders of a Mute Swan and a dog, both wearing a shirt, tie and waistcoat, and below it is a row of books in a specially built outside bookcase. I discovered the pub in 2011 and was completely baffled by the name and the sign. It turns out[7.23] that it was originally called *The Feathers* but was renamed after Swan & Edgar, a former department store on Piccadilly Circus, about two miles away, itself closed in 1982. Presumably (though none of the websites explicitly says so) the department store was named after the proprietors (Mr Swan and Mr Edgar) though why poor Mr Edgar (if it is indeed him) should be depicted as a dog on the inn sign is not clear. It was a pub from 1899 until its closure in 2013 and was known for its unusual interior, having varnished books as wall cover – hence the row of books below the sign. As far as I know this is the only humorous entry for Mute Swans – being regal birds "We are not amused" comes to mind.

Swan and Edgar, Marylebone, London

The *White Swan and Cuckoo* in Shadwell (London) again is no more, but it has been resurrected as *The Dockers Inn*[7.24]. The original sign appears not to have survived re-branding in an act I can only describe as vandalism. It had a lovely plaster-moulded Mute Swan above the name, and a similarly constructed Cuckoo below. As to the origin of the name, my best guess is that it used to be two pubs that merged. The same is probably true of the *Bull and Swan* in Stamford (Lincolnshire) but not of the *Swan and Rushes* in Leicester, which depicts a bit of natural history, except that the plants look more like Flag Irises to me, not Rushes.

White Swan and Cuckoo, Wapping Lane, London

Finally, there is nothing like a good mystery. The sign for *The Swan and Mitre* in Bromley clearly has heraldic origins (Chapter 2). The current sign is an ecclesiastic coat of arms depicting a shield topped by the bishop's mitre. The shield has a Swan on it, a Bohun Swan to be precise[2,8], except that it's black. Just like their wild relatives, Bohun Swans are supposed to be white (Chapter 2). Ecclesiastic heraldry is a specialised branch of a very specialised subject that I do not pretend to understand. But a mitre signifies that the bearer of the coat of arms was an Anglican bishop[7.25]. The pub is an old coaching inn although accounts as to how old vary, from as early as ca 1670 to "early 19th

The Swan and Mitre, Bromley

century"[7.26]. Websites show that the Swans on earlier signs were Mute Swans with one from 1992 showing a bishop, in purple robes and apparently on a stage, being attacked by a Mute Swan and losing his mitre in the process. The pub reopened in 2015 after refurbishment, which I guess is approximately when the current sign was installed. But I cannot find out why the pub is called *The Swan and Mitre*, who the bishop was or why the Swan is now black. None of the references to, or pictures of, Bohun Swans that I can find[2.8] show one that is black. And notice that the bird on the shield does not have white primary feathers, which it should have if it was a real Black Swan. Perhaps this is indeed a reference to Chris Perrins' suggestion[5.6] that Black Swans pre-dating their discovery by Europeans may get their name from Karelian and Finnish oral folklore in *The Kalevala*. Someone much better versed in heraldry than I must understand this symbolism.

Eagles

With the noted exception of the somewhat raunchy and highly dubious story of the *Eagle and Child* (Chapter 2) Eagles (both specific and unspecific) lead solitary lives except for the *Eagle and Sun* in Droitwich (Chapters 2 and 5). That single pub is roughly 3% of the non-child rearing Eagles. No Eagles share their pub with any other bird.

Single pub birds

Five of the commonest pub birds go it alone (or four if you accept that the Swan on the current sign of *The Swan and Mitre* is a Black Swan). In numerical order they are Black Swan (28), Falcons (specific and non-specific, 26), Ravens (17), Peacocks (12), and Pigeons and Doves (12) – a total of 95 pub birds. Many of the other rarer species join them. For example, nothing else is paired with Kingfishers (11, or 12 if we include *The Halcyon* in Peterborough), or Wrens (8). The commonest state by far for a pub bird is to go it alone. From all the other species and kinds of pub birds the only ones paired with anything are in Table 3.

Table 3

Summary of all the rarer (outside the 13 'baker's dozen') pub birds that share their names with another bird, animal, person or object. The birds are arranged in the (recently superseded) conventional taxonomic order used for my main database[7.27]. We have previously encountered all but one of them.

Species or kinds of birds	Number of pubs	Number paired	Names of paired pubs
Mythical	8	1	*Crown and Liver,* Hawarden
Pelican	14	2	*Fox and Pelican,* Grayshot *Ship and Pelican,* Heavitree
Grey Heron	7	1	*Pike and Heron,* Hornsea, now renamed *New Inn*
White Stork	7	1	*Fox and Stork,* Bolton, now renamed *Stork Tavern*
Vulture	2	2	*George and Vulture* (2) Castle Court and Pitfield Street, London
Puffin	2	1	*Pig and Puffin,* Tenby, now closed
Parrot	8	5	*Dog and Parrot* (2) Newcastle upon Tyne and Nottingham *Frog and Parrot,* Sheffield *Hook and Parrot,* Bridlington *Magpie and Parrot,* Shinfield
Cuckoo	9	3	*Goose and Cuckoo* (2) Llangadog and Upper Llandover *White Swan and Cuckoo,* Shadwell, London
Owl	15	4	*Owl and Hitchhiker,* Holloway, London *Owl and Pussycat* (3) Leicester, and Northfields and Shoreditch, London
Lark	5	1	*Linnet and Lark,* Hull
Woodlark	1	1	*Lamb and Lark,* Limington
Blackbird	2[1]	1	*Bush, Blackbird and Thrush,* East Peckham
Song Thrush	5	1	*Bush, Blackbird and Thrush,* East Peckham
Carrion Crow	12	1	*Crow and Gate,* Crowborough.
Canary	2	2	*Canary and Linnet,* Little Fransham *Cat and Canary,* Canary Warf, London
Linnet	3	3	*Canary and Linnet,* Little Fransham *Linnet and Lark,* Hull *Railway and Linnet,* Middleton, Manchester[2]

The data in the table have been augmented by additional web searches.

1. Some *Blackbird* pubs may not be Blackbirds (see Chapter 4) and have not been included here.
2. We have not previously encountered this pub.

The only pub in Table 3 we have not previously encountered is the *Railway and Linnet* in Middleton, Manchester. Linnets are small Finches and are also paired with Canaries and Larks. The females are dull versions of the subtly beautiful males, which have russet-brown backs, grey heads with a red forehead, and a breast suffused with rose-pink. When both sexes fly, they flash silver steaks on the edges of their primaries. Probably more than any other 'small brown bird' novice birders are astonished when they see a male Linnet clearly for the first time, and often mis-identify them (a common mistake is Red-backed Shrike – look at their picture in a bird book and you'll see why). The *Railway and Linnet* is close to the long-closed Middleton Junction railway station[7.28] but exactly why the pub is so called is unclear from anything I can find on the web. Did two pubs merge, and if not, why was a railway paired with a Linnet?

Paired pub birds are the exception

The simple conclusion from all this is that pub birds paired with anything are the exception, not the rule. The data in Table 3 are compiled from a sample of 220 pubs and involve 97 species, kinds of birds and paraphernalia; only 16 species and kinds of birds (16.5%) in my entire database are paired with anything – just 27 pubs (12.3%), all of which makes all those pubs called *The Dog and Partridge* statistically truly exceptional; we might even call it a "Black Swan event"[2.22]. Why is another matter. Does it reflect the crucial importance of Grey Partridges as birds of quarry within historical memory[2.57 & 2.58]? I really have no idea.

One thing does strike me about paired pub birds is that the pubs so named tend to stand out from the crowd (Chapter 2). Perhaps not as much as the mythical ad-man's joke about a pub called *The Kangaroo and Sewing Machine*, but maybe they are distinctive enough to give the pub an edge over its competitors.

In the world of 'real' birds many species naturally occur together in mixed feeding flocks or breeding colonies, but these associations bear little or no resemblance to those encountered in pub birds. The exciting, mixed colonies of breeding seabirds (Chapter 3) on our coasts don't really count in this context, because the two Yorkshire pubs called *The Seabirds* are just that, not *The Gannet and Guillemot* or any other pairing. In winter, mixed flocks of Tits (particularly Blue, Great, Coal and Long-tailed) are one of the pleasures of a birding woodland walk. The birds benefit from there being more eyes to see predators whilst competition for food is reduced because each species has a specialised way of feeding[7.29]. But despite Blue Tits being one of the few birds with a pet name (Tom Tit)[1.15 & 5.11] there are no pubs named after a single species of Tit, never mind two. You can probably work out why.

In the real world, some birds form feeding associations with animals other than birds. Cattle Egrets forage on the insects disturbed by Cows and other grazing animals (both wild and domestic). The close, attractive association between Robins and human gardeners probably has its origin in the Robin's habit of following Wild Boars and other animals rooting around on and under the forest floor and disturbing worms and other creepy-crawlies[5.12]. *The Gardener and Robin* might just catch on; *The Pig and Robin* probably wouldn't (although the enigmatic *Pig and Puffin* clearly did). I would love there to be a pub called *The Meercat and Hornbill*, but there is no chance. They associate in the Kalahari Desert in South Africa where I watched with amusement a pair of Southern Yellow-billed Hornbills following a family of Meercats that was digging in the sand for Termites, which the Hornbills skilfully pinched from under the Meerkats' noses. They were tolerated by the Meercats because, perched on thorn bush, the Hornbills were much better placed to spot an approaching Eagle.

Unlike these co-operative feeding associations in nature, the associations of pub birds are often antagonistic, predator-prey interactions, such as Dogs and Foxes or the *Pike and Heron*, although the *Owl and the Pussycat* seem to rub along together very well. For all the others there are a variety of possible explanations for the pairings, from pub mergers to heraldry (Chapter 2), though often I do not know where the name comes from.

A Closing Miscellany

There is no great logic to this final group of tailenders. They are simply pub birds that we have encountered earlier because I thought they deserved one last say.

Ducks

There are two new Ducks (Mallards) in this section. Although I had passed the *Duck and Drake* in Leeds several times I only recently noticed the sign. It is unusual: I think it is the only pub bird in which the two sexes are explicitly recognised in the name, with the cartoon sign showing one Duck apparently flying into the backside of another (male and female unidentified). It joins several other 'Duck pubs' with amusing signs (Chapter 2).

Duck & Drake, Leeds

I can find out essentially nothing about the *Drookit Duck* in Falkirk (Stirlingshire) but I love the name. *The Scotsman* website[7.30] says that 'drookit' is one of 15 words that can be used to describe Scottish weather. It means "absolutely drenched". I once spent a week on Skye with the intention of birding with a friend. It rained very hard for several days and we gave up. We were drookit. At the post office in Kyleakin the postmistress greeted us with the memorable "Morning, boys. Bonny day. Wee bit damp." Apparently, in that part of the world, it's a "bonny day" if you can stand up against the wind and see across the street.

Crafty Crow, Nottingham

Crows

Carrion Crows are not something that birders actively seek out. They are common and ubiquitous and simply add one more species to a day or year list. But they are also highly intelligent and adaptable, as well as being hated by gamekeepers. Three Crow pubs have not made it into the book yet. One is a play on words. The sign for the *Scared Crow* in West Malling (Kent) is a Crow startled by a scarecrow[7.31]. The *Crafty Crow* in Nottingham has a stylised Crow in flight as a sign. The pub is owned by the Magpie Brewery and sells Magpie beers[7.32] and I cannot help wondering if "crafty" is also a play on words for craft beers.

The *Crow Pie* in Rugby (Warwickshire) is a bit more complicated. From the pub's website it looks as though it was originally called just *The Crow* with a sign depicting a slightly stylised Crow in flight[7.33]. It is an intriguing name to choose for a pub. "To eat crow pie" is an American expression for admitting you were wrong, apparently derived from a 15th-century ballad about a woman who was raped and sought compensation from her attacker[7.34], and if I have understood correctly the "pie" may actually be a reference to Magpie, historically one of the bird's names borrowed from French[1.15]. So, I do not think this is the route by which the *Crow Pie* got its new name. Rather it seems much more likely to be a reference to pies as food[7.35]. Apparently the renowned children's author Beatrix Potter wrote to her publisher about the forthcoming Crow-shooting season and was looking forward to Crow pies. The same website[7.35] cited T.T. Wilkinson's *Lancashire Folklore* of 1867, in which is said that children throughout Lancashire and Yorkshire recited:

"Crow, crow, get out of my site.
Or else I'll eat thy liver and lights." ("lights" are lungs.)

I was born in Lancashire and have lived most of my adult life in Yorkshire, and I have never heard anybody recite that. But at least somebody still makes Crow pie (although I doubt the eponymous pub does so). When Alex Robinson was content editor of *Outdoor Life* he hunted American Crows in Southern Minnesota[7.36] and found that their breasts made a pie that was "nothing short of scrumptious". He also recalls the nursey rhyme "Four and twenty blackbirds baked in a pie", and suggests that they were not Blackbirds but Crows. The potential confusion is exactly the same as deciding whether a pub called the *Three Blackbirds* really refers to a Blackbird (Chapter 4) or one of several other possible black birds, including Crows. However, recall that the nursery rhyme goes on: "When the pie was opened the birds began to sing." Crows caw. Blackbirds sing. Draw your own conclusions.

Nightingale

Blackbirds can sing. Nightingales sing magnificently. One of the first very lovely pub birds I encountered away from the North of England was *The Nightingale* in Egdon, near Spetchley, just outside Worcester. If anything, the current sign on the pub's website is even better than the one I photographed in 2011. The central Severn Valley is (or was) on the north-western edge of the bird's breeding range in England[2.25]. On that day in 2011 I had unwittingly played *Ticks and Tipples* (Chapter 3) because I had heard Nightingales singing from a coppice a few miles down the road from the pub. Sadly, Nightingales are in deep trouble. The core of their world range is in the Mediterranean and warmer parts of south-west Europe, and with climate change they ought to be increasing in Britain. But they are not. Their range is contracting south and east towards Kent, Sussex and Essex. The

The Nightingale, Egdon

2007–2011 *Bird Atlas*[2.25] reported a 90% decline in numbers in the last 40 years and the decline is ongoing. I do not know if I could play *Ticks and Tipples* for this species any more from Spetchley, without a great deal more travelling to find the real bird.

Yellow Wagtail

In Chapter 1 I said that the aviary of 117 species of pub birds doesn't quite range from A to Z, but that the list did run from B to Y, from *The Blackbird* on Earls Court Road in London to a *Yellow Wagtail* in Yeovil (Somerset). We have just re-ticked Blackbirds, so it seems entirely appropriate to finish this last twitch with a Yellow Wagtail. The pub was built in the late 1960s or early 1970s[7.37] and the name was obviously chosen for a reason. When the pub was built Yellow Wagtails almost certainly bred around Yeovil[3.6] and may still do so (just)[2.25]. Their preferred breeding habitats are damp meadows and marshy fields in river valleys, many of which have been lost since the Second World War to agriculture, so like so many farmland birds they are declining[2.57]. However, as probably the most beautiful of our Wagtails they were a good choice for an inn sign. However, the one on the website isn't a 'normal' Yellow Wagtail. The taxonomy of Yellow Wagtails is one of the most complex of all European birds. There are marked geographical differences in their plumage (particularly the males), forming a difficult set of identifiable subspecies and their hybrids and integrades[7.27 & 7.38]. The normal subspecies in the UK is *Motacilla flava flavissima*, which suggests that it is the yellowest of the group. The bird on the sign is not this subspecies. It has a blue-grey crown and ear coverts, a bold white 'eyebrow', a whitish throat and a green back ('ours' has a buttercup-yellow eye stripe and a darker but still yellowish head and back, and a yellow throat). Identification of Yellow Wagtails is tricky and this one looks most like *Motacilla flava bema*, known as Syke's Wagtail. This subspecies breeds from the Volga steppes eastward and birds that at least look like them occur here as vagrants. As sure as heck they don't occur around Yeovil. I can only assume that again the signwriter innocently copied the image from a book, perhaps because it was more colourful than the local birds.

That was quite a twitch to end on.

CHAPTER 8: CLOSING TIME

It's been quite a journey. When I started wondering about Black Swans over a decade ago I had no idea it would lead me to explore things I knew nothing about: how pubs got their names and their links to geography, history, heraldry, art, music and literature. Could I have done this in any other country? Probably no. Pubs are part of our culture and as pictures on boards and walls and even the occasional sculpture, pub birds are a remarkable, eclectic, intriguing flock.

Many of the most abundant pub birds have historical links to mythology, superstition, religion and art and here I am going to delve into this history before looking at the uncontemporary characteristics of pub birds in general.

Pub Birds in the Ancient World

Chapter 2 discussed the Greylag Geese depicted in frescoes in Egypt, where the birds were first domesticated[2.39], dating from about 2000BC, and how these birds were the ancestors of the familiar, usually white 'farmyard geese' with pink bills not the orange-billed wild Greylags from Europe. The funerary (and other) art of ancient Egypt is full of birds, but to keep this section within bounds I am going to skip forward to Jeremy Mynott's scholarly work focussing on ancient Greece[8.1].

Mynott lists 27 species or kinds of birds that appear "among the principal subjects of Aesop's Fables"[8.2]. They are remarkably similar to, but not exactly the same as, the commonest pub birds. Crow (22) tops his list but is closely followed by Eagle (20), Cock/Hen (19) and Pigeon/Dove (11). Six of the remaining baker's dozen in Chapter 2 are there: Goose (4), Hawk, which I take to be Falcon (5), Swan (3), Partridge (5), Peacock (5) and Raven (2). Four are missing (Black Swan for obvious reasons, Duck, Magpie and Pheasant). All the other species in Mynott's list from Aesop appear as pub birds except Buzzard.

The birds listed by Mynott from the plays of Aristophanes is even longer – 41 in total[8.3]. With the exception of Black Swans, Magpies and Pheasants all the remaining baker's dozen species are there. So too are 23 other pub birds[8.3]. Just eight are not pub birds, including two that do not occur in Britain – (Black?) Francolin and a Gallinule (probably Purple Swamphen), Buzzard (again), one for which I have expressed surprise that there is no pub named after them (Jay), and another that I have dismissed as unlikely (Little Grebe).

I find these links with the past astonishing. In simple terms the birds that appear on pub signs have deep historical roots. There is something about them that has appealed to human nature over a time span of 2,000 or more years. In particular they are symbolic of power and aggression, the thrill of the chase, beauty, food and song, as well as being symbols of the seasons (Swallows) and darker emotions (Owls and Ravens).

It's a Male-Dominated World

Even the most superficial look at a sample of inn signs reveals a male-dominated world. Female birds rarely appear on their own; in earlier chapters I identified just four, and (surely by coincidence) all of them are 'Hens' of some sort: the *Peahen* (St Albans); *The Heathcock* (Cardiff) which has, despite its name, what appears to be a female Black Grouse (Greyhen) on its sign; *The Bonny Moorhen* (Stanhope), the sign of which currently has a Moorhen of indeterminate sex but which used to depict another Greyhen; and four pubs with Hens on the sign, which are dwarfed by 36 pubs with Cockerels.

Female birds do little better when sharing the sign with a male, as they do at six pubs: the *Eagles Nest* in Kidderminster; *The Swans Nest* in Exminster; the *Moorcock* (Middleton-in-Teesdale), which has a male Black Grouse (Blackcock) and a Greyhen; the *Riverside* (near Bath), which has a pair of Wood Ducks; *The Marsh Harrier* (Oxford); and *The Duck and Drake* in Leeds. In all except the last of these the males are in front of the female.

Funny Foreigners

I make the case in Chapter 4 that, mostly, publicans have been reluctant to grace their inn signs with foreigners, unless they are edible (Hens but not Turkeys) or have bling (Peacocks). In a nutshell, pub birds are depressingly jingoistic.

Body Size

Inevitably the scientist in me wants the last word. This is not by any means the definitive work on pub birds. There must be much more to discover about the birds on pub signs, the pubs themselves and the human stories surrounding them. There may even be new species of pub birds to discover; I would be amazed if there were not. But it's a start. However, what we can do is make some broad generalisations about the birds themselves using the data we already have, which will probably be robust to the discovery of any additional species.

When I was a working as a scientist one of my favourite occupations was finding and trying to understand patterns in nature. Not necessarily hard-and-fast rules, but discovering what was typical, or generally the case, and why there were exceptions; it is one of the things that scientists do. A book by my late colleague Paul Colinvaux, *Why Big Fierce Animals are Rare*, is a good example[8.4]. Nature is full of similar intriguing patterns and questions, from "Why are there no Penguins in the northern hemisphere?" to "Why do islands have impoverished flora and fauna compared with mainland areas of the same size?" I am not going to attempt answers here, although I did ask in Chapter 4 why there were no pubs named after Penguins. In the search for patterns, pub birds are not a random sample of the world's avifauna. If they were, foreign species would be overwhelmingly represented, and they are absolutely not (Chapter 4). But nor are pub birds a random sample of British species. They are a highly selective bunch.

The most obvious pattern is that the species of birds found on pub signs are bigger than average. Specifically, compared with the body sizes of the species of birds that breed regularly in Britain, larger species are over-represented on pub signs and smaller species are under-represented (Figure 1). For many non-scientists this probably needs unpicking[8.5].

If you are not interested in the details just note that in Figure 1 body size (weight) increases from left to right. The black histograms show the number of breeding species in different weight classes, from tiny Goldcrests on the left to huge Mute Swans on the right. The red bars are the number of species of pub birds in each weight class, again from

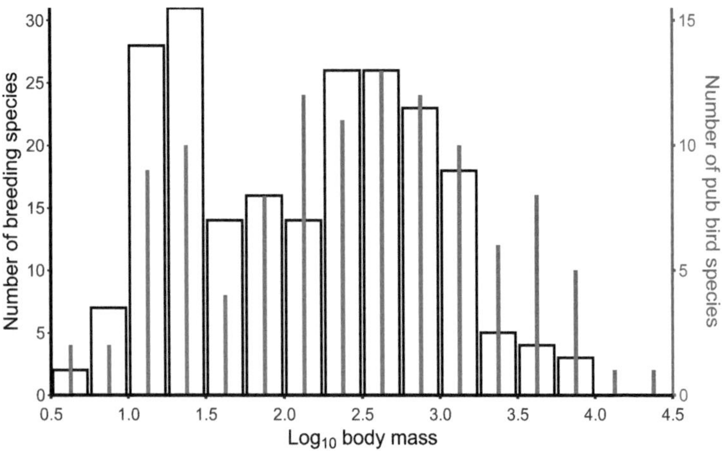

Fig. 1. Pub birds (red bars and right-hand axis) tend to be larger on average than British breeding bird species (black histograms and left-hand axis). See text for details

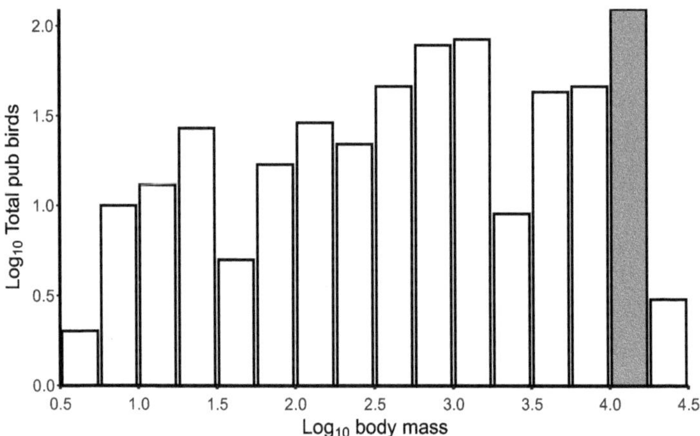

Fig. 2. Total number of pubs named after birds in 16 weight-classes, from the smallest birds on the left to heaviest on the right. The total number of pubs in each weight class on average increases as birds get heavier. The grey histogram is made up of just one species – Mute Swan

tiny species on the left to large species on the right, the heaviest being an Ostrich, which of course is not a British breeding bird. Each species is counted only once, irrespective of how many pubs are named after it. The scales on the vertical axes *are NOT the same*; the maximum number of breeding species (left-hand axis) is just over 30 and the maximum number of pub-bird species (right-hand axis) is 15. What matters are the proportions. Small pub-bird species are proportionately rarer than their real counterparts, and larger pub-bird species are proportionately commoner than their real equivalents. This pattern was more obvious in the paper in *British Birds*[1.7] because that was based on a (roughly) random sample of pubs[1.8]. For this book I concentrated on finding as many species of pub birds as possible, and this inflates the numbers of the smaller species. But the pattern is still apparent.

The dominance of larger birds is clearer if we look at the *total* number of pubs named after birds in each weight class (Figure 2). All I have done here is add up the number of pubs for all the species in each weight class (using the same weight classes as Figure 1). The vertical axis differs from Figure 1 in being a logarithmic scale[8.6]. Without doing any fancy statistics the general trend is for the total number of pubs named after birds to increase as the birds get larger. Mute Swans are the only species in the shaded weight class. The two other species of Swans (Black and Whistling) and Great Bustards are in the weight class immediately before Mute Swans. An increase in abundance as organisms get larger is unusual from an ecological point of view. In general, as Paul Colinvaux explained, in the real world, big fierce animals are rare. Or more generally, larger-bodied species in any group of animals tend to be rarer (they occur in lower densities) than smaller-bodied relatives. The numbers of small birds are generally higher than the numbers of large birds. Kestrels occur at higher densities than Golden Eagles, and Robins at higher densities than Crows. It isn't always so[8.7], but the exceptions are unusual. The general rule makes sense. Larger-bodied species need more food, more space and more resources of all kinds than smaller species; the bigger the individual, the larger area it needs to support it. Not, apparently, pub birds, though, but why should they? It's very simple: pub birds don't need feeding.

What is it about larger species that make them attractive as pub birds? In many human endeavours size matters. Big is butch. So it is hardly surprising that none of the 13 species in the baker's dozen of most frequent pub birds are small[8.8]. They also share other desirable characteristics – usually some combination of royal, fierce, edible and hunted. The argument doesn't just apply to pub birds. Emilio Berti and colleagues[8.9] assembled a data set for 13,680 species of animals (including birds, mammals, amphibians and reptiles) and used a standardised measure of charisma to show a positive correlation between charisma and body size. Berti is quoted as saying: "The bigger you get the more sublime reactions humans have [towards the animal in question]." As with pub birds, there are exceptions – small can be cute, for example (Wrens for instance), but those birds are the exceptions that prove the rule.

One consequence of this human tendency appears to explain why whole swathes of the British avifauna never (or hardly ever) make it as a pub bird. Some missing birds are big and heavy and their absence may have more to do with lack of familiarity than anything else. They include Divers, Shearwaters, Gannets and Skuas among seabirds (W.D. Alexander's favourite group of birds). But a predilection for large over small almost certainly explains why many passerines (perching birds) are missing from the aviary. Passerines are currently the most diverse avian order, with over 6,000 species in 128 families that make up almost 60% of all living birds[8.10]. Somewhere between a third and a half of all the pages in the numerous British bird books on my shelves are devoted to passerines. But most passerines are small. Many of our most familiar garden and countryside birds are passerines but these small species have only one or a small handful of pubs named after them (Finches, Robins, Sparrows, Starlings, Swallows, Thrushes and Wagtails for example). Others have none (Buntings and Pipits – both ultimate 'little brown jobs' much loved by expert birders, but not publicans). There are exceptions, as we have seen. Nightingales and particularly Wrens are popular pub birds. Corvids (Crows and their relatives) are big passerines and unlike their smaller relatives, Carrion Crows, Magpies and Ravens, all have numerous pubs named after them, although the equally large black Rook and smaller grey-capped Jackdaw have just two each. 'Our' wonderfully colourful Jay has none. Choughs, with their striking red legs and bills, and heraldic links, only manage five.

Warblers are particularly telling. There are 13 regular breeding species in Britain and despite many being fine songsters they are all small and mostly boringly coloured in brown, buff, green, olive or grey. Unsurprisingly they are almost entirely ignored as pub birds, with the Dartford Warbler (*The Furze Wren*) and the generic *Warbler on the Wharf* in Milton Keynes their sole representatives. Yet birders love real Warblers because they can be hard to identify, and many of our breeding species look similar (or even almost identical) to other much rarer relatives, so there is the thrill of the chase when you encounter

The Rook and Gaskill, York

one on the east coast in autumn; it might just be a rarity. In my case when I find 'something interesting' it usually isn't. Blackcaps are one of our commonest Warblers (a pair nest in the nettles and brambles in my orchard in most years). The males (grey with a black cap) are fine songsters but unlike Nightingales have no pubs named after them. Steve Shaw[1.5] has a *Blackcap* in Camden in London on his list, but he marks it with an asterisk to show that although it has a bird's name "it refers to something else". Because judges used to don a black cap when sentencing somebody to death I thought it might be another example of gallows humour (*The Rook and Gaskill* in York for example[1.11]) but no. The pub dates from at least 1751 and was originally called *The Mother Black Cap*. It still exists and is reopening after being shut for five years[8.11]. It isn't named after the bird but after a witch in a local legend. And I nearly forgot to mention it. It's a famous gay bar.

Dunnocks (aka Hedge Sparrows or more grandly Hedge Accentors) have incredibly complicated mating behaviour. You can find a brief account in *Birds Britannica*[1.22] and there is a whole book devoted to their behaviour and social evolution by my colleague Nick Davies[8.12]. Nick says their name has its origins in Old English, with "dun" meaning brown and "ock" signifying little – the ultimate little brown bird. In the Acknowledgements to the book, Nick writes: "I did not realise how much my life has been dominated by a little brown bird until I saw how Hannah [one of his daughters] had filled in a school form, entering father's occupation as 'dunnocks'. " Yet they are anything but dull. They mate exceptionally frequently compared with other small birds (once or twice an hour over a ten-day period) and whilst there are simple pairs (monogamy) there are also some bizarrely complicated marital set-ups, or as Nick formally describes them "mating systems". They are polygyny (one male and two females), polyandry (two males and one female) and polygynandry (two males *usually* with two females). Nick quotes the Reverend F.O. Morris, writing in 1856: "Unobtrusive, quiet, retiring, without being shy, humble and homely in its deportment and habits, sober and unpretending in its dress…the dunnock exhibits a pattern which many of a higher grade might imitate, with advantage to themselves and benefits to others through improved example." How wrong can you be? And yet despite a secret life to rival the wild excesses of a rock star, a bird is most likely to feature in the name of a pub if it is large, royal, edible, exciting to hunt or with other sporting connotations, fierce and impressive. If you are a Dunnock, forget it.

Perhaps we should all have one for the road (providing you are not driving).

Cheers and goodnight.

NOTES

Chapter 1

1. The list only includes pubs in England, Wales and Scotland. I have only been to Northern Ireland once and know nothing about the history of its pubs, bars and inns. Accordingly, it felt unwise to include this part of the UK in my database.
2. Alexander, W.B. (1953–54). 'The Ornithology of Inn Signs'. *Bird Notes* 26, Winter 1953–54, 26–29. I am grateful to my long-standing friend and colleague Professor Chris Perrins FRS for directing me to this paper.
3. Fitter, R.S.R. (1955). 'Bird Inn Signs'. *Birmingham Daily Post,* 22 March 1955.
4. Hyde-Parker, T. (1940). 'Birds and inn signs'. *The Naturalist*, 783, October 1940, 241–243.
5. Shaw, S. (2005). 'Birds in public houses'. Appendix 3, pp. 473–476 in *Birds Britannica*[1.22]. Unfortunately, I cannot find out anything about him. The email address given in *Birds Britannica*, which was published in 2005, no longer works.
6. Betraying my career as a professional ecological scientist, the scientific names of all the species of birds mentioned in the text are in Appendix 1; if you are not interested, you don't have to worry about them.
7. Lawton, J. (2020). BB eye. Pub Birds. *British Birds* 113, 432–435.
8. In a rigorous statistical sense, the sample is more haphazard than random.
9. Pubsgalore.co.uk/stats/pubs/pub-names. Pubs Galore is a comprehensive listing site for pubs and pub lovers, kept up to date by its members. I first accessed it in July 2020; the data used in this book were downloaded in October 2020.
10. For the record it is impossible to say exactly how many pubs bear the names of the commonest pub birds. Take Mute Swans as an example. The first bird of any species on the pubsgalore list (ranked seventh, with 287 pubs) is just plain *Swan*, followed (at 40th, with 109 pubs) by *White Swan*. There are also Mute Swans gracing pubs with much fancier, often 'double-barrelled' names (see Chapters 2 and 7), taking the total number of pubs named after Mute Swans to at least 450, possibly more. *Birds Britannica*[1.22] says that Steve Shaw's list[1.5] has "770 names with swan titles" and claims that nearly a quarter of the pub birds on his list are Mute Swans. But I don't understand how these numbers were arrived at; 114 of the "770" are in fact Black Swans (a different species), leaving just 656 potential Mute Swans. But when I go through Shaw's actual list in Appendix 3 of *Birds Britannica,* I find 708 swans that are not Black Swans. A substantial number of Shaw's swans were already, or will have since, closed. So the best I can do is suggest that the number of Mute Swan pubs during the period covered by this book lay between 450 and possibly as many as 550.
11. *The Rook and Gaskill* used to be called *The Queens Head*, but was re-christened in 2020 by York Brewery, continuing the tradition of its two other pubs called *The Last Drop Inn*

and *The Three Legged Mare* (the latter a type of gallows). Somebody in the brewery has a dark sense of humour.

12. Cooper, T.P. (1897). *The Old Inns and Inn Signs of York.* Delittle & Sons, City Press, York.
13. Jack, A. (2009). *The Old Dog and Duck. The Secret Meanings of Pub Names.* Particular Books, The Penguin Group, London.
14. It is easy to see if a pub has a sign if it is real, not virtual. Pub websites surprisingly often do not feature the sign (if it has one) or give no indication of whether the pub has a sign (other than the name) or not. For others the image is too small to see what it is. Under these circumstances I again must be pragmatic and take the name on face value, because checking them all individually would have involved an impossible amount of travelling.
15. Lockwood, W.B. (1984). *The Oxford Book of British Bird Names.* Oxford University Press, Oxford.
16. Jenkins-Jones, D. & Elphick, J. (2005). 'Welsh names of birds'. Appendix 4 pp. 477– 482 in *Birds Britannica*[22].
17. Alexander, H.G. (1974). *Seventy Years of Birdwatching.* T. &. A.D. Poyser, Berkhamsted. There is an obituary of W.B. Alexander by E.M. Nicholson (1966) in *British Birds* 59, 125–128. I also consulted his entry in *Wikipedia* in October 2020.
18. Alexander, W.B. (1928). *Birds of the Ocean.* Putman & Sons, New York.
19. Harriers are small dogs used to hunt hares, but they can also be a type of fighter aircraft and also what we would now call cross-country runners. In my own searches I encountered *The Merrie Harrier* (with no sign) in Llandough, Cardiff. Dogs and aircraft are not "merrie", so it could be a reference to a human athlete. Steve Shaw[5] marks a *Harrier* in Birmingham as not referring to a bird.
20. Fitter, R.S.R. (1945). *London's Natural History.* The New Naturalist, Collins, London.
21. The two books are:

    Fitter, R.S.R. & Richardson, R.A. (1952). *Collins Pocket Guide to British Birds.* Collins, London.

    Fitter, R.S.R. & Richardson, R.A. (1954). *The Pocket Guide to Nests and Eggs.* Collins, London.
22. Cocker, M. & Mabey, R. (2005). *Birds Britannica.* Chatto & Windus, London.
23. Cocker, M. & Tipling, D. (2013). *Birds and People.* Jonathan Cape, Random House, London.
24. Whitbread & Co Ltd. (1948). Inn-Signia. Adprint for Holden and Co Ltd, London and Birmingham.

    "Insignia" in my dictionary is defined as "a distinguishing sign or mark", which the Inn Sign Society (note below) applies specifically to the collective names for inns, pubs and their signs.
25. The Inn Sign Society www.innsignsociety.com. See Chapter 5. I am ashamed to say I am not a member.

Chapter 2

1. CAMRA, The Campaign for Real Ale is considered to be one of the most successful consumer organisations across Europe. It was founded by four real ale enthusiasts in 1971 and today has over 190,000 members across the UK. It sets the gold standard for beers and the pubs in which we drink them. If CAMRA treats a hostelry as a pub, that's good enough for me.
2. Wikipedia (accessed June 2020).
3. One example of the sheer scale of the importance of Mute Swans as food will suffice. In Christmas 1251 Henry III (in my home city, York) prepared a banquet which

involved 351 Mute Swans (about three tons of meat) gathered from all over northern England[1.22].

4. All the websites I accessed, including Wikipedia, support this origin of "Two Necks" as a corruption of "Two Nicks", even though *Birds Britannica* says[1.22] "Others dispute the idea, partly on the grounds that none of the pubs so called occurs near the Thames", and suggests instead that the name may have an heraldic origin. Both may be true. The Worshipful Company of Vintners has on its crest a Swan with two nicks[1.24].
5. Birkhead, M. (1982). 'Causes of mortality in the Mute Swan *Cygnus olor* on the River Thames'. *Journal of Zoology* 198, 15–25.
6. Yalden, D.W. and Albarella, U. (2009). *The History of British Birds.* Oxford University Press, Oxford.
7. Lever, C. (2005). *Naturalised Birds of the World.* T. & A.D. Poyser, London.
8. Wikipedia (December 2020) tells us that the Lancastrians' Swan was a Bohun Swan, an heraldic badge depicting a Mute Swan with a gold crown round its neck attached to a gold chain. Despite its striking appearance it has not been used, as far as I am aware, for an inn sign in the north of England. It is, however, the Swan depicted on the very beautiful, early 15th century, carved wooden sign on *The Swan Inn* at Clare in Suffolk[1.22].

   For more on Bohun Swans see wikiwand.com/en/Bohun_swan
9. The account on Red Junglefowl in *Birds and People* [1.23] is the longest for any species in the entire book, which alone speaks volumes for the interplay between Hens and humans. Most of the information in the paragraphs that follow on Cockerels and Hens is taken from *Birds and People.*
10. del Hoyo, J. & Collar, N.J. (2014). *HBW and BirdLife International Illustrated Checklist of the Birds of the World.* Volume 1: Non-passerines. Lynx Edicions, Barcelona.
11. The figures for the number of Hens currently killed for food in the UK, and the global percentage of Hens reared on intensive farms, are taken from an advertisement placed by The Humane League charity in *New Scientist* on 23 January 2021, p. 23.
12. The six are: *Famous Cock* (Highbury Corner, London), *Fighting Cocks* (Durham City), *Fighting Cocks Inn* (Diss, Norfolk), two *Olde Fighting Cocks* (St Albans, Hertfordshire and Arnside, Lancashire) and *Game Cock* (Austwick, Yorkshire).
13. Woodward, I., Aebischer, N., Burnell, D., Eaton, M., Frost, T., Hall, C., Stroud, D. & Noble, D. (2020). 'Population estimates of birds in Great Britain and the United Kingdom'. *British Birds* 113, 69–118.
14. Whitfield, D.P. & Fielding, A.H. (2017). 'Analysis of the fate of satellite tracked Golden Eagles in Scotland'. *Scottish Natural Heritage Commissioned Report No 982.* Scottish Natural Heritage.

    For more information on persecution of birds of prey of all kinds (not just Golden Eagles) in Scotland and the response of the Scottish Government to the report by Whitfield and Fielding see:

    Pitches, A. (2020). News and Comment. Scottish grouse moor management report published. *British Birds* 113, 64–65.

    RSPB (undated) 'The Illegal Killing of Birds of Prey in Scotland' 2015–2017 – shorturl.at/mwzV5

    Werritty, A. *et al.* (2019). Grouse Moor Management Review Group. *Report to Scottish Government.* November 2019.
15. A pair nested above Hawswater in Riggindale in the English Lake District for several years in the early 1970s. The 2.5in Ordnance Survey map has (remarkably) both an Eagle Crag and a Heron Crag ("Heron" could easily be a corruption of "Erne" or "Ern", Middle or Old English for Eagle) in the vicinity of their chosen nest site; Eagles had been

here before! I watched this lone pair twice from the safety of a car park in March 1974 and 1975. When the female died (of natural causes) the male hung on for many years, without finding a new mate. Eagles have now gone again from Lakeland.

16. Harris's Hawk breeds in the south-western United States and south of there to Chile. I became very familiar with the species in 1979 when I was working in New Mexico and Arizona. It is a large and very beautiful chestnut-and-white bird of prey with striking yellow legs that hunts collaboratively, with groups surrounding and flushing prey for one of their members to catch. They are also popular falconers' birds, often used to scare pigeons and other birds away from football stadiums and airfields in the UK.
17. Wikipedia, accessed January 2021
18. Bald Eagles also feature on the signs of the *Spread Eagle* (Driffield, East Yorkshire), and two *Eagle* pubs (one in Egglescliffe, Stockton on Tees, and one in Cambridge).
19. The 13 pubs called *The Eagle and Child* are in: **Billinge**, **Bispham Green**, **Bury**, Doncaster, **Leyland**, **Liverpool**, **Ormskirk**, Oxford, **Ramsbottom**, Stavely, **Warrington**, **Weeton** and York. Places in bold are in the historic county of Lancashire.
20. The folk story of the Eagle and Child is from Wikipedia, as is the genealogy of the Stanley Family and the Earls of Derby (November 2020). The genealogy is not easy to follow, but the broad details are, I hope, correct.
21. Wikipedia, and information on the pub website (December 2020).
22. Wiens, J. (2012). 'Black swans and outliers'. *Bulletin of the British Ecological Society* 43(1), 42–43.

    Taleb, N.N. (2007). *The Black Swan: the impact of highly improbable events.* Random House, New York.
23. This date is much earlier than that given by J.L. Long (*Introduced Birds of the World,* David & Charles, 1981) in which the date of introduction is "as early as 1851".
24. Marchant, J. and Thewlis, R. (2011). 'Monitoring non-native species. Here to stay'. *BTO News* January–February 2011, 8–9.
25. Balmer, D.E., Gillings, S., Caffrey, B.J., Swann, R.L., Downie, I.S. & Fuller, R.J. (2013). *Bird Atlas 2007–11: the breeding and wintering birds of Britain and Ireland.* BTO Books, Thetford.
26. Eaton, M., Holling, M. and the Rare Breeding Birds Panel (2020). 'Rare breeding birds in the UK in 2018'. *British Birds* 113, 737–791. The data for Black Swan are in Appendix 2, p. 788.
27. Rackham, O. (1986). *The History of the Countryside.* J.M. Dent & Sons Ltd, London.
28. Pubs Galore[1.9] has 58 pubs called *The Sportsman* (rank 82) and 21 called *Dog and Gun* (rank 221). Metaphorically killing things is big business on pub signs.
29. Avery, M. (2019). 'The Common Pheasant: its status in the UK and the potential impacts of an abundant non-native'. *British Birds* 112, 372–389.
30. Pitches, A. (2020). 'News and Comment. Wild Justice wins legal victory on gamebird releases'. *British Birds* 113, 734.

    The legal challenge was not about the morality or otherwise of shooting. It was about the potential environmental damage caused by these massive and unregulated activities. I am not personally against shooting things but do not want to do it myself for 'pleasure' or 'sport'. I have no objection to those who do, providing it is done legally and does not damage the environment.
31. I am grateful to John Headon for bringing this pub to my attention and for telling me its history.

32. Steve Shaw makes this mistake in his epic list of *Birds in Public Houses*[1.5], calling it *The Strawberry Duck* in Entwistle, Lancashire, but goes on to add "(2)", which means there was another one of the same (or similar) name elsewhere. I assume the second pub is the real *Strawberry Duck* in Clayton.
33. The name and sign may have been based on a 'real' Falcon and falconer or in some cases (if the publican wished to advertise their loyalty to the throne) from the badge of Elizabeth I, which depicts a Falcon[1.24].
34. The ancient art of falconry does still have practical relevance in the modern world in, for example, using a trained bird of prey to scare birds away from locations where they might be a nuisance (Feral Pigeons in football stadiums) or dangerous (wading birds, Gulls or Geese on or near airfields, where a collision with an aircraft may be fatal for the people on board).
35. shorturl.at/moxHO. Accessed 16 January 2021.
36. The original search located 30 pubs, but eight of them either no longer exist (despite appearing in the initial search) or do not have an active website. The pub birds in this search are not included in the main database.
37. Ratcliffe, D. (1993). *The Peregrine Falcon. 2nd Edition.* T. & A.D. Poyser, London.
38. From a low of about 350 pairs at the height of the pesticide crisis to an estimated 1,750 breeding pairs in 2014[2.13], and still increasing.
39. Lack, D. (1974). *Evolution Illustrated by Waterfowl.* Blackwell Scientific Publications, Oxford.
40. Websites accessed in January 2021.
41. Cramp, S. & Perrins, C.M. (eds.) (1994). *The Birds of the Western Palearctic* Vol. VIII. Oxford University Press, Oxford.
42. Ratcliffe, D. (1997). *The Raven.* T. & A.D. Poyser, London.
43. Mabey, R. (ed.) (1988). *The Natural History of Selborne. A new edition, with engravings. Gilbert White.* Century Hutchinson Ltd, London.

    I have a treasured first edition of the book, which was published in 1789, and a large collection of the many subsequent editions. References to Gilbert White in *Inn Search of Birds* are from the edition edited by Richard Mabey, one of the most attractive and best annotated of the modern editions. It includes a comprehensive index which greatly facilitates finding White's comments on particular species and places.

    Selborne is in Hampshire, where White was the vicar and where he made an astonishing number of acute natural history observations that make up the book, which is compiled as a series of letters to two of the leading biologists of the day, Thomas Pennant and the Honourable Daines Barrington. In his second letter to Pennant White describes the fate of a Raven killed whilst sitting on her nest in an oak tree as it was felled for timber.
44. www.friendsofravenscourtpark.org.uk. Accessed January 2021.
45. Koeppel, D. (2005). *To See Every Bird on Earth.* Michael Joseph, Penguin Books, London. He writes (p. xvi): "I hope that this book shows how the pursuit of birds relates to – and grows from – science's quest to explain our existence…the same reason Darwin chose finches to illustrate his theories."
46. Kricher, J. (2006). *Galápagos. A Natural History.* Princeton University Press, Princeton & Oxford.
47. Darwin thought the Cactus Finch was a North American Blackbird (in the family Icteridae), the Warbler Finch a kind of wren and all the rest basically the same species of 'Finch'.
48. del Hoyo, J. & Collar, N.J. (2016). *HBW and BirdLife International Illustrated Checklist of the Birds of the World.* Volume 2: Passerines. Lynx Edicions, Barcelona.

49. David Lack (who succeeded W.B. Alexander as director of the Edward Grey Institute in 1945 – see Chapter 1) coined the name "Darwin's Fiches" in 1947: Lack, D. (1947). *Darwin's Finches.* Cambridge University Press, Cambridge. Re-issued with an introduction and notes 1983.
50. Grant, P.R. (1986). *Ecology and Evolution of Darwin's Finches.* Princeton University Press. Princeton.

    Grant, P.R. & Grant, B.R. (2014). *40 Years of Evolution. Darwin's Finches on Daphne Major Island.* Princeton University Press, Princeton.
51. The quotes are taken from pp. 15–16 of my own copy of the 6th (1894) and last edition of *The Origin of Species.*
52. I'd like to think that the *Dead Pigeon* in Rochester referred to at the end of Chapter 1 is a Feral Pigeon. It features a stylised silhouette of a pigeon lying on its back, which seems appropriate given the distain with which Feral Pigeons tend to be held.
53. More generally it is not unusual for pub signs and names to feature triplets of objects: *Three Tuns* (large wine barrels), *Three Horseshoes* (for a pub frequented by farriers), *Three Compasses* (ditto carpenters), *Three Cups* (probably not a reference to tea) and the only other bird in triplets, *Three Cranes* (in York, see Chapter 3). Why three is not at all clear in many (but not all) instances[1.13 & 1.24].
54. Cheke, A. (2019). 'A long-standing feral Indian Peafowl population in Oxfordshire, and a brief survey of the species in Britain'. *British Birds* 112, 337–348.
55. Birkhead, T.R. (1991). *The Magpies.* T. & A.D. Poyser, London.
56. bbc.co.uk/news/uk-england-suffolk-57747683
57. Newton, I. (2017). *Farming and Birds.* The New Naturalist Library, Harper Collins, London.
58. Potts, G.R. (1986). *The Partridge. Pesticides, Predation and Conservation.* Collins, London.
59. These numbers puzzled me and on checking on Google (September 2021) the small number of pubs called *The Dog and Partridge* in my own database was clearly an error. In the main, if you search for "pubs called Partridge", most of those called *Dog and Partridge* do not appear. A new Google search revealed no less than 36! I have not added them to the core database but it confirms that there are still numerous pubs called *Dog and Partridge.*
60. The paltry six *Dog and Partridge* pubs in my database are in Ascot (Berkshire), Calf Heath (near Wolverhampton, West Midlands), Nottingham (with the epithet *Old*), Preston (Lancashire), Tosside (Lancashire–Yorkshire border) and Whitehaven (Cumbria).

Chapter 3

1. The sample of pubs in Glasgow and Edinburgh and the Central Borders was taken very early in the research for this book, during a visit in January 2011 and using old-fashioned *Yellow Pages* and *Thomson Directory* entries for pubs, bars and inns. In Glasgow the only pub bird was *The Black Sparrow.* In Edinburgh and environs the eight pubs were *Doocot* (the pub from which I was chased away – Chapter 1), *Eagle, Eagle Inn, Gulls Nest, Phoenix, Robins Nest, Swan Tavern* and *White Swan.* I have more recently discovered two other pub birds, one in each city: the *Jack Snipe* in Cumbernauld, Glasgow and the *Merlin* in Edinburgh.
2. The most useful lists of pubs, bars and inns on these Scottish Islands (accessed in February 2021) are provided by the beerintheevening.com websites for each island, plus additional information on the websites for the tourist boards for some islands, and yell.com. Information on the closure of *The Puff Inn* on St Kilda is from the website of *The Scotsman* newspaper (www.scotsman.com).

3. All the information on the oldest pub birds came from searching for the name of the pub on Google and either getting the information from the pub's own or other appropriate websites, or from Wikipedia, accessed between June and November 2020 and February and June 2021. It isn't foolproof. I have to have at least some basis for knowing or thinking the pub may be old before I look it up. Some checked in that way had no evidence of age, and there must be others that I have missed completely. Some information is very vague (e.g. "a 17th century coaching inn") and I have largely, but not entirely, ignored these in this section.
4. Dash, M. (2010). mikedashhistory.com
5. Holloway, S. (1996). *The Historical Atlas of Breeding Birds in Britain and Ireland: 1875–1900*. T. & A.D. Poyser, London.
   (See also note 2.26).
6. Sharrock, J.T.R. (1976). *The Atlas of Breeding Birds in Britain and Ireland*. British Trust for Ornithology, Irish Wildbird Conservancy. BTO, Tring.
7. The *Lion and Pheasant* was host to the last recorded cockfight in England, as discussed in Chapter 2. References to the two letters were taken from a website early in my research on pub birds, and unfortunately it no longer appears to exist. To add to the confusion, the pub's current website says it was "originally built in the 16th century".
8. There is (October 2021) a short history of the pub on the wall outside the front door.
9. There is an interesting historical thread here. Chris Perrins succeeded David Lack as director of the Edward Grey Institute of Ornithology in Oxford. David Lack had (as explained in Chapter 2) succeeded W.B. Alexander – the EGI's first director. And as explained in Chapter 1, it was Chris who first put me on to Alexander's original paper on pub birds. Chris, by the way, is tea-total.
10. Merriam-Webster.com/dictionary
11. According to Wikipedia (March 2021) The Bullington was (and still is) a "private, all-male dining club for Oxford University students. It is known for its wealthy members, grand banquets and occasional bad behaviour, including vandalism of restaurants." You do wonder if that is why the pub changed its name.
12. The *Tern Inn*'s entries on Google (March 2021) explain that the pub has been closed for some time because the owner is in dispute with South Gloucestershire Council over a planning application to demolish it and build houses on the site. The council has issued a community asset order to try and maintain it as a pub.
13. Standbury, A. & UK Crane Working Group. (2011). 'The changing status of the Common Crane in the UK'. *British Birds* 104, 432–447.
14. Hengeveld, R. (1989). *Dynamics of Biological Invasions*. Chapman and Hall, London.
15. My friend and work colleague Alastair Fitter was taken by his father (the distinguished naturalist Richard Fitter – Chapter 1) to see the birds nesting in "substantial grounds with plenty of trees" when he was seven. In his words: "There was quite a gathering; my recollection is that several of the big names in ornithology were there, but I cannot remember who they were." What he can remember "was the great feeling of excitement among the whole party and that we viewed the nest from a substantial distance". He also remembers staying with his sister in Sale on the outskirts of Manchester, less than ten years later and about 165 miles from Cromer when Collared Doves had become 'garden weeds' and thinking "What was all the fuss about?" I added Collared Dove to my life list north of Manchester on 12 August 1962 after cycling through a place called Midge Hall just west of my home in Leyland. I was with my birding friend Sam and we were on our way back home from the Ribble Marshes. There were three birds – two adults and a fledged youngster, and we were very excited. But (like Alastair) the

excitement soon wore off, as they became one of the commonest birds on the edge of town.

16. Joemasonspage.wordpress.com (accessed March 2021).
17. Newton, I. (2020). *Uplands and Birds.* The New Naturalist Library, William Collins. London.
18. W.B. Alexander has "Blackcock" as one of his pub birds and unlike "Moorcock" this is unequivocally a reference to Black Grouse. Alexander lists his pubs "beginning with the commonest" (Table 1, Chapter 2), which I have taken to mean from the commonest to the rarest in order of abundance. On his list "Grouse (or Moorcock)" (i.e. Red Grouse) comes well ahead of "Blackcock". We don't know how many *Blackcock* pubs he had on his list, but one of them (or it) could well have been *The Blackcock Inn* in Falstone; it is certainly old enough. Steve Shaw's list does not add much clarity. It has nine pubs called *Black Cock* (two words) in a group of other pubs where for most (but not all) of them "Cock" appears to be a reference to Cockerel, but when writing this I discovered that at least two pubs so named still exist, both old, in the right localities and most likely named after Black Grouse (one in Broughton-in-Furness on the edge of the Lake District and the other in Llanfihangel Talyllyn, Wales. The latter has had its Facebook page blocked for being "racist". Neither has a sign, which doesn't help). Shaw also lists *The Heathcock* in Cardiff, which I had also overlooked. Its sign does not depict a male Black Grouse but seems to show (surprisingly) a female, although Heathcock implies a male. Another vernacular name for female Black Grouse is Grey Hen, and Shaw does have a *Grey Hen* in South Shields among his (puzzlingly) short list of Hen pubs. He also has 11 pubs called *Moorcock*, which as we have seen could be either Red or Black Grouse and he groups *The Bonny Moorhen* in Stanhope (see main text and note 19 below) with *The Three Moorhens* ('real' Moorhens) in Hitchin. Don't worry. It's not you. It is very confused and confusing.
19. Keith Bowey, personal communication, September 2020.

    When I was writing this section six months after Keith had written to me I was re-consulting *Birds Britannica* to check the Black Grouse entry and discovered that a similar mix-up between (in that case Moorcock and Moorhen) is repeated (p. 159–60) for a pub "now closed" in Manchester.
20. Cramp, S. (chief ed.) (1980). *Handbook of the Birds of Europe and the Middle East and North Africa. The Birds of the Western Palearctic.* Volume II. Hawks to Bustards. Oxford University Press, Oxford.

    The section on Black Grouse is on pp. 416–428.
21. Mather, J.R. (1986). *The Birds of Yorkshire.* Croom Helm, London.
22. John R. Mather, letter dated 16 August 2020.
23. A remnant population may survive on Dartmoor. They also still breed south of the Peak District in the Welsh uplands[2.25].
24. Webb, N. (1986). *Heathlands.* The New Naturalist, Collins, London.
25. Mearns, B. & R. (1988). *Biographies of Birdwatchers.* Academic Press, London.
26. *The Natural History of Selborne* is made up of 44 letters to Pennant followed by 66 to Daines Barrington. All the letters to Barrington are dated, but the first nine to Pennant are not, and the general consensus among Selborne fans is that the initial nine to Pennant were written explicitly by Gilbert White to 'set the scene' for the book. It is not clear to me whether White ever actually sent these nine letters to Pennant.
27. Wikipedia, accessed March 2021.
28. In letter VI to Pennant, White records that there was a "species of game in this [Woolmer] forest, now extinct which I have heard old people say abounded much

before shooting flying became so common, and that was the heath-cock, black-game, or grouse…. The last pack remembered was killed about thirty-five years ago."

29. Gulls are in the taxonomic family Laridae. In the UK there are six common breeding species. In order of size from the largest to the smallest they are: Great Black-backed, Herring, Lesser Black-backed, Common, Black-headed Gulls and Kittiwake, which are a shade larger than Black-headed Gulls. Of these, Common Gulls are actually the least common breeding species. The non-birder is most likely to call all of them "seagulls".
30. Coulson, J.C. (2019). *Gulls.* The New Naturalist Library. William Collins, London.
31. Waders (as their name implies) live in and around water, both on the coast and inland. Three different taxonomic families of pub birds are involved: Oystercatchers (Haematopodidae), Plovers (Charadriidae – the family to which Golden Plover and Dotterel belong) and a varied group in the family Scolopacidae. Pub birds in the Scolopacidae family include Common Sandpiper, other indeterminate "Sandpipers", Dunlin, Snipe, Woodcock, Curlew and Turnstone.
32. Wernham, C., Toms, M., Marchant, J., Clark, J., Siriwardena, G. and Baillie, S. (eds.) (2002). *The Migration atlas: movements of the birds of Britain and Ireland.* T. & A.D. Poyser, London.
33. Professor John Lea reported the pub to me in September 2012. In June 2021 the current use of the building was described at www.god-unlimited.org
34. Wikipedia May 2021.
35. greatbustard.org (May 2021)
36. Keith Bowey, personal communication, September 2020.
37. Although 'pub names road' is probably the usual way round, 'road names pub' does happen. *The Marsh Harrier* on Marsh Road in Oxford may be a counter-example, and *The Crow Bar and Kitchen* (see later) definitely is.
38. "Loke" is a local term for a small lane in eastern England.
39. From Wikipedia, May 2021. Pigot's Directory was a major British directory started in 1814 by James Pigot. The directories covered England, Scotland and Wales in the period before official civil registration began. They are a valuable source of regional information on, among other things, major professions, trades and occupations, including taverns and public houses.
40. Wikipedia: *Pigot & Co's National Commercial Directory for 1828–9.* London. However there is a bit of a mystery here. The pub is not in London and Pigot's Directory for Kent was not published until 1839. I cannot clarify which source is correct.
41. Accessed February 2021.
42. Sadly I have forgotten who the cartoon was by, or where it was published, but the picture has stuck in my mind.

Chapter 4

1. Alexander did not record "fabulous monsters with some…bird-like attributes such as Phoenix, Wyvern, Griffin and Cockatrice". On Fitter's list "Heraldic birds or feathered creatures [were] squeezed in by the back door" to give him "numerous" Griffins and Phoenixes. Shaw has no text to explain what he did, and the only mythical bird on his list is a Firebird. I did not records Griffins, but do have Phoenix, Liver Bird and Firebird on mine (the latter cheating slightly on date), plus Martlets.
2. Wikipedia (accessed November 2020).
3. Laver (*Porphyra*) seaweed grows as purplish-red, slightly crinkled, irregularly shaped sheets 10–25cm long and attached to rocks and stones. In parts of Wales it is a popular food that is fried or rolled in oatmeal and known as laverbread.

4. Wikipedia's entry on the Phoenix was accessed in 2010 when I first became interested in pub birds and discovered *The Phoenix* pub in York. There is also a good account in *Birds and People*[1.23]. The two accounts do not always agree about the details.
5. Wikipedia accessed May 2021 provided information on a range of different pub birds used throughout this chapter.
6. According to Wikipedia, Saint Vincent de Paul was a French Catholic Priest born in 1581 who dedicated himself to serving the poor. I cannot find any explanation for why a pub in Yorkshire should be named after him or why the coat of arms features a Martlet.
7. Jobling, J.A. (1991). *A Dictionary of Scientific Bird Names*. Oxford University Press, Oxford.
   Real Swifts of course do have legs and feet but they are small and hidden in the lower breast feathers. Swifts are one of the world's most aerial birds and on the ground can at best manage a shuffling walk.
8. Alan Tilmouth, *BirdGuides* website 27 June 2019.
9. Moss, S. (2019). *The Twelve Birds of Christmas*. Square Peg, Random House, London.
10. www.foodsofengland.co.uk
11. Lever, C. (1977). *The Naturalised Animals of the British Isles*. Hutchinson, London.
12. Blue and Gold Trust Official Website. *A "brief" history of Kings Lynn F.C.* www.thelinnets.co.uk (accessed May 2021).
13. Nick Reynolds (personal communication September 2021). Obviously this particular *Bird in Hand* has nothing to do with falconry (Chapter 2). The original sign was painted by a friend of Reynolds's father and is based on a captive Macaw in the adjacent bird garden. And see www.birdinhandhayle.co.uk.
14. Juniper, T. & Parr, M. (1998). *Parrots. A Guide to the Parrots of the World.* Pica Press, Sussex.
15. Freestone, P. & Lowen, A. (2019). Dalmatian Pelican in Cornwall: new to Britain. *British Birds* 112, 401–406.
16. Hagemeijer, W.J.M. & Blair, M.J. (eds.) (1997). *The EBCC Atlas of European Breeding Birds: Their Distribution and Abundance.* T. & A.D. Poyser, London.
17. The information in this section on the pubs called *The Pelican* or *Pelican Inn* (several go by both names) is compiled from entries in whatpub.com or the pub's own website. Old pubs are in bold, with approximate dates. They are in Addlestone, London; Chew Magna, Somerset; **Devises, Wiltshire** (coaching inn – no date); **Foxfield, Wiltshire** (dates from at least 1773); **Gloucester** (dates from 1679); Hull, Yorkshire; **Newcastle Emlyn, Carmarthenshire** (looks old, but age unknown; the bird is a North American Brown Pelican); Nottingham; **Pamper Heath, Hampshire** (dates from ca 1860); **Stapleford, Wiltshire** (dates from 18th century); **Tacolneston, Norfolk** (early 19th century; the sign is lovely but slightly 'cartoony', and the bird has a grey not white back and a huge blue-grey pouched beak inside of which is what looks like a blue Koala Bear!) W.B. Alexander noted that the *Pelican* as a pub name "seems to be commonest in Hampshire and Wiltshire", without offering an explanation. I cannot provide one.
18. Information on the Pelican in her Piety on the old sign for the *Fox and Pelican* in Grayshott was kindly provided by the manager Lauren Green and by John Childs, vice-charman of Grayshott Heritage. The sign is currently on display in Grayshott Pottery. More generally, Wikimedia Commons (accessed June 2021) has 166 heraldic images depicting pious Pelicans from the crests of families of the great and good. I cannot find out which Ogmore by Sea family is linked to the pub.
19. *Prospect of Whitby* website accessed June 2021.
20. www.fobb.org.uk/history/the-ostrich-inn (accessed June 2021)
21. www.norfolkparadise.com/post/why-ostriches-were-chosen-for-north-norfolk-pub-signs (accessed June 2021)

22. Borrow, N. & Demey, R. (2001). *Birds of Western Africa*. Helm Identification Guides. Christopher Helm, London.
23. whatpub.com (accessed June 2021).
24. As Lockwood[1.15] expertly explains, "Wind Fucker" and "Fuckwind", although potentially offensive to modern readers, may have an entirely innocent origin. In Dutch and German "fokken" and "ficken" can mean to "knock" and "beat" respectively. The birds are literally "wind beaters".
25. There is a Dodo Pub Company in England that has five pubs but none called *The Dodo*.
26. Hume, J.P. & Walters, M. (2012). *Extinct Birds*. T. & A.D. Poyser, Bloomsbury Publishing, London.
27. According to Wikipedia (June 2021) the Dodo in *Alice's Adventures in Wonderland* has been described as an "affectionate self-portrait" of the author, Lewis Carroll, whose real name was Charles Dodgson. It is said that Dodgson stammered and often introduced himself as "Do-do-dodgson". One of the famous illustrations by John Tenniel in the book has Alice shaking hands with a Dodo (the bird standing upright like a Penguin – which it could never have done) that is carrying a cane.
28. For example, Storrington in West Sussex is derived for the Saxon Estorchestone – "the village of Storks". A pair of Storks still feature on the village emblem. See the website for the Knepp Estate in West Sussex for further information – knepp.co.uk/white-storks
29. Strangely, neither Richard Fitter nor W.B. Alexander have Storks on their lists.
30. Information about all the Stork pubs is taken from the pubs' own websites (June 2021)
31. I am grateful to Sir Charlie Burrell for additional information about the Storks on his estate at Knepp, and for discussions about their historical status in Britain.
32. The entire August 1962 volume of *British Birds* (55 No.8, pp. 281–384) was devoted to the Hastings rarities. The two key papers are those by the distinguished applied statistician J.A. Nelder (pp. 283–298) and two of the leading ornithologists and birdwatchers of the day, E.M. Nicholson and I.J. Ferguson-Lees (pp. 299–384), and were followed by other extensive (and intensive) discussions in the birding literature.
33. The "unacceptable records" are listed in Appendix A of *British Birds* 55 (8).
34. The list of foreign pub birds used to calculate these numbers (with the number of pubs) includes:

    American Kestrel (1)
    Blue Jay (1)
    [Canada Goose] (1)
    Canary (2)
    Dodo (1)
    [Golden Pheasant] (2)
    Jacobin Cuckoo (1)
    [Little Owl] (2)
    Ostrich (3)
    Parrot species (8)
    Red-cheeked Cordonbleu (1)
    [Ruddy Duck] (2)
    [Snow Goose] (2 or 3)
    Toco Toucan (1)
    Whistling Swan (1)
    Vulture species (2)
    Wood Duck (1)

    Species in square brackets have (or have had) feral breeding populations in the UK.

35. End of July 2021.
36. It is impossible to be more exact because there are species of pub birds that some would include and others would not. For instance, should I include or exclude *The Three Cranes* in York, *The Bustard Inn* in Lincolnshire or *The Snowy Owl* in Cramlington, Northumberland? The first now has a well-established breeding population after being extinct for 100s of years. The second used to breed in Britain, also went extinct and is

now the subject of a reintroduction programme, and the third is a scarce winter visitor that for a time had a single breeding pair on the island of Fetlar in Shetland. When *Birds Britannica*[1.22] was published in 2005 the British List stood at 575 and Mark Cocker and Richard Mabey chose to include 350 species as British birds in the text including many scarce but not rare visitors. Even if we include all 350, it makes little difference to the argument that foreign and unfamiliar species are rare as pub birds compared with the overwhelming number of 'native' species.

37. There are eight rejected records of Sociable Plover in the Hastings rarities.
38. Condors are New World Vultures with several species in North and South America. They are in the same family as Turkey Vultures, which gave their name to *The Bald Buzzard* in Leighton Buzzard (Chapter 3).

Chapter 5

1. Wikipedia (accessed July 2021)
2. The Owl could be a Long-eared or Short-eared Owl. One way to tell is the colour of the Owl's iris – yellow in Short-eared, Orange in Long-eared. But the picture is not accurate enough to tell. The length of the 'ears' suggests Long-eared, and of course the 'ears' on Owls such as Short- and Long-eared, and Eagle Owls, are not ears at all but tufts of feathers. Owls' real ears lie buried and normally invisible along the left and right edges of the Owl's face (technically its facial disc).
3. I read all five books in the 'trilogy' as they came out (the first one in 1979) but that was 40-odd years ago and I had to rely on my grown-up kids, Anna and Graham, to remind me about *The Horse and Groom.* They tell me that it also makes an appearance later in *So Long, and Thanks for the Fish*, but I don't remember that at all.
4. The ten Shakespearian plays and the 15 or 16 species of bird mentioned in them, as summarised by *Birds Britannica*, are:

A Midsummer Night's Dream	Possibly Jackdaw
Coriolanus	Osprey
Hamlet	(House) Sparrow, Woodcock
Henry IV part 1	Starling
King Lear	Carrion Crow, Chough, Cuckoo, Hedge Sparrow (= Dunnock), (Red) Kite
Love's Labour's Lost	Tawny Owl, Woodcock
Macbeth	(Barn) Owl, Martlet (= House Martin), Magpie
Measure for Measure	(House) Sparrow, Lapwing
The Winter's Tale	(Red) Kite, Turtle Dove
Troilus and Cressida	(House) Sparrow

Only Dunnock (Shakespeare's Hedge Sparrow) and Turtle Dove do not make appearances as pub birds.

5. *The Three Pigeons* is a popular name for fictitious pubs. Real pubs of this name (Chapter 2) can be found in Bishop's Tawton (Devon), Bolton and Warrington (both Lancashire), and *Three Pigeons Inn* in Ruthin, Denbighshire. Shakespeare's use of the name is clearly generic.

According to Wikipedia (accessed in 2020) an imaginary *Three Pigeons* has also been used as a setting by other playwrights in the past, including Oliver Goldsmith in *She Stoops to Conquer* (1773), Ben Jonson in *The Alchemist* (1773) and W.S. Gilbert in *Creatures of Impulse,* which is both a short story (1870) and a musical fairy tale (1871) (see also www.gsarchive.net).

Pub birds that are literary creations (i.e. are not real pubs) are interesting, even fun, to discuss and I have included them in this chapter, even though they cannot possibly fall within the time period I set in Chapter 1. Nor have I included them in the main database.

6. Wikipedia (accessed July 2021). Professor Chris Perrins (who introduced me to W.B. Alexander's paper[1.2]) also alerted me to this possible explanation for the origin of some *Black Swan* pubs.
7. Wikipedia (accessed July 2021).
   www.thenorthernecho.co.uk/news/7030541.abbey-cradle-kings
8. www.culturalindia.net/indian-folktales/jataka-tales (accessed March 2010)
9. bevshistoricalyarns.wordpress.com/2018/01/05/the-origin-of-the-bohun-swan
10. http://read.gov>aesop
11. Other British birds which *Birds Britannica* refers to as having 'personalised nicknames' include:

    Jackdaw (from *Jack* Daw). Daw or Dawe is a traditional name for the bird[1.15].

    Magpie (from *Mag* i.e. Margaret, Pie). Pie "is the ultimate source of most English names for Magpie"[1.15].

    Robin (from *Robin* Redbreast). The birds were originally called, among other names, Redbreasts[1.15].

    All three are, appropriately, also pub birds.
12. Lack, D. (1970) *The Life of the Robin*. Fontana New Naturalist, London.
13. The poem is cited at the head of Chapter 7 of David Lack's *Life of the Robin*. It is undated but was probably written by Blake towards the end of the 18th century or early 19th (Wikipedia for once is unhelpful).
14. Wikipedia (accessed August 2019) associates Minerva/Athena with knowledge and wisdom. Reference to Athena as the goddess of war is in:

    Mynott, J. (2018). *Birds in the Ancient World*. Oxford University Press.
15. Eagles and Falcons include relevant pubs called *Bird in Hand* (Table 2), and Owls include the *Owl and Hitchhiker* and three pubs called *Owl and Pussycat*. Specific and non-specific "Owls" number just 11.
16. Birkhead, T. (2013). *Bird Sense. What It's Like to Be a Bird*. Bloomsbury, London.
17. Owl pubs not so far encountered include:

    Barn Owl
    The Barn Owl, Exeter, Devon
    The Barn Owl Inn, Newton Abbot, Devon
    The Old Barn Inn, Bickington, Devon
    Is it a coincidence that there are three in one county, I wonder?
    The Owl at Hambleton, near Selby, Yorkshire. The sign used to be a Barn Owl (p. 131) and is now an amusing cartoon resembling something between a mermaid and an Owl (p. 147).

    Tawny Owl
    The Tawny Owl, Balderton, Newark

    Non-specific Owls
    Oadby Owl, Oadby, Leicestershire

    We have already encountered an Eagle Owl (*The Minerva*, this chapter), the *Snowy Owl*[4.36], two Little Owls (p. 106 and p. 107) and a *Tawny Owl* that isn't (Chapter 1).
18. King, R.J. (2013). *The Devil's Cormorant. A natural history*. University of New Hampshire Press, Durham, NH.
19. This quote from John Steinbeck is from *Sea of Cortez: A Leisurely Journal of Travel and*

Research written jointly with his friend the marine biologist Ed Rickets and published in 1941 shortly after their trip. Steinbeck went on to publish the much more famous *The Log from the Sea of Cortez* in 1951, based on material from the earlier book (Wikipedia accessed July 2021).

20. exclassics.com/ingold/ingintro.htm and Wikipedia (accessed October 2020).
21. artuk.org
22. www.jackdawdenton.co.uk
23. Wikipedia and pub's own website (accessed July 2021)
24. hopkinspoetry.com/study-guides/individual-poems
    www.jdwetherspoons.com
25. Kesey, K. (1962). *One Flew Over the Cuckoo's Nest.* Viking Press & Signet Books.
26. The quotes are from my own 1894 (6th) edition of Darwin's *Origin of Species by Means of Natural Selection*, p. 198.
27. Wikipedia (accessed July 2021) and www.penguinrandomhouse.com
28. www.londonfictions.com and Wikipedia (accessed January 2015).
29. You can find out more at: charlesdickenspage.com/charles-dickens-our-mutual-friend.html (accessed June 2022).
30. www.hulldailymail.co.uk and Wikipedia (accessed July 2021).
31. www.classicfm.com/composers/purcell/guides/purcell-facts/purcell-ode
32. The Honourable Daines Barrington was one of Gilbert White's correspondents[2.43]. Barrington's 1773 letter to the Royal Society on bird song was published in *Philosophical Transactions* and quoted by David Lack on page 38 of *The Life of the Robin*[5.12].
33. whatpub.com/pubs/CRO/11627/nightingale-sutton, and Wikipedia (accessed July 2021).
34. Coward, T.A. (1956). *The Birds of the British Isles and their Eggs.* Series 1. Revised by A.W. Boyd. Frederick Warne & Co. London.

    There are three volumes in this classic series, which was first published in 1920, and many subsequent editions and reprints. I acquired my three volumes at the age of 13 in 1957. They were at the time the most precious books I had ever owned. I still have them.
35. Michael Hall (personal communication October 2021), who owns the image and to whom I am very grateful for the chance to liaise with the artist.
36. Wikipedia (accessed October 2021).
37. flickr.com/photos/25229906@N00/33277568978 (Roby Virus). It was rebuilt in 1900.
38. "Eggle" may be derived from Latin "ecclesia" – church (Wikipedia accessed October 2021).

Chapter 6

1. Wikipedia (accessed July 2021) describes Nash as a surrealist painter and a war artist of both the First and Second World Wars. He was also among the most important landscape artists of the first half of the 20th century and a "designer of applied art" including stage scenery, fabrics and posters. It is in applied art that I had hoped to find an interest in pub signs, but of this possibility there is no mention. His views on pub signs in *Inn-Signia* may have had as much to do with the fact that he was very famous and died in 1946, just before *Inn-Signia* was published, rather than him having any particular expertise on the subject.
2. Some *Spread Eagle* and some *Stork* pubs that I have not seen or found pictures of may have nests or nest-like cribs on their signs. But it will not be many.
3. Cramp, S. (1983) chief editor. *Handbook of the Birds of Europe and the Middle East and North Africa. The Birds of the Western Paleartctic Volume III, Waders to Gulls.* Oxford University Press, Oxford.

According to the account on Woodcocks in this wonderful book, W.B. Alexander wrote extensively on the question of whether Woodcocks can carry their young, in a series of papers in the ornithological journal *Ibis* between 1945 and 1947. This remarkable behaviour has been much debated and disputed, but now appears to be genuine. See: gwct.org.uk/game/research/species/woodcock/breeding-woodcock

4. Davies, N. (2015). *Cuckoo. Cheating by Nature.* Bloomsbury, London.
5. Nidicolous baby birds hatch naked and blind and are fed in the nest by the parents until they are fully feathered and can fly. Nidifugous chicks hatch covered in down and with their eyes open (think chickens). They leave the nest almost immediately.
6. Long, J. & Schouten, P. (2008). *Feathered Dinosaurs. The Origin of Birds.* Oxford University Press, Oxford.

   Benton, M. (2021). 'China's dinos'. *New Scientist* 3356 (16 October 2021), 43–45.
7. The Jurassic period was 201–145 million years ago and the Cretaceous 145–166 million years ago.
8. Roberts, A. (2021). *Ancestors. The Prehistory of Britain in Seven Burials.* Simon & Schuster, London.
9. Wikipedia (accessed August 2021).
10. *The Three Feathers* is a 19th-century German folk story by the Brothers Grimm. I do not think it has anything to do with the name of this pub.
11. The book was a gift from the author Professor Tetsukazu Yahara of Kyushu University when I was in Japan in 2004. It is entirely in Japanese, except for the names of the birds in English and an English translation of the title: *The Feathers of Japanese Birds in Full Scale*. I have no idea when it was published.

Chapter 7

1. We have encountered three other species of finch: *The Spink's Nest* (Chaffinch), *The Canary and Linnet*, *The Cat and Canary* and *The Linnet and Lark*.
2. Birkhead, T. (2008). *The Wisdom of Birds. An Illustrated History of Ornithology.* Bloomsbury, London.
3. www.hexam-courant.co.uk
4. www.audubon.org/news/what-seahawk-anyway
5. Witherby, H.F. *et al.* (1943). *The Handbook of British Birds Volume III.* H.F. & G. Witherby Ltd, London.
6. This brief history of the Loch Garton Ospreys is taken from an RSPB leaflet *Ospreys on Speyside*, which was published in 1965 and which I still have. It says that RSPB membership then was "one guinea per annum (or 10s. if under 21 years of age)" – £1.05 and 50p in decimal currency. Happy days.
7. This ambiguity is in quite a different category to (for example) the species above (*The Seahawk*) where I have no picture to go on, just a name and the name is ambiguous.
8. www.redstartpub.co.uk, whatpub.com/pubs/MAI/12/redstart-barming, and a general search on Google.
9. Pub's own website and www.visitlancashire.com/food-and-drink/the-sparrowhawk-p7347, both accessed in August 2021.
10. Newton, I. (1986). *The Sparrowhawk.* T. & A.D. Poyser, Calton.

    Village, A. (1990). *The Kestrel* T. & A.D. Poyser, London.
11. Wikipedia (accessed August 2021).
12. Ferguson-Lees J. & Christie, D.A. (2001). *Raptors of the World.* Christopher Helm, London.

13. www.mcmullens.co.uk/warbleronthewharf and pub website (accessed August 2021).
14. Wikipedia (accessed September 2021).
15. The concluding line of the Christmas carol *The Twelve Days of Christmas* (which is a list of gifts received from an unidentified true love) is "A Partridge in a Pear Tree", one of Steve Moss's 12 Christmas birds: Moss, S. (2019). *The Twelve Birds of Christmas.* Square Peg, London.
16. The *Plum and Partridge* just outside York used to be called *The Orchard Inn.*
17. In my database there are pubs called *The Dog and Duck* in Babbacombe (Devon), two in and around Beverley (East Yorkshire), two in London (Soho and Walthamstow) and one in North London between Edmonton and Whetstone, plus a *Royal Dog and Duck* in Flamborough, North Yorkshire. A Google search for *Fox and Duck* (September 2021) came up with six, including the one already in my database in Petersham, Richmond.
18. www.coleshill.org/history/buildings/pubs/79-magpies.html
    yelp.com/biz/harte-and-magpies-amersham
19. According to the pub's website the tiny house measured just 6ft wide by 14ft long. In the 19th century eight children are reputed to have lived there. The father had to ascend the stairs to the upper floor sideways. The last occupant moved out in 1925 and the house was absorbed into the pub in 1952.
20. www.cockandwoolpack.co.uk
21. Wikipedia (accessed September 2021).
22. There are pubs called *The Dog and Pheasant* in Bromsgrove (Worcestershire), Brook (Surrey), Castlefields (Shropshire), Colchester and East Mersea (both Essex) and Godalming (Surrey).
23. Wikipedia (accessed August 2021)
    whatpub.com/pubs/NLD/5966/swan-edgar-london
24. dockersinn.co.uk
25. Wikipedia (accessed October 2021)
26. dover-kent.com/2014-project/swan-and-mitre-Bromley.html
    whatpub.com/pubs/BRO/12484/swan-mitre-bromley
    wikiwand.com/en/Bohun_swan
27. Beaman, M. & Madge, S. (1998). *Handbook of Bird Identification for Europe and the Western Palearctic.* Christopher Helm. A. & C. Black, London.
28. whatpub.com/pubs/ROB/726/railway-linnet-middleton-junction
29. Lack, D. (1971). *Ecological Isolation in Birds.* Blackwell Scientific Publications, Oxford.
30. www.scotsman.com/whats-on/arts-and-entertainment/15-words-which-can-only-be-used-describe-scottish-weather-1478371
31. www.scaredcrow.co.uk
32. *The Crafty Crow* closed in January 2022'
33. www.pubsinrugby.co.uk/list-of-pubs-in-rugby/rugby-south/bilton/the-crow-pie
34. Wikipedia (accessed September 2021)
35. This idea comes from a now defunct website
36. www.outdoorlife.com/blogs/cast-iron-chef/cooking-crow-meat-recipe-blackbird-pie
37. whatpub.com/pubs/TAU/533/yellow-wagtail-yeovil
38. The taxonomy of the Yellow Wagtail complex is under constant review and revision. For present purposes the account in Beaman and Madge (note 7.27 above) is sufficient. They recognise "10 perhaps 12 races", and the identification of the bird on the sign is based on

their descriptions. If it had a yellow throat, it would be *M.f. flava* known as Blue-headed Wagtail, which occurs close to us on the European mainland, but its throat is white.

Chapter 8

1. Mynott, J. (2018). *Birds in the Ancient World.* Oxford University Press, Oxford.
2. Aesop's Fables were written in the mid-to-late 6th century BC.
3. Aristophanes' plays were written around 400BC (Wikipedia, November 2021).

   The 23 other pub birds to make an appearance in the plays of Aristophanes are Blackbird, Coot, Crane, Crow, Cuckoo, Gull, Heron, Jackdaw, Kestrel, Kingfisher, Kite, Lark, Nightingale, Ostrich, Owl, Sparrow, Stork, Swallow, Thrush, Vulture, Warbler, Woodpecker and Wren.
4. Colinvaux, P. (1978). *Why Big Fierce Animals are Rare: An Ecologist's Perspective.* Princeton University Press, Princeton. Colinvaux was born in the UK but spent most of his working life at Ohio State University where he was held in very high esteem as a teacher.
5. The number of British breeding species of birds in Figure 1 is taken from Gaston, K.J. and Blackburn, T.M. (2000). *Pattern and Process in Macroecology.* Blackwell Science, Oxford. (Page 216, Figure 5.10). Kevin Gaston did his PhD and a postdoc with me; Tim Blackburn was also one of my postdocs.

   To understand Figure 1 in more detail the weight classes increase logarithmically. That is, the bird's weights (their body masses) are grouped as follows:
   3.2–5.6 grams (as $\log_{10}$ 0.50–0.75)
   5.6–10.0 grams ($\log_{10}$ 0.75–1.00)
   10.0–17.8 grams ($\log_{10}$ 1.00–1.25).
   And so on, all the way up to:
   10,000–17,782 grams ($\log_{10}$ 4.00–4.25).
   Body weights are taken from a quite remarkable book (not a bedtime read but incredibly useful for nerds like me): Dunning, J.D. (1993). *CRC Handbook of Avian Body Masses.* CRC Press, Boca Raton.
   In a small proportion of the species we have encountered the males and females differ in size. In many birds of prey (Eagles, Falcons and Hawks) mature females are bigger than males. In a few other species (Black and Mute Swans, for example) the males tend to be bigger than the females. Mostly this doesn't matter because even though they are different sizes both sexes are in the same weight class. Where they differ, I have used the male's weight in Figure 1, because almost invariably males rather than females dominate inn signs.
   The sharp eyed among you will have spotted two pub birds heavier than any British breeding species. The lighter one is Mute Swan because the body mass used by Kevin and Tim is slightly less than the average male in John Dunning's book. The largest bird (Ostrich) is not of course a British breeding species.
6. Translate the vertical axis of Figure 2 as:

   0.5 is log10 for roughly three pubs in total
   1.0 = 10 pubs in total
   1.5 = about 32 pubs in total
   2.0 = 100 pubs in total
7. There are other forms of the abundance–body size relationship, as Kevin and Tim point out, but positive relationships like that in Figure 2 are a minority (Fig. 5.23 in their book).
8. There are 16 weight classes in Figure 2. The smallest birds in the baker's dozen are Magpies (in the 8th class). Pigeons and Doves, and Partridges are in weight class 9. The other ten species are all larger than this.

9. *Biological Conservation*, doi.org/ghjjcd, reported in *New Scientist*, 5 December 2020.
10. Reilly, J. (2018). *The Ascent of Birds*. Pelagic Publishing, Exeter.
    Passerines (technically Passeriformes) have three toes pointing forward and one (the hallux) pointing back and a tendon that automatically closes the toes to grip a branch when the legs bend as the bird perches.
11. www.pinknews.co.uk/2021/06/10/london-gay-bar-black-cap-camden-high-street-reopen-historic-pub
    Wikipedia (accessed November 2021).
12. Davies, N.B. (1992). *Dunnock Behaviour and Social Evolution*. Oxford University Press, Oxford.

APPENDIX 1

Scientific names of the bird species mentioned in the text

Those in square brackets are species discussed in the text but which have not been identified as pub birds (as a definite or possible ID), either by me or by W.B. Alexander in his pioneering 1953–54 paper[1.2], Richard Fitter in his short 1955 note[1.3] or Steve Shaw in his Appendix in *Birds Britannica*[1.5]. A "?" signifies a probable (but not certain) identification.

Amazon, Yellow-headed *Amazona oratrix*
[Avocet *Recurvirostra avocetta*]
[Bateleur *Terathopius ecaudatus*]
Bittern *Botaurus stellaris*
Blackbird *Turdus merula*
[Blackcap *Sylvia atricapilla*]
[Bluebird, Eastern *Sialia sialis*]
[Booby, Nazca *Sula granti*]
[Budgerigar *Melopsittacus undulatus*]
[Bulbul, Common *Pycnonotus barbatus*]
Bullfinch *Pyrrhula pyrrhula*
Bustard, Great *Otis tarda*
[Buzzard (Common) *Buteo buteo*]
Canary *Serinus canaria*
Chaffinch *Fringilla coelebs*
Chough, (Cornish or Red-billed) *Pyrrhocorax pyrrhocorax*
[Alpine] *Pyrrhocorax graculus*]
[Cisticola, Zitting *Cisticola juncidis*]
Cockatoo, ?Sulphur-crested *Cacatua galerita*
Condor sp. *Gymnogyps*
Cordonbleu, Red-cheeked *Uraeginthus bengalus*
Cormorant *Phalacrocorax carbo*
Coot *Fulica atra*
Crake, [Spotless *Porzana tabuensis*]
[Little *Porzana parva*]
[Spotted *Porzana porzana*]
Crane (Common) *Grus grus*
Crow, [American *Corvus brachyrhynchos*]
Carrion *Corvus corone*
Cuckoo, (Common) *Cuculus canoris*
Jacobin *Oxylophus jacobinus*
[Yellow-billed *Coccyzus americanus*]
Curlew *Numenius arquata*
Dodo *Raphus cucullatus*
Dotterel *Charadrius morinellus*
Dove, Collared *Streptopelia decaocto*
Domestic – see Pigeon, Feral
Stock *Columba oenas*
[Turtle *Streptopelia turtur*]
Duck, [Mandarin *Aix galericulata*]
Ruddy *Oxyura jamaicensis*
[White-headed *Oxyura leucocephala*]
Wood *Aix sponsa*
Dunlin *Calidris alpinus*
[Dunnock *Prunella modularis* aka Hedge Sparrow]
Eagle, Bald *Haliaeetus leucocephalus*
Black (Verreaux's) *Aquila verreauxii*
Golden *Aquila chrysaetos*
?Harpy *Harpia harpyja*
?Martial *Polymaetus bellicosus*
[White-tailed *Haliaeetus albicilla*]
[Egret, Cattle *Bubulcus ibis*]
Falcon, Peregrine *Falco peregrinus*
[Finch, Zebra (Australian) *Taeniopygia castanotis*]
[Flamingo, Lesser *Phoenicopterus minor*]
[Francolin, Black *Francolinus francolinus*]

[Fulmar *Fulmarus glacialis*]
[Gallinule, Common *Gallinula galeata*]
[Gannet *Morus bassanus*]
Goldcrest *Regulus regulus*
Goldfinch *Carduelis carduelis*
Goose, Brent *Branta bernicula*
Canada *Branta canadensis*
Greylag *Anser anser*
Snow *Anser caerulescens*
Swan (Chinese) *Anser cygnoides*
Goshawk *Accipiter gentilis*
Grebe, Great Crested *Podiceps cristatus*
[Little *Tachybaptus ruficollis*]
Greenfinch *Chloris chloris*
Grouse, Black *Lyrurus tetrix*
Red *Lagopus lagopus scotica*
[Willow *Lagopus lagopus*]
[Guillemot *Uria aalge*]
Gull, [Black-headed *Chroicocephalus ridibundus*]
Common *Larus canus*
[Great Black-backed *Larus marinus*]
[Herring *Larus argentatus*]
[Lesser Black-backed *Larus fuscus*]
[Gyrfalcon *Falco rusticolus*]
Harrier, Marsh *Circus aeruginosus*
[Hawk, Grey (or Grey-lined) *Buteo nitidus*]
[Harris's *Parabuteo unicinctus*]
Heron, Grey *Ardea cinerea*
[Purple *Ardea purpurea*]
Hobby *Falco subbuteo*
Hoopoe *Upupa epops*
[Hornbill, Southern Yellow-billed *Tockus flavirostris*]
Jay, Blue *Cyanocitta cristata*
[Eurasian *Garrulus glandarius*]
[Junglefowl, Grey *Gallus sonneratii*]
Red *Gallus gallus* (as Cock, Cockerel, Hen or Chicken)
Kestrel, American *Falco sparverius*
Common (European) *Falco tinnunculus*
Kingfisher *Alcedo atthis*
Kite, Red *Milvus milvus*
Kittiwake *Rissa tridactyla*
Lapwing *Vanellus vanellus*
Linnet *Carduelis cannabina*
Macaw, Scarlet *Ara macao*
Magpie *Pica pica*
Mallard *Anas platyrhynchos*
Martin, House *Delichon urbica*
Sand *Riparia riparia*
[Meadowlark, Eastern *Sturnella magna*]
Merlin *Falco columbarius*
[Minivet, Scarlet *Pericrocotus flammeus*]
Moorhen *Gallinula chloropus*
Nightingale *Luscinia megarhynchos*
Nightjar *Caprimulgus europaeus*
[Niltava, Small *Niltava macgrigoriae*]
Nuthatch *Sitta europaea*
Osprey *Pandion haliaetus*
Ostrich *Struthio camelus*
Owl, Barn *Tyto alba*
Eagle *Bubo bubo*
Little *Athene noctua*
?Long-eared *Asio otus*
[Short-eared *Asio flammeus*]
Tawny, *Strix aluco*
Oystercatcher *Haemotopus ostralegus*
Partridge, Grey *Perdix perdix*
[Red-legged *Alectoris rufa*]
Pelican, Brown *Pelecanus occidentalis*
[Dalmatian *Pelecanus crispus*]
White *Pelecanus onocrotalus*]
Penguin, [Emperor *Aptenodytes forsteri*]
[Jackass *Spheniscus demersus*]
[King *Aptenodytes patagonicus*]
Petrel, Storm *Hydrobates pelagicus*
Pheasant (Common) *Phasianus colchicus*
Golden *Chrysolophus pictus*
Pigeon, Feral *Columba livia* (also unspecified Doves and Domestic Pigeons)
[Nicobar *Caloenas nicobarica*]
Wood *Columba polumbus*
?Pintail *Anas acuta*
Plover, Golden *Pluvialis apricaria*
?[Sociable *Vanellus gregarius*]
Puffin *Fratercula arctica*
Quail *Cotumix coturnix*
Raven *Corvus corax*
[Razorbill *Alca torda*]
[Redshank *Tringa totanus*]
Redstart, American *Setophaga ruticilla*
(Common) *Phoenicurus phoenicurus*
Robin *Erithacus rubecula*
Rook *Corvus frugilegus*
Sandpiper, Common *Actitis hypoleucos*
Shelduck *Tadorna tadorna*
[Shrike, Red-backed *Lanius collurio*]
Skylark *Alauda arvensis*
Snipe, Common *Gallinago gallinago*
Jack *Lymnocryptes minimus*
[Solitaire, Rodrigues *Pezophaps solitaria*]
Sparrow, House *Passer domesticus*
[Tree *Passer montanus*]
Sparrowhawk, Accipiter nisus

[Spoonbill *Platalea leucorodia*]
Starling *Sturnus vulgaris*
Stork, White *Ciconia ciconia*
Swallow, Barn *Hirundo rustica*
[Swamphen, Purple *Porphyrio porphyrio*]
Swan, [Bewick's *Cygnus columbianus bewickii*]
Black *Cygnus atratus*
Mute *Cygnus olor*
Whistling (Tundra) *Cygnus columbianus columbianus*
[Whooper *Cygnus cygnus*]
[Swift *Apus apus*]
[Teal *Anas crecca*]
Tern, [Arctic *Sterna paradisaea*]
[Common *Sterna hirundo*]
Little *Sternula albifrons*
Thrush, ?Mistle *Turdus viscivorus*
Song *Turdus philomelos*
[Tit, Blue *Cyanistes caeruleus*]
[Coal *Periparus ater*]
[Great *Parus major*]
[Long-tailed *Aegithalos caudatus*]
Toucan, Toco *Ramphastos toco*
Turkey *Meleagris gallopavo*
Turnstone *Arenaria interpres*
Vulture, Hooded *Necrosyrtes monachus*
Turkey *Cathartes aura*
Warbler, Dartford *Sylvia undata*
[Reed *Acrocephalus scirpaceus*]
Whinchat *Saxicola rubetra*
Woodcock *Scolopax rusticola*
Woodlark *Lullula arborea*
Woodpecker, [Great Spotted *Dendrocopus major*]
Green *Picus viridis*
[Pileated *Dryocopus pileatus*]
Wren *Trolodytes troglodytes*

APPENDIX 2

Technical details

The core database

Most of us have encountered the resident pub bore, preaching from a bar stool about the best way to get from Preston to York via Ilkley, except on a Friday evening when.... At this point I usually move seats. But for those of you who want to know exactly what is in my core database, here are the numbers.

The book is based on information accumulated in various ways between 2010 and the end of August 2021. In summary it contains:

Total pubs: 711

They include:

12 named after bird 'paraphernalia' (birdcages, Duck decoys, dovecotes, and Hen houses)
13 unidentified feathers, nests and eggs
10 unspecified called *Bird in Hand.*

TOTAL: 35 pubs

Total of pubs with an identifiable species of bird or non-specific kind of bird (Owl, Duck etc. or just bird): 676 (i.e. 711–35)

They include:

117 identifiable species (excluding mythical species)
17 non-specific kinds of bird
4 mythical species.
TOTAL: 138

Of the total 676 pubs:

560 have one (rarely two, and in one instance three) of the 117 identifiable species
106 have one of the 17 non-specific kinds of birds
10 have mythical species.

The 117 "identifiable species" are the birds I can identify from the pub sign (or just the pub's name if it has no sign) with absolute or reasonable certainty.

In a few instances I have supplemented this core database with extra searches on the web, when my existing information appeared to be inadequate. I have not added these additional searches to the main file but make clear in the text when I have undertaken an additional web search. And whilst I am on the subject, it gets tedious to keep saying "in the main database there are *x* pubs with *y* characteristics", so often it is implicit and I simply say, "there are *x* pubs…", leaving you to mentally fill in the fact that I am referring to my data base, not all the pubs in this country.

GENERAL INDEX

Pub birds and other pubs, and places in the UK are listed in separate indexes. This index covers everything else (including birds that do not make an appearance as a pub bird).

INDEX TO PLACES IN BRITAIN

Index to places in Britain (villages, towns, cities, regions, counties, and countries).

INDEX OF PUBS

An index of all the pubs mentioned in the text. Most are pub birds. As explained in Chapter 1 a few pubs are not apparently named after a bird but have a bird on their sign; or the pub bird on the sign is not the same as the pub's name; or the bird can be identified to species more precisely than the name implies; the identities of these pub birds are in parentheses after the name of the pub. Pubs in square brackets appear to be named after a bird but are not. Other 'non-bird pubs' are included for a variety of reasons (e.g. their name before it was changed to a pub bird). Pubs marked * are fictitious (in literature etc.). Some names (e.g. White Swan) refer to several different pubs with the same name. The page on which the pub is illustrated is *in italics*. Definite articles (*The* White Swan) are omitted.